WILTSHIRE

THE

WILTSHIRE DOMESDAY

ALECTO HISTORICAL EDITIONS
LONDON
1989

ISBN for Wiltshire volumes: 0 948459 48 4
ISBN for this volume: 1 871118 11 5

Printed in England

ALECTO HISTORICAL EDITIONS
46 Kelso Place, London W8 5QG, England

CONTENTS

PREFACE

THIS is the tenth volume of the Alecto County Edition of Domesday Book to be published. In the manuscript, eleven folios constitute the section for Wiltshire of which the first is blank on the recto. Although Wiltshire comes sixth in the order of counties, the spacing and style of the main scribe's writing show that its folios were written towards the very end of the programme in which the thirty counties were inscribed.

Wiltshire shares with the south-western counties of Cornwall, Devon, Dorset and Somerset the advantage of having some of its description in Domesday Book amplified by the Liber Exoniensis or Exeter Domesday, the manuscript usually abbreviated as Exon. Apparently in the custody of the authorities of Exeter Cathedral since the eleventh century, Exon contains a somewhat fuller and differently arranged version of the matter which was entered in Domesday Book itself. Unfortunately almost all the section in Exon which related to Wiltshire is lost: indeed, the entry for only one manor has survived. However three Geld Rolls (tax returns) of almost contemporary date are incidentally bound up with the manuscript and these are of great value for delineating the hundred-boundaries within the shire, since the evidence for them in Domesday Book itself is unusually sparse.

Throughout this edition the names and extent of the counties are those which obtained prior to the restructuring of the counties in 1974. Since their traditional boundaries had remained virtually unchanged since the time of the Domesday survey, there seemed little purpose in following recent, arbitrary innovations which have neither historical justification nor useful function in this context. Although Wiltshire itself has been fortunate to escape such tampering almost entirely, the relationship of the neighbouring counties to one another has been much altered. Thus Oxfordshire for the first time shares a boundary with Wiltshire having now absorbed the north-western part of Berkshire, while Gloucestershire and Somerset, previously contiguous, have been separated by the invented county of Avon. On the associated county map we retain the pre-1974 boundaries which had remained substantially the same for a thousand years or more.

The three volumes that constitute each part of the County Edition are designed to be mutually supportive and are separated in this way for the reader's convenience. For instance, it is desirable for the facsimile folios to be present in one book and the parallel translations in another so that both can be consulted side by side. For the same reason the key to the symbols employed in the translations for Great Domesday's marginal notes and signs (Appendix I), and the list of abbreviations found in the manuscript (Appendix II) are best incorporated in the third volume, *Domesday Book Studies*, so that they, too, can be used in conjunction with the folios of translations and facsimile to which they refer. A fourth separate element is the large-scale county map which is provided as a loose-leaf folded sheet in order to be spread out near at hand if required.

Besides the book containing the facsimile folios and the maps, the division of text into two further self-contained volumes reflects the character and scope of their contents. *Domesday Book Studies* (which is common to the entire County Edition) is a book of essays on topics concerning Domesday Book in general, while this volume contains all matter specific to the locality in question. The translations are put at the end, unusually after the indices, where they are easiest to find and where their pages can be matched with the facsimile of the manuscript by the same folio numbers without disrupting the pagination of the rest of this book.

In a project so closely bound up with local history, place-name identification will constitute a salient feature affecting all its aspects, especially in the translations, indices and maps where their occurrences must always be consistent. By chance, the present publication was first set in motion towards the end of a period when the place-names recorded in Domesday Book had come under particular scrutiny, but not always with unanimously accepted results. The only recourse was to log every mention of a name on to a card index and enter into it all dissident opinion. This organized body of raw material was then submitted to F. R. Thorn, appointed for his special knowledge of the Domesday hundreds and place-names, and who has also established their position on the map. Dr Thorn in turn wishes to acknowledge the generous assistance with the Wiltshire place-names afforded him by T. Foulds and the help of his wife Caroline at every stage of indexing, mapping and writing the material for this county.

Those responsible for the making of the facsimile and for the production of this volume are noticed in the acknowledgements printed in the accompanying *Domesday Book Studies*, though special mention should be made of Westerham Press for the complex task of setting the translations to match the Latin text of the manuscript with such success. The database for the manipulation of the place- and personal names has been developed at the same printing-house under the supervision of James Brennan. The design and typography for this, as for the rest of the work, is by Ian Mortimer, I. M. Imprimit, London.

Our thanks are due especially to Elaine Shaughnessy who has controlled the editing of this volume overall, to Basil Harley for guiding the diverse elements through the press, to Brian Martin for overseeing production at Westerham Press, and also to the following for their diligence in the accomplishment of its various parts:

Bibliography: Dr David Bates, for rearranging his *Domesday Bibliography* already published; editing, Patricia Gibson.

Indices: Jenny Page for keying-in the material for the database from which both Indices are derived; Douglas Matthews for the compilation of the Index of Persons; Cyril Simsa and Elizabeth Mostyn-Owen for editing.

Translation: initial standardization, Eric Hemming, Paul Francis and Stephen Wilson; copy-preparation at Oxford University Press, George Tulloch; editing, Christine Shaw, Caroline Thorn; typesetting at Westerham Press, Clive Logsdon.

Map: assistance with the design, Tom Phillips; compilation and editing, Frank Thorn, Des Seal, Cyril Simsa; drafting, Sheila Hodson; overseeing production at Cook Hammond and Kell Ltd, Jackie Hoy.

Finally, at Alecto, for the myriad incidental activities that such a project requires, we must thank Sarah Burton, Henrietta Pearson and Emma Wells-Cole.

Ann Williams, *Editor-in-Chief*

R. W. H. Erskine, *General Editor*

The following is a list of abbreviations which are used throughout this edition. References to other publications are given in their abbreviated form if they occur in the county bibliography. The county volumes in this series which have already been published are cited in full at the end of the bibliography, as references to them are also abbreviated.

AntJ	*Antiquaries Journal*
ArchJ	*Archaeological Journal*
ASE	*Anglo-Saxon England*
BAR	British Archaeological Reports
BL	British Library
CA	*Current Archaeology*
DB	Domesday Book
EconHR	*Economic History Review*
EETS	Early English Text Society
EHR	*English Historical Review*
EPNS	English Place-Name Society
Exon	Exeter Domesday Book
GDB	Great Domesday Book
HMSO	Her Majesty's Stationery Office
JBAA	*Journal of the British Archaeological Association*
JMH	*Journal of Medieval History*
LDB	Little Domesday Book
MA	*Medieval Archaeology*
MS, MSS	Manuscript(s)
MS	*Mediaeval Studies*
NGR	National Grid Reference
N & Q	*Notes and Queries*
PBA	*Proceedings of the British Academy*
PRO	Public Record Office
TRHS	*Transactions of the Royal Historical Society*
VCH	*The Victoria Histories of the Counties of England*

INTRODUCTION

AN INTRODUCTION TO THE WILTSHIRE DOMESDAY

N. A. HOOPER

WILTSHIRE is a region of two contrasting areas as different as chalk and cheese. The sparsely populated chalk downlands were used mainly as sheep pasture, from which wool, meat and cheese were produced. Certainly by the later Middle Ages dairy farming was well established in the vales of the north-west. The geology of the county consists of four bands, each running approximately south-west to north-east. To the north-west Wiltshire takes in part of the Cotswolds, which here rise to a height of 400 feet. Next is the great clay vale which stretches southwards from the upper Thames. The streams of these two zones drain into the Thames and the Bristol Avon, the watershed being formed by the chalk escarpment which faces north and west, rising to more than 900 feet. Behind it the gently falling dip-slope is deeply dissected by rivers flowing to the east and the south, dividing the uplands into distinct blocks. It is noticeable in this part of Wiltshire how the Domesday settlements are strung out along the rivers and the chalk downs appear as voids. In the east and south-east two areas unsuited to agriculture were thinly populated in the eleventh century and may already have been given over to the royal forests later distinguished as those of Savernake, Chute, Clarendon and Melksham.[1]

The survey of the county occupies ten complete folios and the verso of an eleventh (64v–74v). It is the sixth county in Great Domesday and was surveyed with the four other south-western shires, Dorset, Somerset, Devonshire and Cornwall, by a single group of commissioners. The only one known for certain is William de St Carilef, Bishop of Durham, who possessed no property in the south-west and thus should have had no local connections to distract him. He had already been involved in the collection of the geld levied in 1086, and indeed was active on the main survey.[2]

The Wiltshire folios contain few irregularities. The first column is generally unexceptionable in commencing with a brief account of the Borough of Malmesbury, followed by an accurate index of the Wiltshire landowners, a statement of the payments which the boroughs made to the king and a note of the customary renders from the county. The last item extends into the margins indicating either that it was an afterthought or that insufficient space had been left for it. The account of the rural manors begins at the top of the next column and proceeds in standard form through the lands of the king, church and lay tenants-in-chief. It concludes with lengthy lists of minor tenants, the king's sergeants (*servientes*), thegns and servants (*ministri*).[3] On the whole the text contains few mistakes or omissions. An ink-blot in the account of the royal manor of Amesbury on folio 64v appears to obscure four letters of an erased word, and a misplaced entry for one hide at Coleshill (now in Berkshire) on folio 72v has been written across the foot of the second column. It thus breaks up the entry for the Seagry estate of Drogo fitzPons with no indication where it properly belongs. At the bottom of folio 73 Hugh fitzBaldric's single manor of Marden also runs across the foot of the column, but in this case it is directed to its correct place by transposition signs. There are some omissions. In the account of the Bishop of Winchester's property at 'East Overton' the number of villans was not entered: however, the initials '*rq*' (*require*, 'inquire') indicate that the scribe

[1] For a more detailed geographical summary, see *VCH Wiltshire* and Darby and Welldon Finn (eds.), *Domesday Geography*, 61–4.

[2] R. W. Eyton, *Domesday Studies: An Analysis and Digest of the Somerset Survey (according to the Exon Code), and of the Somerset Gheld Inquest of A.D. 1084*, i (London, Bristol, 1880), 12–13; *VCH Wiltshire*, ii (1955), 42, n.2. William is referred to in the Geld Accounts for Wiltshire, printed and discussed in *VCH Wiltshire*, ii. 173. His activity in Somerset is discussed in Loud, 'An Introduction to the Somerset Domesday', *Somerset Domesday*, 5–6. A leading role in the production of Domesday Book is proposed for him by P. Chaplais, 'William of Saint-Calais and the Domesday Survey', *Domesday Studies*, ed. J. C. Holt (Woodbridge, 1987).

[3] M. Gullick, 'The Great and Little Domesday Manuscripts', *Domesday Book Studies*, eds. A. Williams and R. W. H. Erskine (London, 1987), 100, fig. 9.

was aware of this.[1] In the chapter for Amesbury Abbey on folio 68v no name was supplied for the two hides seized by Robert, Count of Mortain. A marginal sign identifies them with land at Winterslow in the count's chapter (probably West Winterslow).

There are in Wiltshire Domesday some references to the ways information was collected, or at least checked, for the great survey. The 'men' (*homines*) who put the value of Damerham (now in Hampshire) at £45, although it paid £61, probably represent the villagers giving testimony in the hundred court. In other instances the special session of the shire court, where the commissioners presided, is referred to.[2] For example, 'all the thegns of the shire' gave witness to the seizure of land at Chedglow, and the 'testimony of the shire' was given for a usurpation at Calne. These instances reflect one task allotted to the commissioners; that is the settlement of disputes over land, many of which had arisen in consequence of the plantation of a new aristocracy in England after 1066. References to disputes appear in the text in the Wiltshire survey under the estates to which they pertain rather than being collected into one section. There is evidence from Somerset that the royal estates were surveyed separately, and the tenants-in-chief may also have been responsible for the returns from their possessions.[3]

The process by which the final text of Great Domesday was arrived at is elucidated for the south-western circuit by the survival of a collection of documents bound together and now kept at Exeter Cathedral and known as the Liber Exoniensis, usually abbreviated Exon.[4] First in this manuscript are different versions of a sworn inquest made for a tax raised late in William's reign. These state for each hundred the total hides, the demesnes of the king and tenants-in-chief and the amount of money the collectors had actually received.[5] One achievement of this inquest was the identification of a number of 'lost' hides whose owners had succeeded in eluding the payment of geld for many years. These were subsequently included in the Domesday survey. The major part of Exon Domesday consists of the survey of the five south-western counties from which the account in Great Domesday was compiled. Even at this preliminary stage the returns were in 'feudal' form, the information for each shire being organized by fiefs and not by hundreds. Since the hundred-names were omitted in both surviving versions of the south-western circuit the Geld Accounts are indispensable for the identification of many places and the reconstruction of the administrative structure of the county. Finally the Exon text contains summaries for the complete circuit of the fiefs of certain tenants-in-chief, and it is certain that more have been lost.[6]

For Wiltshire most of Exon Domesday has been lost, and all that survives of the county survey is the description of William de Moyon's manor at Sutton Veny. Nevertheless, this will suffice to demonstrate how the returns were treated when Great Domesday was compiled, as a comparison of the two versions of the Sutton Veny account shows. First, here is the description in Exon Domesday (f.47):

> W(illiam) de Moyon has 1 manor which is called Sutton Veny which Cola held on the day when King E(dward) was alive and dead and now W(alter) Hosed holds from (William). It paid geld for 5 hides in the time of King E(dward). 4 ploughs can till these. Of them W(illiam) has in demesne 3 hides and 1 virgate and 2 ploughs and the villans 2 hides less 1 virgate and 2 ploughs. There W(illiam) has 3 villans and 6 bordars and 3 slaves and 1 horse and 300 sheep and 1 mill which pays 4*s.* each year and 4 acres of meadow and pasture half a league long and one furlong wide and 2 acres of wood (*nemoris*). This vill is worth 100*s.* and it was worth £4 when W(illiam) received it.

[1] C. Thorn, 'Marginal Notes and Signs in Domesday Book', *Domesday Book Studies*, eds. Williams and Erskine, 124–6 and figs. 11–12.

[2] For the procedure employed, see H. R. Loyn, 'A General Introduction to Domesday Book', ibid. 3–7.

[3] J. H. Round, *VCH Somerset*, i (1906), 427.

[4] See also *VCH Wiltshire*, ii. 44; V. H. Galbraith, *Domesday Book: its Place in Administrative History* (Oxford, 1974), 49–50 and 68–9.

[5] The date 1084 is often favoured, although 1086 has its supporters (e.g. Galbraith, *Domesday Book*, 64–8). Those for Wiltshire were printed and discussed by R. R. Darlington, *VCH Wiltshire*, ii. 218–21.

[6] *VCH Wiltshire*, ii. 219–21; Darby and Welldon Finn (eds.), *Domesday Geography*, 2.

The equivalent passage in Great Domesday (f.72) reads:

> William de Moyon holds Sutton Veny of the king and Walter (holds) of him. Cola held it TRE, and it paid geld for 5 hides. There is land for 4 ploughs. Of this 3 hides and 1 virgate of land are in demesne, and there are 2 ploughs, and 3 slaves; and 3 villans and 6 bordars with 2 ploughs. There is a mill rendering 4*s*., and 4 acres of meadow, and 2 acres of woodland (*silvae*), (and) pasture half a league long and 1 broad. It was worth £4; now 100*s*.

The terminology of the latter has been streamlined and the statistics for the livestock—which the English chronicler thought so shameful to collect[1]—have been omitted. Another common feature is the removal of the bynames which elsewhere are an indispensable aid in identifying landowners in Great Domesday. The less compressed language of Exon clarifies two matters which are not clear in the terser final version: the earlier of the two values for land relates to a date after the Conquest, normally when the new tenant received it, and the peasants' ploughs are assigned to the villans. The most important difference in this example lies in the amount of pasture recorded, a considerable discrepancy which is perhaps due to the omission of the word for furlong (*quarentena*) when copying took place. It is a reminder that Great Domesday is not infallible and that there is seldom any way of checking its accuracy.

Nevertheless, let us take this as an entry typical of Wiltshire. It does not refer to the whole vill of Sutton Veny, for William fitzGuy and Nigel the physician also had manors there (ff.72 and 73). The entry gives the name of tenant, subtenant and hidage, as the instructions to the commissioners required, and a statement of the number of ploughs which could work the land. In many cases it appears that this figure has been arrived at simply by adding together the numbers of ploughs actually at work. Next comes the division of the land between the lord and the peasants. On this manor the demesne (the lord's home farm) accounted for the bulk of the land, where there were three slaves with two ploughs. At least for the tax which gave rise to the Geld Accounts in the Exon manuscript the demesne land was exempt from payment. The remainder was held by nine peasants of differing degrees, of whom the villans had two ploughs and their oxen, and all would have been required to spend part of their time working the lord's portion. The account finishes with a list of the other resources of the manor and its value at two dates. There are variations throughout the shire in the formulae employed to express some of this information, but the overall pattern does not vary greatly. For the lay estates the hidage of the demesne was not always entered, but the numbers of demesne ploughs were always stated.[2]

Other manors, while following much the same pattern as Sutton Veny, were much larger and tenurially more complex. In these cases the subtenancies had to be listed in addition to the demesne and the peasants' farms. There was greater opportunity here for disagreements to arise. At the Bishop of Salisbury's huge estate at Potterne parts of the manor had been leased out before the Conquest, and each subtenancy was listed with the statistics of the estate. Information about the terms on which the land had been held was given in order to safeguard the church's title, which often came under threat. In the case of Potterne it indeed turns out that one tenancy had been usurped after 1066 by Ernulf de Hesdin (ff.66, 69v–70).

One difficulty with Wiltshire Domesday lies in determining the number of estates which were entered twice. There are at least eight examples, like that of Potterne, where land in dispute was entered under the heading naming the owner as well as that of the man actually in possession. Two Wiltshire manors were duplicated in the manuscript even though they were not in dispute. Land which William Scudet and Hervey of Wilton held of the royal estates of Westbury and Netheravon was also described in the list of royal sergeants. The royal manor of Melksham presents difficulties because, according to Domesday, Melksham with its appendages was assessed at eighty-four hides, and there was another small holding of three hides. The Geld Account assigned eighty-six hides to the hundred of Melksham, which included places listed separately in Domesday with an assessment

[1] Loyn, 'General Introduction', 1. [2] In ninety-two of 261 entries: see Darby and Welldon Finn (eds.), *Domesday Geography*, 14.

of forty hides. R. R. Darlington was probably correct in suggesting (although he advanced the explanation with 'great hesitation') that the hidage of the appendages was entered twice; both at Melksham and at the individual estates which made up the parent manor.[1]

On the whole, Wiltshire Domesday contains most of the information that the commissioners were directed to collect. Different tenurial conditions in the south-west account for the absence of the 'free men' and sokemen who occur so commonly elsewhere, and the only major deviation from the terms in the Inquisitio Eliensis was the failure to state the information for three dates, the one missing being the time of King Edward.[2] Woodland (*silva*) is normally recorded in linear measurements, with its length and breadth stated in leagues and furlongs, but frequently also in acres. There are a few references to forest, but most of the great royal forests known from the next century are not mentioned, the only indication of their existence being the sparsity of occupation in their areas. Meadow (*pratum*), almost always measured in acres, was found mainly in the river valleys, while pasture (*pastura*) was recorded for two-thirds of Wiltshire manors. Like woodland it could be measured by length and breadth or by acreage. What these figures mean is difficult to interpret. That they were usually estimates is shown by the use of round numbers, and they cannot in any case be converted into modern measures. The indications are, however, that while meadow was restricted and probably inadequate for the needs of agriculture, most villages possessed a share of downland pasture.[3]

The categories of rural inhabitants show a greater diversity than the terms preserved in the Ely Inquest allowed for. The Sutton Veny entry noted the presence of villans, bordars, and slaves. The largest group are the villans who varied greatly in substance, sometimes possessing greater holdings than free men and sokemen. Many of them were probably still personally free if economically dependent, as they were to remain until the next century. The bordars form part of a larger group of less well-off peasants which included cotsets, of whom 80 per cent of the recorded total in Domesday were in Wiltshire, and a handful of cottars. The differences between them are obscure and were probably ignored in many counties where all were lumped together as bordars or cottars. It is notable that in the summary of the Glastonbury estates in the Liber Exoniensis some of the cotsets were called bordars instead. But the Wiltshire jurors did consider the differences between them worthy of mention in the first place. At the foot of the social scale were the slaves who were often listed with the demesne ploughs which they may have worked. The record of slaves is irregular. They were most numerous on royal manors where they formed one quarter of the population. Other large manors had no recorded slaves. This may represent sympathetic landlords who had manumitted their slaves, but is more likely to be a failure to report or to record the presence of slaves on those manors. Slightly above the slaves in status were the *coliberti*, of whom half the total in the whole of Domesday Book are found in Wiltshire and Somerset. They occur mainly on royal manors and those of the large monastic houses. Lastly there are the miscellaneous rural inhabitants, among whom the largest groups were swineherds, beekeepers, and the potters at Westbury, although *potarii* may be an error for *porcarii* (swineherds). Many more of these essential rural 'tradesmen' are found in the Exeter text, but in Great Domesday they were lumped together with the other peasantry.[4]

While Domesday Book furnishes a broad outline of the mixed agricultural resources of eleventh-century Wiltshire, it is almost bereft of details. Several charters from the tenth century refer to common open fields cultivated in strips and there are also references to private, presumably consolidated, holdings. Darlington concluded 'it is probable that the open-field system of agriculture was prevalent in tenth-century Wiltshire'. The distribution and density of population and ploughs and the variations in values give some indication of the prosperity of different parts of Wiltshire, so long as it is remembered that Domesday entries may represent more than one settlement on the ground. R. Welldon Finn concluded that: 'the most densely occupied areas lay in

[1] *VCH Wiltshire*, ii. 193–4.

[2] Loyn, 'General Introduction', 5.

[3] For these resources, see Darby and Welldon Finn (eds.), *Domesday Geography*, 33–45.

[4] *VCH Wiltshire*, ii. 53–5; Darby and Welldon Finn (eds.), *Domesday Geography*, 27–9; H. C. Darby, *Domesday England* (Cambridge, 1977), 64–82.

the lower valley of the Bristol Avon, the Vale of Pewsey and the valley of the Salisbury Avon . . . The areas with densities below the average for the county were the forest areas of the east . . . and the south-west, the Grovely-Great Ridge area, the north-west of Salisbury Plain, the Braydon Forest district in the north of the county and the Cotswolds in the north-west . . .'. On a number of manors, mainly royal ones, it is noted that the estate was paying more than the value. No reasons are specified in Wiltshire, but it is well documented that estates were farmed out for fixed sums of money. A good indication of this practice is the use of *reddit* ('it renders') instead of the usual formula that an estate *valuit* ('is worth'). In many cases values rose, perhaps as the result of a more exploitative managerial regime, but in a few cases they actually fell. The county was 60 per cent downland, thinly populated but rich in sheep and wool and still heavily forested, but it was basically good farmland. Place-names recorded from the eighth to the sixteenth centuries show that assarting in 'the old forest areas of Braydon, Chippenham, Melksham, Pewsham, Savernake, Chute, Clarendon, Melchet, Grovely and Selwood' was extensive over a long period.[1]

Anglo-Saxon Wiltshire

The first references to Wiltshire are in two sources compiled in the late ninth century, and record events which took place in *Wiltunscir* and involved the *Wilsætan*, the men of the region, after 800. The latter form means 'dwellers on the (river) Wylye' and may represent an early tribal unit in the south around which the shire was formed subsequently. However, the dependence of the region on Wilton, from which the shire took its name, may date to before 700. Early Wessex consisted of a number of kingdoms each with its own dynasty, one of which was normally dominant, and it may well be that the shires of the ninth century are the descendants of these early provinces.[2]

The conquest of the region by Germanic invaders and settlers appears to be charted in a series of sixth-century annals in the Anglo-Saxon Chronicle. This highly selective account relates the establishment of the West Saxons around Southampton Water in the late fifth and early sixth century. In 552 and 556 they defeated the British at the hill-forts of *Searobyrg* (Old Sarum near Salisbury) and *Beranbyrg* (Barbury Castle near Swindon). These could as well be raids as conquests and it would be unwise to see in these events the piecemeal conquest of Wiltshire. Nevertheless, two decades later the Chronicle records the West Saxon acquisition of Gloucester, Cirencester and Bath following the battle at Dyrham in Gloucestershire. West Saxon expansion north of the upper Thames was brought to an end by the growing power of Mercia under Penda and his descendants, and it may have been this check which caused them to turn some of their energies westwards to the conquest of Somerset, Dorset and Devonshire. For a time before 700 part of northern Wiltshire came under Mercian authority, and the battle at *Woddesbeorg* ('Woden's barrow', now Adam's Grave in Alton Priors) in 715 may represent a failed Mercian attempt to regain that influence. This bald and one-sided list of battles leaves unanswered many questions about the nature and circumstances of the Anglo-Saxon settlement. In particular the relations of the newcomers with the native inhabitants is obscure, although there is a significant survival of British place-names in Wiltshire which suggests that peaceful coexistence may have been as important as war. In truth, the historical and archaeological remains are too sparse to attempt any adequate reconstruction of the origins of Wiltshire. The dates, if not the events themselves, of the fifth and sixth century were guesses probably made in the ninth century when the early legends were woven together in the Anglo-Saxon Chronicle. Despite the efforts of many scholars to synthesize this fragmentary information,

[1] *VCH Wiltshire*, ii. 11–13; Darby and Welldon Finn (eds.), *Domesday Geography*, 32; *VCH Wiltshire*, iv (1959), 1; Gover *et al.*, *Place-Names of Wiltshire*, 417 and maps. Some of these names are no longer associated with woodlands.

[2] *VCH Wiltshire*, ii. 1–2; H. M. Chadwick, *Studies on Anglo-Saxon Institutions* (Cambridge, 1905; repr. New York, 1963), 282–90; F. M. Stenton, *Anglo-Saxon England* (3rd edn., Oxford, 1971), 294–5, 336–7; P. H. Sawyer, *From Roman Britain to Norman England* (London, 1978), 43–7.

there is no reason to modify Kemble's observation of 1849 that 'I look upon the genuine details of the German conquests in England as irrevocably lost to us'.[1]

During the eighth century Wessex was at times subject to the authority of the Mercian overlords and for some time lost control of Berkshire and of significant areas of Somerset, and perhaps of north Wiltshire too. In the mid-750s the great Mercian king Æthelbald granted land at Tockenham in a transaction witnessed by Cynewulf of Wessex. It may be significant of a change in the border in the north-west that Sherston, in Wiltshire in 1066 but west of the Fosse Way which forms the boundary for some distance, was said to be 'in Hwicci', that is, in Mercia.[2] But Wessex survived to overthrow Mercian overlordship in the years 825–9, and its resistance later to the Viking 'Great Army' was decisive in the emergence of a single kingdom of England and the consolidation of the modern nation. Several of the battles by which this was achieved were fought in Wiltshire. The victory of the men of Wiltshire over the Mercians at Kempsford in Gloucestershire in 802 marked a stage in West Saxon emancipation from domination by the Midland kingdom; Mercian power over southern England was shattered at the Battle of *Ellendun* (near Wroughton) in 825. Although Alfred was forced to buy peace from the Danes in 871, it was only after hard fighting which included a defeat at Wilton. The decisive stage of the war came at the end of 877 when the rump of the Danish host seized Chippenham and Alfred was driven to seek refuge at Athelney in Somerset. But he counter-attacked and besieged the Danes in Chippenham after defeating them at Edington (near Westbury).

Wiltshire's position as a land-locked inland county did not save it during the second Viking era, which culminated in Cnut's conquest of England in 1016. Although little is known of the eleventh-century road system, it is clear that Wiltshire lay astride roads followed by the Danish invaders, and that its towns also attracted them. In 1003 the Danes under King Swein moved inland and, upon the failure of the ealdorman to lead the men of Wiltshire and Hampshire against him, sacked Wilton and possibly Salisbury too. The Anglo-Saxon Chronicle reports under the year 1011 that much of Wiltshire had been ravaged, a reference to the previous year when Thorkil's army marched as far as Cannings Marsh (near All and Bishops Cannings) before returning to its ships. In 1013 Swein's host traversed Wiltshire on its way from Wallingford to Bath, and in 1015 his son Cnut ravaged inland from the mouth of the Frome. The climax of the war was reached in 1016. In the winter Cnut and his English ally Ealdorman Eadric marched through Wiltshire to cross into Mercia at Cricklade. In the summer the Danes were defeated near Gillingham in Dorset, close to the Wiltshire border, before another inconclusive struggle at Sherston in the vicinity of Malmesbury. In many cases a combination of major Roman roads and ancient trackways forms the link between these places.[3]

The Domesday County

The backbone of royal government in medieval England was the framework of shires and hundreds, both of which were well established by the end of the tenth century. The county probably paid tax on around 4,000 hides in 1066,[4] but there were large areas not assessed to tax at all. These were the six royal manors discussed below. Domesday Book mentions only three

[1] For these 'events', see *VCH Wiltshire*, i (2) (1973), 468–80; *VCH Wiltshire*, ii. 2–3; J. N. L. Myres, *The English Settlements* (Oxford, 1986), esp. Ch. 6. Kemble is quoted from P. Sims-Williams, 'The Settlement of England in Bede and the "Chronicle"', *ASE* 12 (1984), 41.

[2] P. H. Sawyer (ed.), *Anglo-Saxon Charters: An Annotated List and Bibliography*, R. Hist. Soc. Guides and Handbooks, 8 (London, 1968) (henceforward cited by number preceded by S.), S.96; Stenton, *Anglo-Saxon England*, 203–4; *VCH Wiltshire*, ii. 4–5. See also for Sherston, B. Thorpe (ed.), *Florentii Wigorniensis Monachi Chronicon ex Chronicis*, i (London, 1848), 174, a statement from the early decades of the twelfth century at latest. Sawyer (ed.), S.1257 (D. Whitelock (ed.), *English Historical Documents, c.500–1042* (abbr. *EHD*), i (2nd edn., London, 1979), 506–7), for Offa's acquisition of land in Somerset hard by the Wiltshire border.

[3] This is apparent on a small scale from the map in *Britain before the Norman Conquest* (Ordnance Survey).

[4] F. W. Maitland, *Domesday Book and Beyond* (Fontana paperback edn., 1960), 464, counted 4,050 hides. Welldon Finn, 'Assessment of Wiltshire in 1083 and 1086', 383, counted 4,084$\frac{7}{8}$ hides and 74 acres. There were also a number of carucates in the Geld Accounts, possibly newly cultivated land, which did not pay tax (Darby and Welldon Finn (eds.), *Domesday Geography*, 16).

Wiltshire hundreds, the administrative subdivisions of the shire for fiscal, military, police and judicial purposes. Each hundred had a court which should have met monthly,[1] and much of the work involved in compiling Domesday Book employed the hundred officials and assembly. It is only due to the fortunate survival of the account of the 1084 geld that we know there were forty or so of them (although the three versions differ in detail). Because the Geld Accounts existed for purposes very different to Domesday Book, however, it has been difficult to combine information from the two in order to arrive at confident reconstructions of the Wiltshire hundreds. In the detailed study by F. R. Thorn in this volume on pp.31–45 below, the problem has been tackled more thoroughly than previously with auspicious results.

Despite the coincidence between the assessment and the number of hundreds the latter were not regular units, like so many in the Midlands, of one hundred hides each, or a mixture of full, half- and double-hundreds. It is difficult to see beyond the varied figures of the Geld Account hundreds and determine whether this was ever the case in Wiltshire. The Wiltshire hundreds varied in size from nearly 200 hides ('Selkley' and Kinwardstone) to less than twenty ('Frustfield' and Collingbourne Ducis). In two cases, however, Anglo-Saxon charters show areas called Downton and Chalke (equivalent to the Geld Accounts' Stowford), both granted as round hundreds of hides in the tenth century, although they accounted for less in 1086.[2] There is clear evidence that the assessment of the county had fallen since the early tenth century. A list of West Saxon fortresses includes four in Wiltshire, to which 4,800 hides were assigned to provide for their defence. Another list of hidages repeats this figure for Wiltshire.[3] When the reduction to the Domesday figure took place and on what principles is unknown.

In origin many hundreds were areas, often ancient estates, which took their names from king's *tunas* from which they were administered by royal reeves. A number of Wiltshire hundreds were named after manors in 1086. Of these, four had been held by King Edward TRE and were still royal manors (Calne, Chippenham, Warminster, Amesbury), while two manors which had formerly been in the possession of Earl Harold and his sister had been taken into royal hands by that date (Melksham, Westbury). Cricklade was named after a borough held partly by Westminster Abbey, and partly by the king. Mere, Highworth, Heytesbury and Alderbury Hundreds must also have been named after royal *tunas* but by the time of the survey the royal presence is only attested indirectly.[4] Before the Conquest kings had already begun to grant rights over hundreds to favoured churches and persons. About a quarter of the Wiltshire hundreds may have been granted away by the king by the time of Domesday Book. They were a source of profit to their holders, but they did not amount to a serious diminution of royal control, for serious crime was not included in the rights alienated. Where they exist, charters are usually vague about these rights before the twelfth century, but there is little reason to doubt that where hundredal manors or complete hundreds were not in royal hands, some or all of the jurisdiction over the hundred had also been transferred.

Several hundredal manors had been taken out of royal hands by the time of the Domesday survey. All of Ramsbury Hundred belonged to the Bishop of Salisbury, and his manor of Bishops Cannings was conterminous with the hundred of the same name.[5] Damerham was granted to the Abbey of Glastonbury as a round hundred of hides, although by 1086 its holding had been reduced to fifty-two out of a total of sixty-three, and at Downton the Bishop of Winchester held the full

[1] Whitelock (ed.), 'The Hundred Ordinance', *EHD*, i. 429–30; for hundreds in general, see H. R. Loyn, 'The Hundred in England in the Tenth and Eleventh Centuries', *British Government and Administration*, eds. H. Hearder and H. R. Loyn (Cardiff, 1974), 1–15.

[2] See p.14, n.3, and p.17, n.5 below. Collingbourne Ducis, when used as a hundred-name, is cited elsewhere in this volume and in Box 1 of the accompanying map as Collingbourne (Ducis). For simplicity, however, the suffix is not enclosed in parentheses when used in the body of the text, even when the hundred-name is intended.

[3] For the Burghal Hidage, see S. Keynes and M. Lapidge (eds. and trans.), *Alfred the Great* (Harmondsworth, 1983), 193–4, 339–41. The County Hidage is not securely dated: see Sawyer, *Roman Britain to Norman England*, 228–9; D. Hill, *An Atlas of Anglo-Saxon England* (Oxford, 1981), 96–7.

[4] Sawyer, *Roman Britain to Norman England*, 199–200. In 1255 Mere Hundred was held with the manor by the king's gift (*Rotuli Hundredorum*, ii (Record Commission, London, 1818), 230); although there were no royal estates in Highworth or Heytesbury in 1086 and the manors were not surveyed separately, their churches were both royal; similarly, the main holding at Alderbury was not surveyed but the church was royal.

[5] The hundred of Bishops Cannings may have been created out of a larger unit for the benefit of the bishop (Gover *et al.*, *Place-Names of Wiltshire*, 249). Bishops Cannings, like Collingbourne Ducis (see n.2 above) is used without parentheses in the text of this article.

hundred hides in the tenth century. It is possible that the grant of Bradford on Avon to Shaftesbury in 1001 included the lands that later made up the hundred (ninety-nine hides in the Geld Account). Although the nuns held only half of it in 1086, the abbess claimed in the thirteenth century that they had held the hundred too.[1] Curiously, the small manor of 'Frustfield' (divided between four minor lay holders in 1086) also named a hundred, though there is no evidence of either a royal or ecclesiastical presence there.

The remaining hundreds were named after natural features, often their ancient meeting-places, and about them little is known. Kinwardstone Hundred belonged to the manors of Wexcombe and Bedwyn from 1255, and as Bedwyn was one of the royal manors assessed for the 'farm of one night' it is likely that the hundred had always been dependent on this estate.[2] The hundred of 'Cawdon' may have been dependent on the royal manor of Britford which lay within it. A few more hundreds were, or were claimed as, private jurisdictions in the eleventh century. There is no firm evidence that Wilton Abbey had Stowford before the thirteenth century, but since the previous century it had been named after the manor of Chalke. As this was granted to the nuns in 955 as 100 hides they probably held the hundred with the manor. In 1086 the nuns retained seventy-seven of 105 hides.[3] In 'Whorwellsdown' the Romsey manors of (Steeple and West) Ashton and Edington accounted for seventy of seventy-eight hides in the hundred. Edgar's charter does not mention hundredal rights but this is not unusual and the jurisdiction may well have belonged to the nuns.[4] 'Wonderditch' may have been appurtenant to the Bishop of Salisbury's manor of Salisbury which accounted for fifty of seventy hides in the hundred. He certainly had it by 1084.[5] The Abbey of Malmesbury's claim to have held the three hundreds of Malmesbury, Startley and Chedglow (the Domesday "Cicementone") since before the Conquest must be rejected on the evidence of Domesday. Although the monks held most of "Cicementone" Hundred, it is clear from the survey that the hundreds of "Cicementone" and Startley were still royal in the eleventh century, and that the borough was not yet regarded as a hundred.[6]

The areas of the hundreds were variable not only in proportion to the number of hides in each, but also because the hide was not a fixed measurement of land but a rating for royal dues and public burdens. The agricultural and other resources and the values of estates with the same assessment could vary widely (see the examples in Table 1 opposite). Some manors were heavily assessed, others more lightly. The most extreme example of beneficial hidation in Wiltshire is the royal manor of Britford. Here, land assessed at only one hide for royal services turns out in fact to contain a substantial estate worked by nineteen plough-teams with a recorded population of forty-eight peasants and with the considerable annual value of £30 'by weight'. The power to reduce assessment was used as a political tool after the Conquest, notably by Henry I, and the pre-Conquest monarchs were aware of this possibility too. The subdivisions of the hide, the virgate (quarter-hide) and the acre were also artificial units. The evidence of Wiltshire Domesday suggests that between forty and forty-eight acres were reckoned to the hide for tax purposes.[7] Like many of the counties south of the Thames, Wiltshire was heavily assessed to geld in 1066. But whereas the south-eastern counties had their hidation reduced by between one- and almost two-thirds by 1087, only two reductions are recorded for Wiltshire and one of these was granted before the Conquest (Corsham and Calcutt, ff.65 and 73v). In the next century the county continued to pay heavily when geld was taken.[8]

A comparison of the hidation of estates for which Anglo-Saxon charters survive with their equivalents recorded in Domesday shows a remarkable stability in assessments, apart from some examples cited above. Estates granted in the tenth century and sometimes before have identical

[1] See p.18, n.1 below. *VCH Wiltshire*, v (1957), 46, expresses some doubt about Bradford Hundred.

[2] H. M. Cam, *Liberties and Communities in Medieval England: Collected Studies in Local Administration and Topography* (Cambridge, 1944; repr. London, 1963), 68. Bedwyn presents a problem as it was both a manor and a borough at the time of the survey. Only the manor, which encompassed both Great and Little Bedwyn (NGR SU 2764, SU 2966), is named in DB, but the borough (mentioned indirectly on f.64v) is known from later evidence to have lain at Great Bedwyn alone. For simplicity, Bedwyn is used without affixes where it occurs in the body of this article.

[3] *Rotuli Hundredorum*, ii. 249.

[4] See p.18, n.3 below.

[5] *VCH Wiltshire*, vi (1962), 195.

[6] GDB 64v; *VCH Wiltshire*, vi. 46–7.

[7] See Stenton, *Anglo-Saxon England*, 479; *VCH Wiltshire*, ii. 182–3; Darby and Welldon Finn (eds.), *Domesday Geography*, 14–15.

[8] Maitland, *Domesday Book and Beyond*, 464–7, 530–1, 545–6.

assessments in 1087 as at the time of donation. *Ellendune* ('Elingdon' in Wroughton), for example, was given to Ælfheah in 956 with a hidation of thirty hides, the same as it bore in 1087. Dauntsey's reckoning at ten hides may be traced back as far as *c.*850, if the thirteenth-century copy of King Æthelwulf's charter was based on a genuine diploma.[1] At first sight the Church of Wilton's large manor of Chalke, which consisted of several modern parishes, contradicts this pattern. In Domesday Book its assessment of seventy-seven hides was substantially smaller than the original grant of 100 hides in 955, but it is probable that the missing twenty-three hides, consisting of Tollard Royal and Ebbesborne Wake, had been alienated.[2] While it is not unusual to find inconsistencies between the assessments of estates in Domesday and at some earlier time, there are several possible explanations.[3]

Nearly half the Wiltshire manors were assessed at five hides or multiples of that figure. In many more cases a vill which was divided into several manors had a total assessment of five hides or a multiple (see Table 1 below). And although there is no evidence of this in practice, it is likely that neighbouring vills with odd assessments formed groups with decimal assessments. The nearby vills of Codford and Ashton Gifford, for example, in which there were four manors, add up to fifteen hides. While it was not universal in Wiltshire or the many other counties of England where decimal assessments predominated, this is what Round called 'a vast system of artificial hidation', which is clear from a comparison of the resources of different vills rated at five or ten hides.[4]

TABLE 1: Comparison of resources of some Wiltshire manors

Manor and folio number	Hides	Plough-lands	Ploughs	Population	value TRE as recorded	value TRW as recorded
(?)Bincknoll, 71	5	2	2	8	40*s.*	50*s.*
71	$1\frac{3}{4}$	$\frac{3}{4}$	*	1	*	18*s.*
71	$3\frac{1}{4}$	$1\frac{1}{4}$	*	2	20*s.*	27*s.*
Broad Hinton, 71	10	4	3	11	100*s.*	100*s.*
Colerne, 71	10	12	11	28	£10	£10
Dauntsey, 66v	10	6	6	12	£6	£6
(Great and Little) Chalfield, 70	$2\frac{1}{2}$	2	1	5	£4	50*s.*
Hazelbury, 71	5	5	5	22	£6	£6
Littleton Drew, 66	5	8	7	16	£7	£7
(?Longbridge) Deverill, 66v	10	9	9	52	*	£12
Poole Keynes (now Glos.), 69v	5	5	5	14	100*s.*	£6
Poulton (near Cirencester, now Glos.), 68v	5	8	8	23	£12	£16
Uffcott, 71	$1\frac{1}{2}$	1	1	*	15*s.*	15*s.*
74	$3\frac{1}{2}$	$1\frac{1}{2}$	*	*	*	30*s.*
Yatton Keynell, 70	5	3	2	8	30*s.*	50*s.*

*details not recorded

The estate of five hides had a special significance in later Anglo-Saxon England, for it was considered the appropriate possession of a thegn. Although it is clear that many men who had a thegn's privileges held rather more or less than the ideal, two treatises of the early eleventh century agree that one condition necessary for a free peasant (*ceorl*) to qualify for the thegn's wergeld was land of five hides.[5] In neighbouring Berkshire five hides of land was clearly associated with military service, because of the following custom:

> If the king sent out an army anywhere only one thegn (*miles*) went from (each) five hides, and for his sustenance or pay 4*s.* for two months was given to him from each hide. This money, however, was not sent to the king but given to the thegns.

Exactly how this arrangement worked is not clear and it was complicated by the existence of estates of more and less than five hides. Smallholders may have clubbed together to equip and pay one of

[1] Sawyer (ed.), S.585; GDB 65v; Sawyer (ed.), S.301; GDB 66v.
[2] Sawyer (ed.), S.582; GDB 68; *VCH Wiltshire*, ii. 91.
[3] Darlington examined the pre-Conquest documents for Wiltshire in *VCH Wiltshire*, ii. 85–98.
[4] J. H. Round, *Feudal England* (London, 1895), 49, and the general survey at 44–90. See also Darby and Welldon Finn (eds.), *Domesday Geography*, 16–17, and *VCH Wiltshire*, ii. 48–9. I have counted sixty-two five-hide manors.
[5] *Gethyncthо* and *Northleodalaga* in Whitelock (ed.), *EHD*, i. 468–9.

their number, or they may have found a substitute, or they may have had a lord who provided a soldier from his following. Greater landowners who had the service from many hides need not have taken a man from each five hides, but were free to maintain warriors in their households (the size of a lord's following was a reflection of his wealth and prestige). Moreover, if they did endow their followers with land, it was not incumbent upon them to give the full five hides.[1] The personnel of the late Old English army were well equipped for the warfare of the era. Laws more often represent ideal than reality, but from the end of the tenth century warriors were expected to be mounted (for mobility) and armed with sword, spear, helmet, and shield; and mailcoats were widespread too.[2]

Compared to some English counties, the boundaries of Wiltshire have changed little since the middle of the eleventh century. Some adjustments were made at the end of the nineteenth century when parishes were transferred between neighbouring shires (see Table 2 below). Two places along the Berkshire border were divided at the time of the survey. Of five manors in Shalbourne four were in Wiltshire but over half the assessment (six and a half hides) was in the next county. Coleshill was primarily in Berkshire, with three manors of eight hides each, divided between three holders (ff.59v, 61, 63). A further one hide, however, also divided between three owners, was in Wiltshire (f.72v, at the foot of the second column). This and the way the border between the two counties follows estate boundaries and field patterns suggest that the division between Wiltshire and Berkshire was laid out much later than most West Saxon shires, and ran over existing arrangements. Two parts of Dorset were surveyed in Wiltshire, for reasons which are not apparent, and a fragment of West Tytherley in Hampshire was included in its owner's nearby manor at West Winterslow, probably for convenience. West Dean and Latton were also divided in 1086, with neighbouring Hampshire and Gloucestershire respectively, but have since been wholly taken into Wiltshire.[3]

TABLE 2: Alterations to Wiltshire, 1086–present

Places in Domesday Wiltshire not in the county as restructured in 1974

Poulton (near Cirencester)	65v	to Gloucestershire, 1844
Somerford Keynes	66	to Gloucestershire, 1897
Damerham	66v, 67v	to Hampshire, 1895
Kemble	67	to Gloucestershire, 1897
Long Newnton	67	to Gloucestershire, 1930
Gussage St Michael	69	in Dorset, wrongly included in Wiltshire
Poole Keynes	69v	to Gloucestershire, 1897
North Standen	70	to Berkshire, 1895
'Charlton' (in Hungerford)	71v	to Berkshire, 1895
Ashley	71v	to Gloucestershire, 1930
Standen	72	to Berkshire, 1895
Shorncote	73	to Gloucestershire, 1897
Gillingham	73v	in Dorset, wrongly included in Wiltshire
Bramshaw	74 (x2)	to Hampshire, 1895
Plaitford	74	to Hampshire, 1895
West Tytherley (part)	74	to Hampshire, ?late Middle Ages (parts surveyed in both shires)

Places transferred to Wiltshire since 1086

Bagshot	from Berkshire, 1895
Kilmington	from Somerset, 1896
Latton (part)	from Gloucestershire, ?Middle Ages (parts surveyed in both shires)
Shalbourne (part)	from Berkshire, 1895 (parts surveyed in both shires)
West Dean (part)	from Hampshire, 1883 (parts surveyed in both shires)
Yarnfield	from Somerset, 1896

[1] GDB 56v. There is an extensive literature on this subject. See C. W. Hollister, *Anglo-Saxon Military Institutions on the Eve of the Norman Conquest* (Oxford, 1962), Chs. 3–5; R. Abels, 'Bookland and Fyrd Service', *Proc. of the Battle Conference 1984*, vii (1985), 1–25; J. Gillingham, 'The Introduction of Knight-Service into England', *Proc. of the Battle Conference 1981*, iv (1982), 53–64, esp. pp.61–4; Hooper, 'An Introduction to the Berkshire Domesday', *The Berkshire Domesday*, 18–20.

[2] See N. P. Brooks, 'Arms, Status and Warfare in Late-Saxon England', *Ethelred the Unready: Papers from the Millenary Conference*, ed. D. Hill, BAR Brit. ser. 59 (1978), 81–103.

[3] GDB 69, 73v, 74, 48v, 170.

THE KING'S LAND

The dominant landowner in post-Conquest Wiltshire was King William. The hidation of the royal estates gives no indication of their real value, for the *Terra Regis* had a value of £1,000, nearly a quarter of the total value of land in the county and a significant part of the total royal revenues from land (see Table 4, p.22). These vast lands had been acquired by the Crown in diverse ways over several centuries. The first seven listed had been King Edward's. Six had been organized to pay the 'farm of one night' (*firma unius noctis*), a food-rent considered sufficient to support the royal household for a day and a night. Although it was a type of render to be found in many of the southern counties in the eleventh century, there is no evidence of the form it then took. Two charters, from the late eighth and ninth centuries, refer to food-rents due from estates in neighbouring Gloucestershire. One owed the king three varieties of ale, oxen and wethers, cheeses and cereals. The other rendered ale and beer, honey, bullocks, swine and sheep.[1] Cash values were given for only two of these Wiltshire estates in 1086 when they were worth £110 and £100 (Chippenham and Tilshead), and none in 1066, so it is possible that the rent was still being taken in supplies for the royal court. All were large single manors which included several neighbouring vills not mentioned in Domesday Book. As a result of their extent the area surrounding each appears as a blank on the map. None of the six performed royal services and had never been assessed in hides. Four of them were the heads of hundreds and so their values included the profits of justice from the hundred courts. The greatest of all was Chippenham, whose arable was worked by eighty-three ploughs, although the statement that there was land for 100 suggests it was not being worked to capacity.

The last of Edward's estates was Britford, where he based himself in the crisis at the end of 1065 when the Northumbrians rebelled against Tosti, their earl.[2] It had the purely nominal assessment of one hide, although it paid £30 'by weight' (*ad pensum*). This was a way of ensuring that royal revenue remained buoyant when the weight of the coinage diminished, as it would through wear, clipping or deliberate manipulation by the government.[3] It has been calculated that one pound's weight of the issue of coins in circulation in 1086 consisted of 254 silver pennies (the only coin then in existence), so that at face value Britford would have paid £31. 15*s*.

The second block of royal lands had been the property of the Godwine family and consisted of twelve manors. As earl, Harold possessed 229 hides, of which William kept the majority, 154 hides, with a value of £273. Chief of them was the great manor of Melksham with its hundred. Its value was £111. 11*s*. 'by weight' which with its size makes it look like a former royal manor assessed for the 'farm of one night' before the earl or a predecessor acquired it. Harold's mother Gytha also possessed substantial property in the county (three manors, 100½ hides, £137 in 1086) and his exiled brother Tosti had two estates. At Corsham we see an example of beneficial hidation in the reduction of the assessment from thirty-four to eighteen hides. These lands became available to William early in his reign: Harold and Tosti died in the battles of 1066 and their mother chose voluntary exile with many other women, probably in 1068.[4] Another member of the family holding land in Wiltshire lasted rather longer. Godwine's daughter Edith married Edward in 1045 and probably retained her estates until her death in 1075. Her four manors amounted to eighty-seven hides with a value in 1086 of £190.[5] Winterbourne Stoke was obviously beneficially assessed at two and a quarter hides although there was land for twelve ploughs worth £33. The forty hides at Westbury comprised the whole hundred and the value of £100 hints that this too may have been a great royal estate granted to his wife by Edward.

[1] Sawyer (ed.), S.146 (Whitelock (ed.), *EHD*, i. 507) and S.218 (F. E. Harmer, *Select English Historical Documents* (Cambridge, 1914), 20–2, 53–4, 113–15). See P. A. Stafford, 'The "Farm of One Night" and the Organization of King Edward's Estates in Domesday', *EconHR* 2nd ser., 33 (1980), 491–502. Chippenham, Calne, Warminster and Amesbury were hundredal manors.

[2] F. Barlow, *Edward the Confessor* (London, 1970), 236–40.

[3] See H. R. Loyn, *The Governance of Anglo-Saxon England, 500–1087* (London, 1984), 122–6, 192–4; S. P. J. Harvey, 'Royal Revenue and Domesday Terminology', *EconHR* 2nd ser., 20 (1967), 221–2.

[4] *Anglo-Saxon Chronicle* (abbr. *ASC*), 1067 D, D. C. Douglas and G. W. Greenaway (eds.), *EHD 1042–1189*, ii (London, 1953), 148.

[5] (?West) Lavington was granted by William to Robert Marshal (f.73).

The remainder of the *Terra Regis* consisted of miscellaneous items. For most royal estates in Wiltshire the value of the church was entered with its owner. The most remarkable was that of Netheravon held by Nigel the physician (*medicus*) with one hide. Domesday describes it as derelict and half-ruined, yet it was worth the surprising sum of £32 with its appurtenances, though what there was amongst these which made it so valuable is not divulged by the survey. At the end of this section is a list of eleven royal churches, although the manors were in other hands.[1] There were three other royal estates. There is a blank in the manuscript where the pre-Conquest owner of Ogbourne St George should have been entered. Land there had been bequeathed to his brother in the will of Ealdorman Æthelwold in the middle of the previous century but its subsequent history is unknown.[2]

East Knoyle and Lydiard Millicent were granted to William fitzOsbern, Duke William's seneschal and Earl of Hereford, early in the reign. The king regained them in 1075 when Earl Roger, Earl William's younger son and the heir to his English lands, rebelled and was sentenced to perpetual imprisonment and forfeiture. William fitzOsbern had also held part of the royal manor of Amesbury, but as Domesday Book explains, 'Earl William gave "Quintone" and Swindon and (?Great) Cheverell . . . for land in the Isle of Wight, which belonged to the farm of Amesbury.'[3] Two more Normans had suffered the confiscation of their lands, although they were entered in separate chapters and not under the *Terra Regis*. Odo, Bishop of Bayeux and Earl of Kent, the king's half-brother and a great prince in Normandy and England, held for many years a key role in William's kingdom. He came under suspicion of treason and was arrested and imprisoned in 1082. He briefly recovered his liberty and lands in the reign of William Rufus, before losing them permanently for rebellion. His Wiltshire estates were not extensive and all were held by tenants who weathered their master's downfall. One among them is of particular interest, for the Wadard who held Swindon is depicted on the Bayeux Tapestry and was associated with the bishop in Normandy.[4] Aubrey de Couci, a man with substantial estates in the Midlands, was appointed earl beyond the Tees after the suppression of a rebellion in 1080, but he soon resigned his rule over this turbulent region and forfeited his English possessions in consequence. His Wiltshire lands were listed in a separate chapter with the note that they were 'in the king's hands'. In Warwickshire Aubrey's lands were let out at farm to Geoffrey de la Guerche, a local landowner, but if there was a similar arrangement in this county there is no record of it. His chapter includes the Dorset manor of Gussage St Michael, Aubrey's only possession in that county. This is perhaps an indication that his estates in the south-west were returned as one fief rather than county by county. It is noteworthy also that none of his ten Wiltshire manors was held by any tenant, perhaps an indication of the short time for which he held them.

The chief royal officer in each county was the sheriff ('shire-reeve') who came into greater prominence after the Conquest with the abolition of the great Anglo-Saxon earldoms. He saw to the administration of royal demesnes, overseeing the reeves who ran the individual estates, and collected the various sums due to the Crown. In Wiltshire the 'farm of the shire' consisted of the rents in money and kind from the royal estates, the payments from the boroughs, profits of jurisdiction from shire and hundred courts and the annual 'gift' of money for a hawk, packhorse and hay (f.64v). The only reference to the pre-Conquest sheriff is in Domesday Book, an incidental note that Eadric had leased out a parcel of the royal estate of Chippenham. A writ from early in the reign of King William shows that Eadric, like many Englishmen in local administration, stayed in office, although for how long is not known. The sheriff at the end of William's reign was Edward of Salisbury, whose name indicates that he too was English. He probably paid the king a lump sum (*firma* or 'farm') and kept anything extra he could take. Not surprisingly, some sheriffs were

[1] Bedwyn is an exception: the church appears to have been omitted from the details of the royal estate given on the preceding folio.

[2] Sawyer (ed.), S.1504 (printed in Harmer, *Select English Historical Documents*, 33, 63–4, 116–19).

[3] GDB 64v; *VCH Hampshire*, i (1900), 408.

[4] D. R. Bates, 'The Character and Career of Odo, Bishop of Bayeux', *Speculum*, 1 (1975), 1–20. For Wadard, see N. P. Brooks and the late H. E. Walker, 'The Authority and Interpretation of the Bayeux Tapestry', *Proc. of the Battle Conference 1978*, i (1979), 8, 18 and 192–3 (where his Wiltshire holdings are not noted).

renowned for their rapacity. In Edward's case he was bound to make an extra payment of £60 'by weight', an indication of the scale of profit that a zealous sheriff could make on his own account. From the 'pennies which pertain to the shrievalty' Edward received a considerable amount of foodstuffs, as well as £80 from 'reeveland'. What this consisted of is not clear. It might have been land which the sheriff held so long as he was in office, although whether it was included under the royal demesne or Edward's fief on folio 69 is unknown. Or it could mean that he normally received £80 more than he passed on to the king. Either way, he had the responsibility of making up any shortfall in the revenues of the reeves in a bad year. Edward's reach also extended into neighbouring counties. He farmed the revenues of Bath in Somerset, which he paid with the Wiltshire farm, and he had acquired the farm of Woodchester in Gloucestershire too, although, it is stated, 'unjustly'.[1]

The Land of the Church

The greatest landowner in eleventh-century Wiltshire was the Church, or more accurately, a group of ecclesiastical institutions whose possessions accounted for nearly half of the assessment of the shire. As in every other county, the survey of the lands of the Church stood next to that of the king in Domesday Book and preceded the manors of the lay magnates. The ecclesiastical tenants were listed in strict order: first the bishops, next the native houses of men followed by the nuns, then the foreign house of Bec and finally some miscellaneous clerics. Among the ecclesiastical landlords were houses which went back to the seventh century, almost to the beginnings of Christianity in Wessex, and others of more recent origin. The Norman Conquest had little impact on the Church as landowner in Wiltshire, although of course the rulers of the Old English Church were displaced almost as completely as the lay aristocracy. Three Norman bishops acquired lands in the county. Bishops Odo of Bayeux and Geoffrey of Coutances were great secular lords in England who stood among William's most trusted lieutenants and received rich grants of land. Although they are listed under the clergy, they held their English possessions as lay barons. Gilbert Maminot, Bishop of Lisieux, was a confidant of the king, his chaplain, doctor and friend. The canons of his cathedral also held one manor in the county in 1086, at Kingston Deverill. The only Norman abbey holding as a tenant-in-chief in Wiltshire at the time of the survey was the great monastery at Bec which had Brixton Deverill as a gift from Queen Matilda. However, there were other Norman churches that did profit from the Conquest and which received properties in Wiltshire (see Table 3 below). This was not a process which had ended when Domesday Book was made, for Norman kings and barons continued to make gifts to churches in their homeland. A major gift in Wiltshire was Henry I's gift of Tilshead, worth £100 in 1086, to his mother's church of La Trinite, Caen.[2]

TABLE 3: Norman churches holding in Wiltshire 1086

Church and folio number	holding	held from	value as recorded
Saint-Wandrille, 65	Rushall Church	the king	40*s*.
65v	Sherston Church	the king	28*s*.
65v	Upavon Church	the king	£10 15*s*.
Saint-Etienne, Caen, 65	Corsham Church	the king	£7
Mont-Saint-Michel, 65	Wootton Rivers, two churches	the king	20*s*.
Saint-Pierre, Jumieges, 65	Winterbourne Stoke Church	the king	20*s*.
Sainte-Marie, Bec, 68v	Brixton Deverill	(held as tenant-in-chief)	£12
Canons of Lisieux Cathedral, 68v	Kingston Deverill	(held as tenant-in-chief)	70*s*.
Sainte-Marie, Grestain, 68v	Conock	Count of Mortain	£9
Saint-Etienne, Fontenay, 72v	Middleton	Osbern Giffard	50*s*.
Sainte-Marie, Montebourg, 73	Sutton Veny	Nigel the physician	100*s*.

[1] GDB 64v, 69–69v, 87 (Bath), 164 (Woodchester); *VCH Wiltshire*, ii. 62–3.

[2] H. W. C. Davis *et al.* (eds.), *Regesta Regum Anglo-Normannorum*, ii (Oxford, 1956), no. 1692.

The endowments of the Wiltshire churches were built up over a considerable period through the pious donations of kings and the laity, and through purchase and exchange. For many ecclesiastical estates Anglo-Saxon diplomas have survived, of varying degrees of authenticity, which make it possible in many cases to reconstruct their history, to see how land ownership changed and to improve our knowledge of certain manors.

Two English bishoprics held manors in the county, Salisbury and Winchester. In 1086 Wiltshire was part of the diocese of Salisbury, where the see had only been removed since the Conquest. In 909 the bishopric of Wiltshire and Berkshire was carved out of the territory of Winchester and the new bishop was established at Ramsbury, the centre of a large estate on the border of the two counties. By the eleventh century it was clearly felt to be an unsuitable site, remote and impoverished, and possibly without suitable buildings. Bishop Herman sought self-imposed exile after his attempt to translate the see to the rich monastery of Malmesbury was successfully resisted. He returned in 1058 after the diocese of Sherborne was added to his jurisdiction, and until the move to Salisbury (in fact the hill-fort known as Old Sarum) he may have been based at the monasteries of Sherborne and Wilton. In 1086 there was still a community of priests at Ramsbury, holding a small part of the manor, but nothing more is known of the organization of the diocese before its relocation was authorized at the Council of London in 1075.[1] The great bulk of this see's endowment lay in Wiltshire, where its estates were assessed at 267 hides and their value was put at more than £300. It was made up of no more than five manors, of which Charnage was assessed for only five hides. The remaining four, however, were immense. The least was Salisbury, assessed at fifty hides with a value of £77 and a recorded population of ninety-five peasants with thirty-two ploughs. The greatest was Ramsbury: the value of its ninety hides was put at £70 and the recorded population was 151 peasants with fifty-four ploughs. Each of these contained settlements not surveyed separately in Domesday, but the absence of early charters from the Salisbury archive means that they are difficult to identify and their history cannot be traced.[2]

The Bishops of Winchester retained very extensive lands in Wiltshire, nearly as much as the bishop of the shire. Already by the time of the survey the estates of the see had been formally divided between the monks of the Old Minster and the bishop. By this arrangement the latter had three manors assessed at 110 hides with a value of £125. The largest was Downton which originally consisted of a full hundred hides until five were taken away by Cnut (1016–35). No less than seven diplomas concerning land at Downton were preserved in the Winchester cartulary, the Codex Wintoniensis, the oldest of which purports to be Cenwealh's grant to the Old Minster in the late seventh century. The tradition may be correct, but most of these documents have a poor reputation for authenticity. Æthelræd II, who took land from several churches in his 'period of youthful indiscretions', confiscated it, although the land was restored when, as he is made to say in a charter of 997, he realized the error of his ways as he grew older. The 100 hides appear to have been in two fragments, fifty-five hides of Downton itself and a further forty-five hides along the river Ebble which embraced further settlements.[3]

The manors assigned to the support of the monks came to a little more than 147 hides. Diplomas for many of them were entered into the Winchester cartulary, but it is not often obvious how the estates were acquired from lay owners. Ham was first granted by Athelstan in 931 to the thegn Wulfgar, who later bequeathed it to the Old Minster.[4] Other estates (for example Westwood, 'East Overton' and Bushton) were first granted to laymen by tenth-century monarchs and the preser-

[1] See F. Barlow, *The English Church 1000–1066* (2nd edn., London, 1979), 201; F. Barlow, *The English Church 1066–1154* (London, 1979), 48. The only Anglo-Saxon work at Ramsbury is some architectural fragments difficult to date: see H. M. and J. Taylor, *Anglo-Saxon Architecture*, ii (Cambridge, 1965), 502–3.

[2] GDB 66. Potterne probably contained Worton and Marston; the large parish of Bishops Canning included Bourton, Horton and probably Roundway, as well as the detached Chittoe and possibly the Devizes area; Ramsbury included at least Baydon and Bishopstone; Salisbury included the site of the modern city, Stratford sub Castle and Lower, Middle and Upper Woodford.

[3] GDB 65v. Standlynch (ff.72(x2), 73v), Barford St Martin (f.72) and Witherington (f.74) make up the lost five hides. Charters for Downton: Sawyer (ed.), S.229, S.275, S.393, S.540, S.818, S.821, S.1515 (King Eadræd's will, printed in Whitelock (ed.), *EHD*, i. 554–6), and S.891 (see S. Keynes, *The Diplomas of Æthelred II 'the Unready' 978–1016* (Cambridge, 1980), 225, also 101, 176–86). Sawyer (ed.), S.861 granted five hides of Downton to a thegn while it was confiscated. For the extent, see *VCH Wiltshire*, ii. 84–5.

[4] Sawyer (ed.), S.416, S.1533.

vation of the charters in the Codex argues that they were subsequently bequeathed or sold to the community.[1] Fonthill Bishop was acquired by exchange with Ealdorman Ordlaf at the beginning of the tenth century.[2] Some of the Winchester diplomas refer to lands in Wiltshire which were no longer in the possession of the Old Minster in 1066. In addition to Downton, King Eadræd bequeathed Calne and Damerham to Winchester, but the donation appears not to have taken effect. In 1086 Calne was still royal demesne while Damerham was held by Glastonbury and Cranborne.[3] What kings gave, they or their successors could also take, and there were other ways in which churches could lose or dispose of estates.

On assessment alone the possessions of Malmesbury were the most extensive in the county, although somewhat less valuable than those of Glastonbury (see Table 4, p.22). Some of the Malmesbury estates were very large. Brokenborough was granted as 100 hides, although it was assessed at fifty hides in Domesday Book. It included, in addition to the modern parish of Brokenborough, land at Grittenham (in Brinkworth), Sutton Benger, Rodbourne (near Malmesbury), Corston, Cole Park and Bremilham (in Foxley). Of these, only Corston was mentioned separately in the survey.[4] The documents preserved in the Malmesbury cartulary have often been treated with scepticism. They include a number of obvious fabrications or charters which have at least been doctored in favour of the community. It is also suspicious that most of the grants are from kings and that Malmesbury, almost alone among English monasteries, claimed success in retaining intact most of its early endowment. But copies of charters which purport to date back to the foundation of the house in the late seventh century, perhaps written by the great scholar Aldhelm, do seem to contain early formulae and authentic material. Such diplomas refer to extensive grants at Long Newnton (now in Gloucestershire), in Kemble (now in Gloucestershire) and other places, at Wootton Bassett, Somerford Keynes (now in Gloucestershire) and Great Somerford. They were the gifts of nobles as well as kings, and of both Mercian and West Saxon rulers, a reflection of Malmesbury's location on the fringes of the two kingdoms.[5] Much of the property at the last two places would appear to have been lost by the eleventh century.

In the following centuries the community continued to attract gifts, and the cartulary contains diplomas in the names of Ine, Cynewulf and Æthelwulf of Wessex, and Ecgfrith of Mercia, although few of them are acceptable in their existing form.[6] At the end of the ninth century Alfred appropriated Chelworth (in Crudwell), which was reckoned as part of Kemble at the time of the Domesday survey, with the consent of the community, and leased it to his thegn Dudi for the term of four lives. When the lease expired the land was to revert to Malmesbury. Such short-term loans of land to kings were not always made voluntarily. They represented an easy way by which kings could acquire resources to reward their followers, but it was often difficult for the church to regain possession of land which had been in lay hands. In this case the land passed to Ealdorman Ordlaf as early as 901 and although he agreed to restore Chelworth to the abbot, his price was the lease of another estate for five lives.[7]

Of the tenth-century kings, Athelstan was remembered at Malmesbury as the great benefactor of the community who was reputed to have given it estates, a gold cross with a fragment of the True Cross and other holy relics. It was at his behest that the bodies of his two cousins, who fell in battle at *Brunanburh*, were buried there, and his own body was interred before the high altar, a sign of the esteem in which he held the community. However, none of his diplomas preserved in the

[1] Sawyer (ed.), S.867, S.449 and S.547, S.848. S.846, also for Bushton (AD 983), is spurious as it stands (Keynes, *Diplomas of Æthelred II*, 241–2); Sawyer (ed.), S.427 and S.312–13 are also suspicious. For the hidages, see *VCH Wiltshire*, ii. 85–6.

[2] Sawyer (ed.), S.1284 has suspicious features, but Ordlaf's letter proves that the exchange occurred, see Whitelock (ed.), *EHD*, i. 544–6.

[3] See p.2, n.3 above, and *VCH Wiltshire*, ii. 86–7, for lost estates.

[4] Sawyer (ed.), S.629; see *VCH Wiltshire*, ii. 87–90. Bremhill, Long Newnton (Glos.), Crudwell and Kemble (Glos.) were extensive manors whose dependent settlements were also not surveyed separately in DB.

[5] Sawyer (ed.), S.71, S.73, S.231, S.234, S.1166, S.1169–70. Recent work suggests they have been unjustly rejected; see H. P. R. Finberg, *The Early Charters of Wessex* (Leicester, 1964); H. Edwards, 'Two Documents from Aldhelm's Malmesbury', *Bull. of the Inst. of Hist. Research* 59 (1986), 1–19. Darlington, *VCH Wiltshire*, ii. 3, n.14, commented that only Sawyer (ed.), S.1146 deserves to be entirely rejected.

[6] Sawyer (ed.), S.243, S.149, S.301, S.305, S.320.

[7] Ibid. S.356 (AD 871–99), pronounced authentic by D. Whitelock, 'Some Charters in the Name of King Alfred', *Saints, Scholars and Heroes: Essays for C. W. Jones*, eds. M. H. King and W. M. Stevens (Minnesota, 1979), i. 77–98.

Malmesbury cartulary is authentic. Wootton Bassett, one of the lands he is alleged to have given, was no longer a Malmesbury possession by 1066, but there is no need to doubt the community's tradition that Athelstan was their chief benefactor.[1] His successor but two was Eadwig, who was remembered rather less fondly at Malmesbury. William of Malmesbury accused him of turning the abbey into a 'sty of clerks'. But there had not been monks at Malmesbury for decades, if not longer, and reform came only in the reign of Edgar. Nevertheless, Eadwig granted the considerable estate at Brokenborough.[2] From this time on, the flow of benefactions appears to have dried up.[3] In Æthelræd's reign Abbot Brihtwold was forced to alienate property for small sums of money in order to raise his payments to the Danish tributes.[4]

The richest monastery in eleventh-century England was Glastonbury, the former base of the great reformer St Dunstan. Rather more than a quarter of its total endowment of nearly 800 hides lay in Wiltshire. Most of its estates were large, consisting of twenty hides or more, and were spread across the county. As is to be expected of Dunstan's house, the greatest source of lands was royal generosity. Edmund's first grant to Dunstan, after he became abbot, was the twenty hides at Christian Malford in 940. In the middle of the decade he made over to his second wife Æthelflæd an estate of 100 hides at Damerham for her life, after which it was to pass to Glastonbury—a provision which did not take effect for many years as the lady lived into the last quarter of the tenth century. In Domesday Book Glastonbury still held the whole hundred, although the assessment by then was only fifty-two hides.[5] Edmund's brother and successor Eadræd was responsible for the grant of Badbury in 955, and the last recorded royal gift was of land at Kington Langley in 987. Altogether, these accounted for 121 hides in Domesday Book.[6] Another great source of lands was Ælfwine. Edmund and Eadræd gave eighty-five hides in Wiltshire to his father, the thegn Wulfric, in the years 940–8. He was a wealthy landowner most of whose property lay in the south-west. All his Wiltshire estates, together with some elsewhere, ended up in the possession of Glastonbury when Ælfwine entered the community.[7] Kington Langley was a grant from Æthelræd in 987, while Idmiston and Winterbourne Monkton were presumably left to Glastonbury by lay beneficiaries of royal grants, or their descendants.[8] Estates for which both TRE and TRW values were recorded in Domesday Book show a marked increase, from £104 to £160 by 1086. The monks had their first Norman abbot, Turstin of Caen, to thank for this prudent management of their demesnes, even if his rule was excessively harsh in other respects.

New Minster, Winchester, had lands worth less than half the Glastonbury possessions. It was founded by Alfred's son Edward, very early in his reign, if the charters are to be trusted. Diplomas survive for all their Wiltshire estates, although serious problems are attached to some of them. The bulk of their endowment of 132 hides consisted of the two large estates at Collingbourne Kingston and Chiseldon.[9] Finally the minor Dorset house of Cranborne had twenty hides at Ashton Keynes and one hide at Damerham, representing half of its total endowment.

The two wealthiest and most important nunneries in eleventh-century England were Shaftesbury and Wilton. The latter was in Wiltshire, together with practically all of its lands, while the greatest part of the former's extensive estates were also in this county. In the eleventh century Wilton was an important and influential community and cult centre which attracted a number of important women. Edward the Confessor's wife Edith, the daughter of Earl Godwine, was educated with the nuns. She was also sent there while her family were in eclipse in the years 1051–2

[1] Sawyer (ed.), S.415, S.434–6. The Malmesbury pancarte, dated 1065 but fabricated at a later date, also attributes Wootton Bassett to Athelstan; N. E. S. A. Hamilton (ed.), *Willelmi Malmesbiriensis Monachi De Gestis Pontificum Anglorum* (henceforward *Gesta Pontificum*), Rolls ser. 52 (London, 1870), 394–400.

[2] Hamilton (ed.), *Gesta Pontificum*, 403.

[3] Æthelræd II granted ten hides at Rodbourne (Sawyer (ed.), S.841; see Keynes, *Diplomas of Æthelred II*, 240).

[4] For Brihtwold, see Hamilton (ed.), *Gesta Pontificum*, 411, and K. Lawson, 'The Collection of Danegeld and Heregeld in the Reigns of Æthelred II and Cnut', *EHR* 99 (1984), 721–38.

[5] Sawyer (ed.), S.466, S.513, S.1494 (Æthelflæd's will). GDB 66v, and see, for its original extent, *VCH Wiltshire*, ii. 96. It occurs as another unfulfilled bequest in the will of Eadræd.

[6] Sawyer (ed.), S.568, S.866.

[7] Ibid. S.472–3, S.504; cf. the note on Wulfric in C. R. Hart, *The Early Charters of Northern England and the North Midlands* (Leicester, 1975), 371–2.

[8] Sawyer (ed.), S.775, S.341, S.866. For comparison of hidages, see *VCH Wiltshire*, ii. 95–7.

[9] Sawyer (ed.), S.370, S.366 (cf. Whitelock, 'Some Charters', 90–1), S.359 (of dubious authority, but the tradition may be correct), S.1417, S.470, S.865, S.1505, S.746 (marked as spurious; this place is not identified in *VCH Wiltshire*, ii. 87).

and retired to the nunnery after their fall in 1066: she also caused the church to be rebuilt in stone in pious competition with her husband's work at Westminster. After the Conquest, Harold's daughter Gunnhild was also there for a time, and Matilda, the great-granddaughter of Edmund Ironside and the future wife of Henry I, studied in the convent.[1] The Wilton tradition held that the first founder was the Ealdorman Weohstan of Wiltshire who fell in battle in 802, and that the nuns joined a new community which Alfred established in 890. There is no early evidence to support this story, and if there is any value in the date attributed to Alfred's foundation it is curious that there is no reference to it in the biography written in 893 by his friend Asser.[2] The earliest undoubted reference to a convent at Wilton comes from a charter of Athelstan, granting land at Burcombe to the nuns in 937.[3] Following this the Wilton cartulary contains a series of generally reliable diplomas from tenth-century monarchs which account for all the property the community held in 1066, with the exceptions of Wardour and Washern.

Few of these charters were directly in favour of the nuns, and they consisted largely of grants to lay persons. In most cases it is not explained how Wilton got the land, the exception being the small estate at Ditchampton. According to a diploma of Edward the Confessor in the Wilton cartulary, it was granted to the thegn Thorth in 1045. From Domesday the additional information is supplied that he subsequently gave the land to Wilton when his daughters entered the community, and that after 1066 most of the land was seized by Odo of Bayeux. On the other hand, Athelstan's charter of 933 was forged to improve the title to North Newnton, but as Wilton already had the diploma by which Alfred granted the estate to Ealdorman Æthelhelm, it is likely that one of his descendants gave it to the convent.[4] The 231 hides which belonged to Wilton in 1066 were located mainly in the south of the county, the valleys of the Wylye and Nadder and in the Vale of Chalke. At the centre of this collection lay the hundred of Stowford, which originated as a grant of a hundred hides in the area of Chalke, bestowed upon the nuns by Eadwig in 955. By 1066 the abbess had only seventy-seven hides there, but it seems likely that the balance of twenty-three hides at Tollard Royal and Ebbesborne Wake had been alienated or otherwise lost during the intervening century.[5] An isolated group of manors which lay in the centre of the county, in the valleys of the Kennet and upper Avon, consisted of North Newnton, Stanton St Bernard and West Overton.

The charters show that Wilton had also lost estates by the middle of the eleventh century. A confirmation of lands by Edgar included property at Sherrington and an unidentified *Defereal*, neither of which were held by the abbess in 1066. Eadwig's grant of Upton Lovell to a thegn was copied into the cartulary, which suggests he left it to the nuns, but by the time of Domesday this manor was held by the clerk Gerald of Wilton.[6]

The Abbey of Shaftesbury was established by Alfred, before 893, 'near the east gate' of the fortress. His daughter Æthelgifu was its first abbess, and Asser reports that it was richly endowed by Alfred with lands and a portion of his annual revenues. It is difficult to assign any of the Wiltshire estates to his reign, however, because the Shaftesbury foundation-charter recording the grant of land at Donhead and Compton (Compton Bassett in Wiltshire or Compton Abbas in Dorset) is a transparent forgery. The diploma of 956, for land at Donhead and *Estune*, could represent either its original donation or a later restoration.[7] The nuns possessed charters for all their Wiltshire manors, if the diplomas for Teffont Magna (not in Domesday Book) include the land at Dinton.[8] Donhead,

[1] Barlow, *Edward the Confessor*, 80, 115–16, 232–3; R. R. Darlington (ed.), *The Vita Wulfstani of William of Malmesbury*, Camden Soc. 3rd ser., 40, R. Hist. Soc. (London, 1928), 34; W. Stubbs (ed.), *Willelmi Malmesbiriensis Monachi De Gestis Regum Anglorum*, Rolls. Ser. 90, i (London, 1887), 493.

[2] *VCH Wiltshire*, iii (1956), 231; *ASC* 800 (recte 802), Whitelock (ed.), *EHD*, i. 183.

[3] Sawyer (ed.), S.438.

[4] Ibid. S.1010; GDB 68(x2) and 66—under Odo's fief the TRE holder of Ditchampton is given as Azur, who may have been Thorth's tenant or descendant, unwilling to observe the bequest. Sawyer (ed.), S.424.

[5] Ibid. S.582, whose bounds describe the whole hundred and include six hides at Donhead in the next hundred. Wilton had no land there in 1066, but it may be significant that Shaftesbury had a tenancy of that size there (f.67v).

[6] Sawyer (ed.), S.766, S.642; GDB 68v. See *VCH Wiltshire*, ii. 91–3, for the other Wilton estates.

[7] Keynes and Lapidge (eds. and trans.), *Alfred the Great*, Ch.98, p.105, Ch.102, p.107, and p.272, n.237; Sawyer (ed.), S.357, S.850; *Estune* is represented on modern maps by Easton Farm in Berwick St James parish (NGR ST 9421), and probably corresponds to the six-hide tenancy of Turstin from the manor of Donhead (f.67v); *VCH Wiltshire*, xiii (1987), 89–92.

[8] See *VCH Wiltshire*, ii. 94–5.

Tisbury and Dinton (eighty hides), of which the first two were acquired directly from the Crown at the same hidages as in Domesday, were in the south of the county, intermingled with the Wilton lands. In the west, the small Abbey of Bradford on Avon was granted an unspecified area in 1001 as a refuge from Viking attacks for the nuns and their relics. Among those relics were the remains of Æthelræd's martyred half-brother Edward, which had been translated to Shaftesbury in 979. In 1066 the abbess held half of Bradford Hundred, and two centuries later her successor was to claim that the original donation included jurisdiction over it. There may well be some truth in this claim, for the bounds attached to the charter of 1001 show that it included land in the hundred which the nuns no longer possessed in 1066.[1]

Three more nunneries were holding estates in Wiltshire at the time of Domesday. Amesbury was of little significance, and nothing is known of its early history other than that it was founded by Æthelræd's mother Ælfthryth. Two queens before her had held the royal estate at Amesbury, so it is possible that she was in possession when the convent was founded, although by 1066 it was royal demesne again. Its Wiltshire property of thirty-five hides was concentrated in the hundred of Amesbury. The only manor of any size was the twelve-hide estate at Bulford. The Count of Mortain wrongfully held two hides at West Winterslow in 1086. The house was suppressed less than a century after Domesday, its reputation clouded by scandal.[2] Nunnaminster at Winchester, founded by Alfred's wife Ealhswith, held the bulk of its lands in Wiltshire where the forty-eight hides and one and a half virgates consisted of two large manors in the centre of the county, at Urchfont and All Cannings. The former apparently covered the whole of the modern parish, and possibly included the settlements of Eastcott and Wedhampton. In the absence of early charters it is not possible to say whether they were part of the original endowment. Two estates in Wiltshire granted to Nunnaminster in the will of Eadræd, Bradford on Avon and Shalbourne, were among several of his bequests which were not put into effect. Certainly Bradford was in royal hands in 1001 when it was given to Shaftesbury, while several laymen held Shalbourne in 1066. Romsey also possessed more land in Wiltshire than in its native county. Its two large manors here were at Edington and (Steeple and West) Ashton, and they were assessed at seventy hides. For each the convent had a diploma of Edgar who refounded the house in 967. Edington was granted directly to the nuns in 968, but Ashton is the subject of an interesting charter of 964 by which the king 'booked' the land to himself; that is he converted the tenure to a form known as bookland, which gave him the freedom to alienate it perpetually to whoever he wished.[3]

It is clear from this that a substantial proportion of Wiltshire was made over to the Church by the tenth-century monarchs, and that the total might have been even greater if Eadræd's bequests had been honoured and the Berkshire Abbey of Abingdon had retained the lands granted by Edgar.[4] Up to this time the ecclesiastical demesne in the county must have been vast, even if some of the land was confiscated from previous owners. The primary purpose of this generosity was to secure the 'work of God', especially prayers for the kings and their souls. But there were also burdens associated with them. The lands of the Church were liable for the payment of tax and for the performance of military service. The usual way to provide for the latter was to lease land to laymen for a term of three lives in return for services which were probably well defined, even if written records of them are rare. Land held on these terms is distinguished in Domesday Book by the phrase the 'holder(s) could not be separated from the church' and was often known as 'thegnland'. Military service was not the only duty these men owed. When Bishop Oswald of Worcester set out the obligations of his tenants they included escort duty and riding on their lord's business, hunting service and lime-burning (to produce mortar).[5]

[1] Sawyer (ed.), S.899. The Domesday hundred of Bradford probably embraced the modern parishes of Holt, South Wraxall, Atworth, Limpley Stoke and Winsley. The bounds of the diploma —which are in Middle rather than Old English—also take in Westwood and Wingfield.

[2] GDB 68v(x2). See *VCH Wiltshire*, iii. 242–4.

[3] Sawyer (ed.), S.765, S.727. For the extent of these estates, see *VCH Wiltshire*, ii. 93–4.

[4] Sawyer (ed.), S.688, S.756, a total of ninety-two hides at Bedwyn and Burbage. S.937 relates that these estates were for the support of the king's sons, and so Æthelræd compensated Abingdon with estates elsewhere. There are anomalies in the last two diplomas, but they are not conclusive; see Keynes, *Diplomas of Æthelred II*, 256, but also 96, n.42.

[5] Oswald's terms are translated in R. A. Brown (ed.), *The Origins of English Feudalism* (London, 1973), 133–4.

The identities of the ecclesiastical tenants in Wiltshire in 1066 are rarely given. It was most important to record that they were tenants and not free owners to prevent any loss of land to laymen after the Conquest. However, this did not prevent the Norman successors of Englishmen who held leases of the Church from regarding that land as part of their inheritance. In addition to these, churches also made occasional leases on less strict terms of which there is an example at Highway. Toti bought it from the Abbot of Malmesbury for three lives, but with the freedom to choose his lord. The result was that in 1086 the Church had lost the land which was part of the fief of Ralph de Mortimer. The duty to provide soldiers continued to be a burden on ecclesiastical lands after 1066. Not surprisingly, it was usually the lands which had been leased to Englishmen which were used to endow Norman tenants, although native tenants are also found on these properties. Whether the land was responsible for the same amount of service before as after 1066 is an open question. The quota of knights owed by each church was fixed by William and there is no way of knowing if it was a heavier burden than it had been under the Anglo-Saxon arrangements. Certainly, if the Abbey of Shaftesbury owed soldiers to the host at the rate of one man to every five hides it possessed, it would have owed thirty-three men for its Wiltshire estates alone. Its post-Conquest quota was only ten knights, which represents a considerable reduction, unless the Anglo-Saxon abbesses had been able to negotiate a similarly favourable deal from the king.[1]

Parishes were well developed in the late Anglo-Saxon kingdom. Many of the ecclesiastical parishes which existed in the early nineteenth century preserved Anglo-Saxon estates, as may be seen from the bounds attached to many of the charters. It is a paradox that Domesday Book as a whole records churches so badly, and Wiltshire is no exception. The bulk of the twenty-nine mentioned in the survey were on royal manors or were royal churches.[2] Clearly there were many more churches in eleventh-century Wiltshire than this, ranging in size and importance from the great cathedral of Salisbury (then in Old Sarum) and the monasteries at Malmesbury, Amesbury and Wilton to the tiny church at Bradford on Avon now thought to date to around 1000.[3] Many English churches must have been constructed of wood of which no trace survives. Even stone construction was no guarantee that a church would not be rebuilt later, and less than a dozen Wiltshire churches exhibit signs of Anglo-Saxon work.[4] There is one reference to church-building in the almost boastful record that Sheriff Edward had 'a new church and an excellent house and a good vineyard' at Wilcot (f.69).

Lay Tenants-in-Chief

Domesday Wiltshire contains separate chapters for forty-five lay barons, and in addition there are three sections devoted to the king's thegns, sergeants and servants. In the following discussion the order used will normally be based on the value of their holdings in this county rather than their sequence in the folios.[5] Many important men held land in Wiltshire, but the county was not dominated by great landowners of national importance. Rather, men of all degrees among the new French landowners are represented. Many of those who held property here did so because the English predecessors whose lands they had been allotted had some of their estates in Wiltshire, but there was also a group of barons whose chief holdings lay in the county.

Domesday Book provides a snapshot of the progress of the Norman settlement at a particular point. In Wiltshire it is difficult to say anything about the stages by which the new aristocracy received its lands. It is certain that it did not happen immediately, and the general impression is that

[1] Light is thrown on the knight service of Shaftesbury by A. Williams, 'The Knights of Shaftesbury Abbey', *Proc. of the Battle Conference 1985*, viii (1986), 214–37.

[2] See p.12 above, and Darby and Welldon Finn (eds.), *Domesday Geography*, 49–50.

[3] E. Fernie, *The Architecture of the Anglo-Saxons* (London, 1983), 145–51.

[4] The following have fabric and/or sculpture which is thought to be pre-Conquest work: Alton Barnes, Avebury, Bremhill, Britford, Cricklade, Inglesham, Knook, Limpley Stoke, Netheravon, Ramsbury, Somerford Keynes (now Glos.); see Taylor and Taylor, *Anglo-Saxon Architecture*.

[5] Darlington used the same order in *VCH Wiltshire*, ii. 98–111. Individual references are not made to his detailed survey here.

it was orderly and under royal control. Among the Anglo-Saxon landowners not all were dispossessed for opposition to William in 1066 and subsequent years, and some survived long into the Conqueror's reign. Thus the process of enfeoffing William's French followers was a gradual one and by no means complete at his death. In the reigns of his sons some families were dispossessed for disloyalty, other more recent immigrants and loyal servants were rewarded, and the few remaining English landowners lost their estates. All the significant post-Conquest landholders in Wiltshire are taken individually in the following paragraphs. The figures in brackets after each name refer to the numbering of the chapters in the text in which the fiefs are described (and also to the list of tenants on the preliminary f.64v). The details of these fiefs are set out schematically in Table 4 on pp.22–3, where for convenience the same numbering is supplied on the extreme left.

After the king himself and the ecclesiastical holders, first among the lay tenants-in-chief come the four men of highest rank to hold in the county, although their fiefs in Wiltshire were of little importance compared to those elsewhere. Robert, Count of Mortain (20) was the king's half-brother. His vast fief, second only to the king's, was scattered over twenty counties but was concentrated in Sussex and Cornwall. In the latter he was earl in fact if not in name. The value of his six manors in Wiltshire was paltry beside the total throughout England of more than £2,000 and it is therefore not surprising to find three manors held by his tenant Gilbert, all of which had been the property of the English thegn Godwine. A fourth manor had been granted to the family foundation at Grestain.[1] Roger de Montgomery (21) was Earl of Shrewsbury with substantial possessions in Shropshire and Sussex. He held two of his three Wiltshire manors as successor to the Englishman Osmund, whose lands he also acquired in Hampshire and Surrey. The property of Hugh d'Avranches, Earl of Chester (22), was mainly concentrated in the north of England. In the south he succeeded to the land of Eadnoth the staller, who is discussed below, which accounts for five of his six Wiltshire manors and property elsewhere in the south. All his Wiltshire manors were held by tenants. William Malbanc held two manors here, and four more in Somerset, while Hamo de Masci was the tenant of the other four. Earl Aubrey (23), as we have seen, had forfeited his estates when he resigned his earldom. His fief in Wiltshire, as elsewhere, was assembled from the land taken from Hearding the son of Eadnoth and Azur, with the addition of one manor of King Harold's.[2]

Three more men of the first rank among the new aristocracy held land in Wiltshire, but not on any great scale. After about 1070 Henry de Ferrers (39) was one of the most important men in the realm. His power lay chiefly in Derbyshire, where his descendants became earls, and Staffordshire, where the castle of Tutbury was the centre of his fief. Domesday names the former owner of his two Wiltshire manors as Godric, who is probably identical with the Godric who was Sheriff of Berkshire where Henry acquired six of his estates and became the most powerful lay landowner. Richard (40), the son of Count Gilbert and ancestor of the house of Clare, held the single manor of Sutton Mandeville. His predecessor there was Wulfweard, who may be the man from whom he acquired one of his Surrey properties. Geoffrey de Coutances (5) has already been encountered (p.13 above). He was listed among the ecclesiastical tenants in Domesday, although he held as a baron in England. After his death in 1093 his lands passed to his nephew, Robert de Mowbray, Earl of Northumbria, who forfeited his vast fief in 1095 for rebellion.

The largest fief in Wiltshire was that of the sheriff, Edward of Salisbury (24). His lands here had a value of more than £200 out of his total of £410. Thus he was one of the twenty most wealthy men in England. His origins are obscure. He took his surname from the borough, the custody of whose castle he may have had. It has been observed that his Christian name indicates that he was English, and it would indeed be unusual for a Norman to have used an English name. Nevertheless, while Englishmen continued to serve in the lower levels of royal administration, the rise of an English thegn to this level of wealth is unparalleled. If the origin of Edward is a mystery, the course of the family fortunes was spectacular, as his grandson Patrick was created Earl of Salisbury by the Empress in the 1140s during the civil war.

[1] See D. J. A. Matthew, *The Norman Monasteries and their English Possessions* (Oxford, 1962).

[2] Azur in Oxon. and Northants; Hearding in Leics. and War.

As is to be expected in a fief of this size (193 hides) it was widely scattered, although there were marked concentrations of manors. Nearly half lay in a belt across the centre of the county near Salisbury. A further six were in Chippenham Hundred. For the first three manors in Edward's chapter no pre-Conquest owner is entered, which gives rise to the suggestion that Edward himself held them in 1066. The remainder were, on the whole, acquired from some thirty unimportant English *antecessores*. William gave him Harold's manor of Heddington, and three more manors came from Wulfwynn. She was a wealthy woman with scattered properties in Dorset, Somerset, Middlesex, Hertfordshire and Buckinghamshire (she was described as Wulfwynn of Creslow in that county), but there is nothing to support the suggestion that she was Edward's mother.[1] On these estates he had eighteen tenants in 1086 who represent the sort of following of knights and servants a baron required, especially if he was to perform the king's business and make a profit for himself. One of them, the Hervey who was his tenant on a single hide at Ratfyn, was the Hervey of Wilton who also possessed land as one of the king's servants (*ministri*) and held of the king and Romsey Abbey at Netheravon and Edington. There is also reason to believe that Edward's tenant Robert at Broad Blunsdon was the tenant-in-chief Robert *flavus* ('the Fair').[2] Edward had other lands too. At Tisbury and at Little Langford and Christian Malford he was a tenant of the Abbeys of Shaftesbury and Glastonbury respectively. At Little Langford one of the three hides was held against the will of the abbot. He also had two hides, probably at Broad Blunsdon, 'in the king's hand' which Lang held from King Edward, noted under the chapter headed 'the land of Oda and other king's thegns'. It was convenient for the sheriff that he had his own manor there (ff.74, 69v). He may also be the Edward who held one hide of Wilton Abbey at Burcombe. The tables were turned at Bradenstoke where part of his manor was wrongly in the possession of William fitzAnsculf.

The next wealthiest man in the shire was Alvred of Marlborough (26) who was Norman despite his English name, and was the nephew of Osbern 'Pentecost', one of King Edward's Norman followers. His fief demonstrates how the lands of a single Englishman were allotted to a French baron in their entirety. In Wiltshire, as in Somerset, Hampshire and Surrey, most of his property had belonged to Karli. A significant part of his fief was in Wiltshire, and his other major concentration of land was the group of twelve manors worth £81 in Herefordshire, formerly Harold's, where he had held one manor before the Conquest. He had at least seventeen tenants on his Wiltshire manors, including one unnamed knight. Among them were Wulfmær and Wulfgeat, both of whom held their estates in 1066. The Turstin who held three and a half hides at West Kennett might be Turstin the Fleming who, although deprived of some land for loyalty to Earl Roger in 1075, possibly married Alvred's daughter and became his father-in-law's tenant.[3] Humphrey de l'Isle (27) held as a tenant-in-chief only in Wiltshire, where he was a man of some standing. His lands had belonged to at least eighteen Englishmen and one woman, of whom the names of Leofnoth, Ælfric, Eadric and Edwin stand out. William de Eu (32) had somewhat less than Humphrey in Wiltshire, but he was the son of one of the greatest Norman nobles, Count Robert de Eu. In 1086 his lands were concentrated in three south-western counties, Wiltshire, Dorset and Somerset, and by 1093 he succeeded to his father's substantial lands as well. However, by 1096 he had paid the penalty for persistent rebellion against William Rufus, for which he was mutilated and deprived of his lands and liberty. The bulk of his fief in 1086 came to him in succession to the wealthy English thegn Ælfstan of Boscombe in Wiltshire, whose estates were rated at seventy-seven and a quarter hides with a value of £89. 5*s*. in 1086. They included one hide at Ditteridge which Ælfstan leased from Malmesbury Abbey, and another six and a quarter hides which belonged to the bishopric of Salisbury. Strictly speaking, the land belonged to the churches but Norman barons interpreted the law differently. The same relationship between the landholding of Ælfstan and William is apparent in Somerset, Dorset, Gloucestershire, Hertfordshire, Bedford-

[1] Darlington, *VCH Wiltshire*, ii. 99–100, was less sure of his Englishry than J. Green, 'The Sheriffs of William the Conqueror', *Proc. of the Battle Conference 1982*, v (1983), 132. His predecessors Alric, Alwine, Alweard and Azur qualify for inclusion in Table 5 below.

[2] *VCH Wiltshire*, ii. 75, 106.

[3] F. and C. Thorn (eds.), *Domesday Book: Herefordshire* (Chichester, 1983), note to 19,6; C. P. Lewis, 'The Norman Settlement of Herefordshire under William I', *Proc. of the Battle Conference 1984*, vii. 202–3.

TABLE 4: The tenants-in-chief in 1086: all values to nearest £

	Holder, preceded by chapter-number in Wiltshire Domesday	number of manors held in chief	£ value in 1086	£ value of demesne manors	£ value of subinfeudated manors	£ value of manors held as undertenant in Wiltshire	Approximate values of all manors held in England; or, for some laymen, A–F classification by Corbett and Green†	Significant undertenants in Wiltshire
1	King William	22	1,000	90			12,600	Excludes four manors for which no value is given — perhaps £400
2	Bishop of Winchester	12	270	207	63	—	1,000+	Richer, William Scudet, William, William de Braose
3	Bishop of Salisbury	5	303	221	83	—	600	Many, including Englishmen
4	Bishop of Bayeux	4	21	—	21	—	A	Odo, Robert
5	Bishop of Coutances	7	25	5	20	7	A	Roger, Robert
6	Bishop of Lisieux	2	9	7	2	—		Turstin
7	Glastonbury Abbey	15	225	165	60	—	828	Many, including Edward of Salisbury
8	Malmesbury Abbey	13	182	132	50	—		
9	Westminster Abbey	—	—	—	—	—	584	
10	New Minster, Winchester	5	104	90	14	—	391	
11	Cranbourne Abbey	2	16	16	—	—		
12	Shaftesbury Abbey	6	182	152	30	—		Turstin, Gunfrid
13	Wilton Abbey	20	215	199	16	—		Edward, Gerard, +£11 from borough of Wilton
14	Nunnaminster, Winchester	2	60	57	3	—	65	Knights, including Englishmen
15	Romsey Abbey	2	85	60	25	—		William
16	Amesbury Abbey	6	32	29	3	—	56	Alweard
17	Abbey of Bec	1	12	12	—	—		
18	Gerald of Wilton	1	10	—	—	—		
*	Regenbald the priest	1	9	—	—	—		
19	Canons of Lisieux	1	10	—	—	—		
	Alweard the priest	1	4	—	—	—		
	Osbern the priest	1	1	—	—	—		
	Agenulf	1	¼	—	—	—		
20	Count of Mortain	6	30	15	15	—	A	Gilbert (£6), abbey of Sainte-Marie of Grestain. Held an Amesbury manor
21	Earl Roger	3	32	16	16	—	A	Turold
22	Earl Hugh	6	16	—	16	—	A	William (£5), Hamo (£9)
23	Earl Aubrey	10	76	76	—	—		
24	Edward of Salisbury	42	215	150	65	3	B	Nineteen men, plus food-rents and £80 from reeveland
25	Ernulf de Hesdin	27	81	39	42	§	C	Robert (£12), Eadric's wife (£7), Urse (£4) and many lesser men. § indicates ½ hide from William de Eu
26	Alvred of Marlborough	23	124	68	56	—	C	Ralph (£14), Hugh (£7) and lesser men
27	Humphrey de l'Isle	27	120	67	53	—		Robert (£26), Pain (£8), Ranulph (£5) and others
28	Miles Crispin	12	60	24	36	—	C	Reginald (£30; one entry, £4, is to Reginald Canute), Humphrey (£5)
29	Gilbert de Breteuil	9	43	27	16	—	E	Ansfrid (314)
30	Durand of Gloucester	7	27	16	11	—	F	Roger (£5)
31	Walter Giffard	1	10	10	—	—	B	
32	William de Eu	17	97	25	72	$\frac{3}{10}$	C	William d'Audrieu (£13), Ralph (£13), Bernard (£12), Hugh (£11), Edward (£10), William (£7)
33	William de Braose	1	1	—	1	—	B	
34	William de Moyon	1	5	—	5	—	D	Walter
35	William de Falaise	1	1	—	1	—	E	
36	Walter de Douai	2	10	—	10	—	C	Ralph (£7)
37	Waleran the huntsman	16	46	27	19	—		Walter (£5), Erenburgis (£5)
38	William fitzGuy	1	10	10	—	—		
39	Henry de Ferrers	2	9	9	—	—	A	
40	Richard son of Count Gilbert	1	6	—	6	—	A	Berengar
41	Ralph de Mortimer	10	40	22	19	—	C	Richard (£7+)
42	Robert fitzGerald	10	55	7	48	—	D	Rainer (£19), Joscelin (£10), Robert (£14), Hugh (£5)
43	Robert fitzRolf	2	7	7	—	—		
44	Roger de Courseulles	1	25	25	—	—		
45	Roger of Berkeley	3	4	4	—	—		Information missing for one property

Table 4: Continued

	Holder, preceded by chapter-number in Wiltshire Domesday	number of manors held in chief	£ value in 1086	£ value of demesne manors	£ value of subinfeudated manors	£ value of manors held as undertenant in Wiltshire	Approximate values of all manors held in England; or, for some laymen, A–F classification by Corbett and Green†	Significant undertenants in Wiltshire
46	Bernard Pauncevolt	1	¼	¼	—	—		
47	Berengar Giffard	2	7	7	—	—		
48	Osbern Giffard	12	52	48	5	—	E	
49	Drogo fitzPons	3	9	9	6	—	F	
50	Hugh l'Asne	5	12	2	10	—	E	William (£6)
51	Hugh fitzBaldric	1	10	—	10	—	D	Walter
52	Humphrey the chamberlain	1	3	3	—	—	D	
53	Gunfrid Mauduit	2	5	5	—	—		
54	Alvred d'Epaignes	1	4	4	—	—	E	
55	Aiulf the sheriff	2	7	7	—	—	D	
56	Nigel the physician	6	38	30	8	—	E	Sainte-Marie of Montebourg, also a derelict church valued at £32
57	Osbern the priest	1	2	2	—	—		
58	Richard Puignant	2	12	12	—	—	F	
59	Robert Marshal	2	23	23	—	—		
60	Robert the Fair	1	12	12	—	—		
61	Richard Sturmy	1	2	2	—	—		
62	Reginald Canute	1	1	1	—	4		
63	Matthew de Mortagne	1	3	3	—	—	E	
64	Joscelin Riviere	1	2	2	—	—		
65	Godescal	2	3	3	—	—		
66	The king's sergeants							
	Herman de Dreux	1	2	2	—	—		
	Amalric de Dreux	1	3	3	—	—		
	Ansger the cook	1	4	4	—	—		
	William Corniole	1	2	2	—	—		One manor as king's servant, £2
	Fulchred	1	1	1	—	—		
	Stephen the carpenter	2	5	5	—	—		
	Osmund	1	1	1	—	—		
67	The king's thegns: only men with land worth more than £5, unless of other interest							
	Oda of Winchester	1	4	4	—	—	F	
	Beorhtric	9	37	33	4	—		His brother Alwig held one manor and part of another
	Alweard	3	6	6	—	—		
	Alweard Colling	1	4	4	—	—		
	Ælfric of Melksham	3	5	5	—	—		Edward holds one manor as surety (*vadimonium*)
	Ælfric the Little	4	5	5	—	—		
	Ealdræd	5	11	11	—	—		
	Grimbald the goldsmith	2	18	18	—	—		
	Hearding	2	24	24	—	—		He had lost a further six manors worth £26
	Thorkil	1	5	5	—	—		
	Wulfric	8	8	8	—	—		
	Swein	1	12	12	—	—		
	Ragnburh	1	5	5	—	—		
68	The king's servants: only men with land worth more than £5							
	Richard Sturmy (see 61 above)							
	Ralph de Hauville	3	11	11	—	—		
	John the doorkeeper	6	6	6	—	—		
	William Scudet	1	8	8	—	—		
	Geoffrey	1	5	5	—	—		
	William fitzAnsculf	2	6	6	—	—	C	
	Odin the chamberlain	1	5	—	—	—		

* not numbered, and missing from list of tenants on f.64v.

† Corbett's categories (J. Tanner *et al.* (eds.), *Cambridge Medieval History*, v (Cambridge, 1921), 510–11):
A = £750+ (8 men) B = £650–400 (10 men) C = £399–200 (24 men) D = £199–100 (36 men)
E = £99–50
F = £49–0 } additional categories from Green, 'Sheriffs of William the Conqueror', *Proc. of the Battle Conference 1982*, v (1983), 139

shire, and also on a lesser scale in Berkshire and Hampshire. A further four of William's hides in Wiltshire came from Toli whose contribution to his fief was much more significant in Somerset and Dorset. Two of his manors in Wiltshire were held of him by William d'Audrieu, his cousin and steward who joined his lord and relative in rebellion in 1096 and was hanged for it.[1]

Ernulf de Hesdin (25) was one of two Flemish tenants-in-chief in Wiltshire. Although he held land in eleven counties, the centre of his fief was in Wiltshire and Gloucestershire. Most of his manors in this county were of small or moderate size, the only exception being Keevil. As with many Wiltshire fiefs, his consisted of the land of many minor Anglo-Saxon landowners. Only Beorhtsige held a significant property, Keevil, but three manors belonged to a man called Eadric whose wife was still in possession of two as a tenant in 1086. The name recurs as Ernulf's predecessor for six manors in four neighbouring counties, making it likely that the same man is represented. The other Fleming was Walter de Douai (36), appearing as Walscin in Wiltshire Domesday only, and Walter elsewhere. His two manors were worth only £10, but in Somerset he was a significant landowner with many properties worth more than £100. Miles Crispin (28) was the holder of Wallingford Castle and lands in seven shires, a significant proportion of them formerly belonging to the great English thegn Vigot of Wallingford. In Wiltshire the manors of Rodbourne and Manton had been Vigot's, and Miles was granted in addition three of Earl Harold's estates, and a further three that had been Leofnoth's. Of Miles' thirteen manors, no less than six worth £34 were held by Reginald, although the Geld Accounts identify the tenant-in-chief Reginald Canute as the holder of one of them, Rodbourne. A further two manors (10 hides) were held by Humphrey, and both he and Reginald held of Miles elsewhere.

Robert fitzGerald (42) and Osbern Giffard (48) were both men of influence in Wiltshire where they held the bulk of their lands. Robert's chief predecessor in both Wiltshire and Somerset was Vitalis, but he held also in Dorset, Hampshire and Berkshire. All ten of his manors had been granted to his tenants, Rainer, Robert, Joscelin and Hugh. By contrast, Osbern held a compact fief with only two manors outside Wiltshire. Both belonged to his Wiltshire predecessors Dunna and Trasmund. The two holdings at Elston, although not the largest, were later the *caput* of the powerful barony belonging to Elias Gifford. The practice that a Frenchman claimed all the parcels of land that his *antecessor* had is epitomized in this case by the six acres of meadow at Stanton St Quintin which the Abbot of Glastonbury leased to Beorhtric before 1066. As Beorhtric's successor in the manor of Stanton, Osbern took the meadow land as well. Berengar Giffard (47) who held two manors in Wiltshire is often reckoned as Osbern's brother. Waleran the huntsman (37) was another holder whose lands were restricted to this region. The bulk of his properties lay in Wiltshire, although he had nearly as much in Dorset and sixteen and a half hides in Hampshire.

The focus of the fief of Gilbert de Breteuil (29) was also in Wiltshire where he held lands worth £41 out of his total of some £70. The balance lay mainly in Berkshire. Swallowfield in Berkshire had originally been part of William fitzOsbern's fief and Gilbert had been subinfeudated on it. When Earl Roger forfeited his lands in 1075 Gilbert survived. Alvred d'Epaignes (54) was also an associate of William fitzOsbern who came from a place on or near the earl's Norman lands. In Herefordshire he arrived as Earl William's tenant, but he was an important tenant-in-chief in the south-west where more than half Alvred's lands (valued at some £80, chiefly in Somerset) came from Ælfwig son of Banna. Hugh l'Asne (50) (sometimes designated 'the donkey') seems to have been a tenant of Earl William in Normandy, and in Herefordshire he received many of Thorkil White's manors. The survival of Gilbert, Alvred and Hugh shows they stood by the king rather than their lord in the crisis of 1075, but there is no reason to assume that they received all their lands or any of their Wiltshire estates from the earl.[2] In Herefordshire Alvred of Marlborough also had connections with William fitzOsbern, but again there is no indication that he received his Wiltshire lands other than from the king (see p.21 above).

[1] F. Barlow, *William Rufus* (London, 1983).

[2] For Swallowfield, see Dom S. F. Hockey (ed.), *The Cartulary of Carisbrooke Priory* (Isle of Wight Record Office, 1981), p.xxv and *passim*; for Alvred, see L. C. Loyd, *The Origins of Some Anglo-Norman Families*, Harleian Soc. 103 (Leeds, 1951), 51–2; for Alvred and Hugh, see Lewis, 'Norman Settlement of Herefordshire', 205–7.

Ralph de Mortimer (41) was another important baron to hold in Wiltshire. His most important lands were a compact barony on the border of Wales in Shropshire and in Herefordshire, where the *caput* of the fief was at the now sadly neglected castle of Wigmore. The lands of Cypping which he inherited in Hampshire and Berkshire were also significant. In Wiltshire he was allocated different predecessors. Four of his manors belonged to Alwine, but the most important was Harold's twenty-hide property at Hullavington. The possessions of William's physician Nigel (56) were largest in Wiltshire, and he had smaller fiefs in Herefordshire, Shropshire, Somerset and Hampshire. Most of them had belonged to his *antecessor*, the wealthy English priest Spirites, who lost his estates in 1065.[1] Durand of Gloucester (30) had the most valuable lands of the three sheriffs of neighbouring counties to hold in Wiltshire (Aiulf and William de Moyon were the others). Roger de Courseulles (44) who came from the vicinity of Caen in Normandy, had a single important manor at Fisherton de la Mere but most of his land was concentrated in Somerset. William de Falaise (35) was also an important local landowner in Somerset and Devonshire, but his Wiltshire estate was insignificant. Walter Giffard (31) kept his manor in demesne. He was a major baron and the greatest landowner in Buckinghamshire, of which he became earl in the next reign.

The degree to which these Wiltshire estates were kept in demesne or granted to subtenants varied according to the policy of the individual. In some cases these subtenants can be traced in several counties. Indeed, some of them were as wealthy as the lesser barons holding in chief. Among other things they owed their lords military service as knights, although Domesday Book does not record what that service should entail. Also entered on ecclesiastical and lay estates were unnamed knights (*milites*), men who it is sometimes said were difficult to distinguish from the peasantry. An example on a lay estate is the knight listed with three cotsets at Hartham on only one hide of land (f.68v), but it would be dangerous to press this evidence too far in assigning peasant status to such 'poor knights'. What Domesday Book does not record is their equipment and training at arms (a considerable investment), the payment in money and kind that they received from their lords, or what lands they could acquire for themselves.

The survey of Wiltshire landowners concludes with three more sections of small tenants; the king's sergeants, his thegns and his servants. The reasons for this arrangement are uncertain. The thegns who held in 1086 were practically all Englishmen; that is they bear English or Anglo-Scandinavian names and presumably represent pre-Conquest families. Among these English tenants many are said to be holding the land of fathers or husbands (and in one case a brother) in 1066; in several cases the same individual had held TRE. Darlington suggested that they were all in royal service by 1086, which accounts for their survival and separate entry.[2] Among them Godric, Wulfric (in Exon) and Wulfgeat are named as huntsmen. Few among them were significant either in Wiltshire or elsewhere, Oda of Winchester and his brother Ealdræd excepted. Both the latter held in several southern shires and although they had lost estates since 1066 they found sufficient favour with the king to acquire others.[3] The list of such survivors had gradually been whittled down after 1066. Surviving the terrible years of the Conquest did not guarantee that an English family would retain its lands. Eadnoth the staller, who made his peace with William and fell in battle against the sons of Harold in 1068, had a son, Hearding. If the Wiltshire thegn of that name is the same man, he possessed property there to the value of £24 in 1086, and he had lost as much to Earl Aubrey. Among his properties in 1066 was a five-hide manor at Beechingstoke which he had on a one-life lease from Shaftesbury Abbey, although it is said he terminated the arrangement prematurely and in 1086 one Turstin held it from the abbess. It is possible to suggest that Hearding may have been forced to give up this land, perhaps by Turstin, for he had regained

[1] Barlow, *The English Church 1000–1066*, 135, 156, summarizes what is known of Spirites.

[2] *VCH Wiltshire*, ii. 76. On the significance of these men, see also J. Campbell, 'Some Agents and Agencies of the Late Anglo-Saxon State', *Domesday Studies*, ed. Holt, 210–12, which appeared after this was written.

[3] *VCH Wiltshire*, ii. 71; *VCH Berkshire*, i (1906), 292; *VCH Hampshire*, i. 427.

possession of it by the time of Henry I against the will of the church.[1] Wulfweard White survived until shortly before 1086 but his land did not remain in his family.

The reasons for inclusion in the lists of *servientes* and *ministri* are less clear. The occupations of some of these men are given in Domesday Book or other sources: Ansger, Humphrey and William Scudet were all royal cooks, but the former was a sergeant and the latter two *ministri*. More significantly, Robert fitzRolf and Richard Sturmy had possession both as barons and as *ministri*, while William fitzAnsculf, one of the great barons of the Midlands, is recorded in Wiltshire only as a *minister*. If this suggests that these men held land by both knight service and by sergeanty for some lesser service, there is an additional problem. Some of the properties entered in the list of tenants-in-chief were later held as sergeanties, as it is likely that they were in the eleventh century. Richard's land at Cowesfield, entered in Chapter 61, was held by sergeanty, and the same is true of his Hampshire manors. It is also likely that the lands of Matthew de Mortagne (63) were held for the service of buying for the king's larder. Finally, men who were entered as barons in one county could appear as *minister*, thegn or sergeant in neighbouring shires.[2] This confusion makes it impossible to be sure on what grounds the lesser lay tenants were classified in Wiltshire, other than that many if not all of them were in royal service. It may be that the distinctions between them were less formal in 1086 than they were later to become.

Wiltshire on the Eve of the Conquest

This subject has been left until after the tenurial structure of Wiltshire in 1086 because it was not the purpose of Domesday Book to portray the same for 1066. Nevertheless, it is possible to say that tenurially Wiltshire in 1066 was very different from the county twenty years later. 'On the day when King Edward was alive and dead' the royal demesne consisted of the six large estates rendering the farm of one night and Britford with its nominal assessment. In addition, the forfeited estates of Earl Tosti were probably at his disposal and the property of his queen may more properly be counted royal. Although far smaller than William's demesne it was still the preponderant estate in the county. The position of the Church as landowner barely changed over the period of the Conquest. The next most important layman was Earl Harold with 229 hides which consisted mostly of large manors of ten and twenty hides and the hundred of Melksham, although they show no particular concentration. When he became king they became part of the royal demesne and substantially increased its extent. His mother Gytha had a further 100 hides. By 1065 the Godwine family was not a united one and there is no indication of the side she took in the succession.

Beneath this level it becomes difficult to identify individual landowners because of the absence of surnames, although the practice of allotting all the lands of one Englishman to a single Norman successor makes it possible to make some attempt. Table 5 opposite, which contains more than 100 names, lists all those men and women who possessed property of at least five hides or £5 in value, although the values are those of 1086, and it is possible to distinguish among them a group of significant landowners who held property throughout southern England. In most cases their estates had been assembled over a considerable period through the action of inheritance, marriage and royal gift. An example of the latter is the charter of 1045 by which Edward gave a small estate at Ditchampton to his thegn (*minister*) Thorth. He in turn donated it to Wilton Abbey when his two daughters became nuns.[3] Unfortunately it is usually impossible to trace the history and growth of Anglo-Saxon lay estates.

After Harold, the richest layman was Ælfstan of Boscombe who owned some 230 hides in eight shires. His name shows that he was a native of the county. Karli was the most significant Wiltshire

[1] *VCH Wiltshire*, ii. 66, 71, 98–9. Hearding may also have been Queen Edith's butler: see ibid. 66, and T. J. Oleson, *The Witenagemot in the Reign of Edward the Confessor* (London, Toronto, 1955), 126. The Beechingstoke affair is discussed by Williams, 'Knights of Shaftesbury', 227.

[2] *VCH Wiltshire*, ii. 72–8; for example, Robert fitzRolf, baron and *minister* in Wilts., king's thegn in Berks., and *minister* in Oxon.

[3] Sawyer (ed.), S.1010; GDB 68. But Bishop Odo had it and GDB records (f.66) that Azur had it TRE—perhaps he was Thorth's tenant or descendant.

TABLE 5: The principal pre-Conquest landowners

Holder	Number of manors	Hidage	Value in 1086 £
Royal and comital persons			
King Edward	7	1	630
Queen Edith	4	87	183
Earl Harold	16	229	343
Earl Tosti	2	44	41
Lady Gytha	3	100½	132
Ecclesiastical persons and bodies			
Bishop of Winchester	12	259½	268½
Bishop of Salisbury	4	262	296½
Glastonbury Abbey	14	258	234
Malmesbury Abbey	12	279	165
Westminster Abbey	—	—	9
Winchester Abbey	5	132	103½
Cranbourne Abbey	2	21	16
Shaftesbury Abbey, nuns	—	165	187
Wilton Abbey, nuns	21	231½	234
Winchester Abbey, nuns	2	48	60
Romsey Abbey, nuns	2	70	84½
Amesbury Abbey, nuns	7	35	32
Gerald the priest of Wilton	1	10	10
Laymen with lands of more than £5 or five hides and including those holding less who are of special interest. Bracketed figures after the name indicate the chapter number in the Wiltshire folios			
Ailwacre (36)	1	8	7
Aki (6)	1	10	12
Aki (24)	1	5	3
Algar (3)	1	5	4
Algar (25)	1	3¼	5
Algar (48)	1	5	5
Almær (30)	3	13½	12¼
Alnoth (27)	1	10	5
Alric (24)	2	15¾	11
Alsige (36)	1	5	3
Alsige the monk (2)	1	5	5
Alweald (38)	1	8	10
Alweard (5)	1	5	7
Alweard (6)	1	10	7
Alweard (8)	1	10	6
Alweard (24)	3	8¼	13½
Alweard (25)	2	6½	7
Alweard (52)	1	5	3
Alwig (41)	1	5	7
Alwig (54)	1	5	4
Alwine (24)	2	13½	13
Alwine (41)	4	11	13
Azur (4)	1	2	8
Azur (23)	3	50	50
Azur (24)	3	12¼	33
Ælfgeat (5)	1	5	4½
Ælfric (27)	4	13	14
Ælfric (32)	1	5	4
Ælfric (61)	1	2	1½
Ælfric (68)	2	4	2
Ælfstan (32)	14	77¼	89¼
Æthelgifu (1)	1	30	30
Baldwin (24)	1	7	6
Beorhtmær (42)	2	5½	5½
Beorhtmær (67)	2	10	8½
Beorhtric (17)	1	10	15
Beorhtric (24)	1	6	6
Beorhtric (25)	3	20	29½
Beorhtric (48)	1	18	8
Beorhtric's father (67)	4	37	27½
Beorhtsige (25)	1	16	26
Bondi (44)	1	10	25
Cola (34)	1	5	5
Cuthwulf (67)	1	6	3
Cynewig (27)	1	6	6
Cynewine (24)	1	5	10
Dene (50)	1	6	6
Dodda (30)	1	5	4
Dunna (48)	3	23¼	16½
Eadnoth the staller (22)	5	9½	13
Eadræd (24)	1	7	11
Eadric (25)	3	6	8
Eadric (27)	3	10½	7
Eadric (29)	2	7	18
Eadric (68)	1	5	5
Eadwulf (4)	2	11	8½
Edward (67)	1	6½	6
Edwin (24)	1	7	7
Edwin (27)	3	14	10
Euing	1	5	6
†Gerald the priest of Wilton (18)	1	10	10
God (25)	1	5	5
God (27)	1	6½	4
Godric (1)	1	10	12
Godric (39)	2	6	9
Godric (67)	1	5	5
Godwine (20)	3	9¾	6
Gunnar (58)	1	3¾	5
Hearding (11)	1	5	6
Hearding (20)	1	6½	10
Hearding (23)	6	22½	6
Hearding (67)	3	27½	24
Herlebald (37)	1	6	12
Karli (26)	15	112¾	105
Ketil (20)	1	5	5
Lang (67)	1	10	12
Leofgeat (94)	1	5	4
Leofnoth (27)	3	19½	17½
Leofnoth (28)	4	27¾	20
Leofric (50)	1	5	2
Northmann (37)	1	5	5
Ordwulf (27)	1	5	3½
Osmund (21)	2	18½	15½
Osweard (49)	1	5	2½
Oswulf (37)	1	10	10
Robert fitzWimarc (68)	1	5	2
Sæwine (27)	1	5	3
Sæwulf (42)	1	10	10
Siward (21)	1	5	16
Smala (48)	2	8	8
Spirites the priest (56)	4	43	37
Strami (24, 68)	2	23¾	15
Swein (27)	1	10	10
Swein's father (67)	1	10½	12
Thorbert (68)	1	12	5
†Thorkil (67)	1	6	5
Toki (28)	1	5	2½
Tovi (27)	1	10	8
Trasmund (48)	1	5	5
Vigot (of Wallingford) (28)	2	8	8
Vitalis (42)	3	20+	17+
Wulfgar (27)	1	10	5
Wulfgar (29)	2	14	9
Wulfgar (43)	2	10	7
Wulfgifu (68)	1	5¼	3½
Wulfweard (68)	1	4½	8
Wulfwig (24)	1	7	4
Wulfwine (27)	1	10	4
Wulfwynn (24)	3	17	23
Wynsige (51)	1	10	10
Laymen sharing ownership			
Ælfric, Burghelm, Godgifu (29)	1	15	9½
Beorhtnoth, Alwine (67)	2	13	6½

†continues to hold in 1086

landowner with 112 hides in the county and more than 150 altogether in at least four shires. Apart from Azur, the *antecessor* of Earl Aubrey, and Hearding, no other man or woman can be seen to have had more than fifty hides in Wiltshire. The latter was also a landowner in the Midlands. As in 1086, there were persons who had relatively minor estates in Wiltshire who were none the less significant men in the county, even if their influence rarely extended outside Wessex. Aki, the *antecessor* of Robert Blund (also called *flavus*, *albus*), was a housecarl of King Edward who also held land in Middlesex, Northamptonshire and Suffolk worth nearly £35 in 1086.[1] The property of Beorhtric son of Ælfgar, which Darlington described as vast, went to Queen Matilda, while Beorhtsige was a man of local importance with some fifty hides in Somerset, Dorset and Wiltshire. Robert fitzWimarc, a Norman or Breton who held a court appointment as staller, was referred to as kinsman of King Edward, as was Vigot of Wallingford.[2] The former was a major landowner who was made Sheriff of Essex by William. The latter had eight hides in Wiltshire, but nearly 150 in eleven counties, and his survival after 1066 has already been referred to. The Anglo-Saxon Chronicle records that his son Toki fell at the Battle of Gerberoy in 1079, in King William's service—an indication that the sons of noble Englishmen did not find it impossible to fit into the new society.[3] Wulfweard White who held land in at least ten counties had a toehold in Wiltshire in the shape of the three hides he leased from the Bishop of Salisbury for his own lifetime only. Lastly, the lady Wulfwynn, owner of three manors, had land in six shires, and Toli, with only four hides here, held 100 hides in three counties.

This leaves about 100 Wiltshire landowners who possessed the qualifications of a thegn but often little more. Domesday gives the impression that they had no lord but the king, for it records very few instances of a man commended to another more influential landowner. Wiltshire estates are never described as 'alods'; that is the owner having full rights to sell or bequeath the land, or subject it to another lord. The equivalent description, that an English owner could 'go to whom he wished' is used so rarely as to suggest that so many landowners had this right that it went unrecorded. Nevertheless, passages in the Old English laws and in Domesday Book assumed that many landowners would have superior lords other than the king. Some would have received their land from that lord, others would have sought his lordship voluntarily. This latter bond may not have been very strong in pre-Conquest England, as is suggested by the events of 1051 when Edward was able to transfer to his own allegiance the thegns in the armies of Godwine and Harold.[4] It is inconceivable that the great landowners did not have lesser men commended to them, and the omission of such evidence from the Wiltshire survey severely hampers any attempt to reconstruct the tenurial structure of the county on the eve of the Conquest.

Darlington drew attention to the group of pre-Conquest Wiltshire landowners who bore Scandinavian names. This need not mean that they were of Scandinavian blood. There had been heavy settlement in England in the later ninth and early tenth century, although not in Wessex. One impact of Cnut's conquest may have been to make such names popular, as Norman and French names became popular even among Englishmen after 1066. Earl Godwine's sons, for example, bore Danish names, partly to be accounted for by the blood of their mother Gytha. Gestr (a Scandinavian name) had a brother with the English name Særic, which may indicate mixed parentage. Several of these Wiltshire 'Danes' had land in many counties, like Azur, Aki and Karli mentioned above. Others, like Strami and Kolsveinn, occur rarely, the former only in Wiltshire. Darlington was probably correct to suggest that some of these names occur in this county as the result of grants by the Scandinavian kings who ruled from 1016 until 1042, or in the case of Thorth by Edward. Some may also have been followers of Earls Godwine and Harold. In the absence of detailed evidence, such as exists for Worcestershire, it is impossible to be certain of the significance of these names.[5]

[1] His land was hardly 'extensive' (*VCH Wiltshire*, ii. 66; GDB 130v, 225v; LDB 438–440v). For a recent discussion of the housecarls, see N. A. Hooper, 'The Housecarls in England in the Eleventh Century', *Proc. of the Battle Conference 1984*, vii. 161–76.

[2] Barlow, *Edward the Confessor*, 163, n.1.

[3] *ASC* 1079 D, Douglas and Greenaway (eds.), *EHD*, ii. 159. See also GDB 66 (Potterne) for the English tenant of the bishopric of Salisbury, who was a 'knight by the king's command'. Also N. A. Hooper, 'Edgar the Ætheling: Anglo-Saxon Prince, Rebel and Crusader', *ASE* 14 (1986), 210, 212.

[4] *ASC* 1051 D, E, Douglas and Greenaway (eds.), *EHD*, ii. 123–4; Stenton, *Anglo-Saxon England*, 489–92.

[5] *VCH Wiltshire*, ii. 68–9; A. Williams, '"Cockles amongst the Wheat": Danes and English in the Western Midlands in the First Half of the Eleventh Century', *Midland Hist.* 11 (1986). See also Hooper, 'Housecarls' (n.1 above).

The Wiltshire Boroughs

The towns of Wiltshire have been left until last because they were given very cursory treatment in Domesday Book. Indeed, the Ely Inquest suggests there was some doubt as to how towns (or boroughs) should be dealt with by the survey. Ten places in Wiltshire displayed some of the characteristics of boroughs in 1086.[1] Malmesbury stands at the head of the Wiltshire account as the county borough with an incomplete list of those who held property there. The king had fifty-one properties (*masurae*) in 1086, on each of which could stand more than one house. Of these, twenty-five had houses on them but did not pay geld 'any more than waste land'. That they were not derelict is proved by the payment of 10*d.* from each. The list records another twenty-two and three-quarters *masurae* belonging to sixteen lords, although from the rural manors it is possible to add a further eleven burgesses and five and a half houses. This has been interpreted as amounting to a population of some four to five thousand, possibly more when the monks and their servants are taken into account. It was thus a small town typical of the south-west. Earl Harold had an acre of land with ten plots on it, six of them derelict, which presumably became the king's. It was worth £5 in 1066, although what gave it this high value is not indicated. The two parts of the revenue from the borough which the king received at both dates had not changed, a most unusual circumstance because at most boroughs there had been an increase in value. The £8 recorded included the pleas of two hundreds, "Cicementone" and Startley. The third part of the revenues, £6 in 1086, was also the king's by that date, but must have represented the 'earl's third penny' in 1066. There was a mint worth a further £5, and there is a note of the military privilege enjoyed by the burgesses. They paid 20*s.* to the expenses of the royal fleet or contributed one soldier from each five hides, although the total hidation of the town is not given.

If the information for Malmesbury is sparse and there is no indication of its economic activity, there is even less for the other nine towns. For Wilton, Salisbury, Marlborough, and Cricklade no more than the royal revenues from the 'third penny' are noted. From the surveys of rural manors it is possible to add that Cricklade had 'many burgesses', even if only thirty-three are actually recorded, and that Wilton had at least eighteen burgesses and five houses. However, the king was in receipt of £50 and the Abbess of Wilton nearly £11 from the latter place, which indicates that it must have been a significant and flourishing centre. However, the Iron Age hill-fort of Old Sarum, nearby, was chosen for the site of the royal castle. Evidence for the remaining towns is only incidentally recorded under the rural manors. Bedwyn, Calne, Tilshead and Warminster, the heads of important royal manors, had recorded twenty-five, seventy-three, sixty-six and thirty burgesses respectively (according to Welldon Finn's figures). Urban life is also indicated at Bradford on Avon where the Abbess of Shaftesbury had thirty-three burgesses and a market. This is the only market specifically mentioned in Domesday Wiltshire, although it is likely that the other places referred to above each possessed one.

Three of these places were listed in the Burghal Hidage as fortresses in the early tenth century, although the information probably relates back to the middle years of Alfred's reign. Whether the beginnings of urban activity and defences pre-dated this list is unknown. The areas enclosed were considerable. At Wilton provision was made for a rampart of nearly 2,000 yards; 1,650 yards for Malmesbury on its spur between two streams; and more than 2,000 yards for Cricklade. Chisbury, in the same list, was on a smaller scale, probably being a refurbished Iron Age hill-fort.[2] Well before the time of Domesday Book the exposed site at Chisbury had been abandoned for the royal *tun* at Bedwyn, of which manor it was part. Of the development of the remaining Domesday boroughs there is no indication other than the sporadic existence of mints in the later Anglo-Saxon period at Bedwyn, Marlborough, Warminster and Salisbury. Of these perhaps Salisbury is the most intriguing, given its close proximity to Wilton. Although the burning of the latter is recorded in

[1] The Wiltshire towns are surveyed in *VCH Wiltshire*, ii. 14–23; Darby and Welldon Finn (eds.), *Domesday Geography*, 50–60; J. Haslam (ed.), *Anglo-Saxon Towns in Southern England* (Chichester, 1984), 87–147.

[2] Not Tisbury as was thought until recently; Keynes and Lapidge (eds. and trans.), *Alfred the Great*, 193, 340.

1003 in the Anglo-Saxon Chronicle and the mint at Salisbury began striking about this time, that at Wilton was not abandoned. However, when the emergency had passed, moneyers continued to be active at Salisbury, and in the reigns of Cnut and Edward some signed their coins at both places. It is possible, as Haslam has suggested, that Salisbury became an administrative centre.[1]

The evidence for the Wiltshire towns is most unsatisfactory, then. They were all royal, with the exception of Bradford on Avon, but the nature of the activity which took place in them is not explained in Domesday Book. It is possible that some, like Tilshead and Marlborough, owed their importance to the wool trade.[2]

Conclusion

It is regrettable that the scope of the evidence recorded for Domesday Wiltshire is limited. Tenurially it does not possess the special interest for the historian of the Norman Conquest which Sussex and the Welsh Marches hold, which is to be explained by its location. The campaigns of the reigns of Alfred, Æthelræd II and Stephen demonstrate, however, that it was not spared the rigours of war. Nor is it of special interest to the historian of late Anglo-Saxon England for there is too little incidental information in the survey, and it is not supplemented by monastic records such as the chronicle of Abingdon Abbey which helps fill in the picture for neighbouring Berkshire. Finally, the loss of the Wiltshire folios of Exon Domesday and the deficiency in the accounts of Wiltshire's towns mean that our knowledge of the economic life of the county is disappointingly poor. Nevertheless, what the survey does reveal is a shire which was dominated by the king and a number of wealthy churches. The first detailed examination of the Wiltshire survey was the work of Canon W. H. Jones, published in 1865, which remains of immense value in place-name identification. However, it was undertaken before the modern age of Domesday scholarship was inaugurated by the work of J. H. Round and F. W. Maitland. The main contributions to the study of the Domesday county have been Professor R. R. Darlington's detailed chapters for the *Victoria County History* and R. Welldon Finn's essays (see the Bibliography, pp.49–50 below). Both worked within the modern scholarly approach to Domesday studies, and the debt owed to their work in the present Introduction to the Wiltshire Domesday is immense and much greater than can be properly acknowledged in the notes.

[1] The mint evidence is summarized by Darlington, *VCH Wiltshire*, ii. 17–18.

[2] W. G. Hoskins, *VCH Wiltshire*, iv. 1.

HUNDREDS AND WAPENTAKES

F. R. THORN

UNDER William I, as under the English kings, vills were grouped together for taxation, judicial and other obligations into 'hundreds' or, in former Danish areas, into 'wapentakes'. These administrative units, intermediate in size between the vill and the shire, and laid down before civil parishes came into existence, usually consisted of a single unified tract of territory (in 1086 varying widely between twenty and 300 hides in extent) which could belong to a variety of tenants-in-chief. Often a lord (particularly the king or a church) was paramount in a hundred; or the lordship of the hundred was attached to a particular manor by a system that was developed in the later medieval period. Some hundreds contained a single large manor only, and these and others had but a single tenant-in-chief. A few had isolated detachments and fewer still were ecclesiastical hundreds geographically scattered but owing suit to their church, however remote, and not to some local meeting-place. Vills were sometimes divided by hundred boundaries and the members of large manors were often in several different hundreds. Many of the hundred-names, if not replaced in 1086 by those of manors, refer to the meeting-places, 'moots', which were often at road-junctions, river-crossings, beside barrows or mounds, on hilltops or near isolated trees in a prominent position.

Hundreds cannot be described or mapped on the basis of Domesday Book alone, for the boundaries of estates and hundreds are never indicated, nor can every estate be allocated with certainty to a particular hundred, especially when it is mentioned in passing or is the dependency of some composite manor. The composition of hundreds can be partly restored from internal evidence by noting those places that fall directly beneath a hundred heading in the text and by identifying hundredal groupings which in many counties are inscribed in a standard sequence. However, the later history of the manor and of the hundred as well as geographical probability must also be employed and the hundredal rubrication itself examined, for it can be shown to be sometimes incorrect or deficient. The scribe's not infrequent errors are of only a few types and easily allowed for, and some restoration of missing headings can be made from the evidence of the text; but a decision sometimes has to be made to restore a hundred heading above a place from later evidence alone.

If these restorations are not made, Domesday will seem to allocate such a place to a different hundred, of which it will appear, owing to its geographical position, to be an improbable detachment. Allowance must be made for the fact that places lying close to the boundary of a hundred in 1086 may well be found in an adjacent hundred in the thirteenth-century surveys which are the first to show the composition of hundreds in detail.

Strictly speaking, it is impossible to map eleventh-century hundred boundaries. The hundred is the sum of exploited land and woodland, while 'waste', 'forest', moor and bog are either to be regarded as being outside the hundred, or the hundred boundary through them is ill-defined. Expansion of arable land, assarting, and drainage have all tended to change boundaries considerably. Compared with the number of vills surveyed in Domesday Book, charters with boundary clauses are few, their interpretation difficult and their relation to Domesday estates often indirect. Few estate maps survive from the Middle Ages and the first accurate hundred maps, dating from the early nineteenth century, are at the end of a process of change which may have left the 1086 pattern scarcely recognizable. But by using the evidence, whether certain, probable or supplemented, for the composition of the eleventh-century hundreds, lines can be drawn between manors—which may well contain more than one place and extend over more than one modern parish—according to the hundred in which they probably lay in 1086. In this way it is possible to recover something that approximates to eleventh-century topography and administrative divisions.[1]

THE HUNDREDS OF WILTSHIRE

For most counties surveyed in 1086, the text of Domesday Book provides hundredal rubrication to indicate the hundred in which the estate or estates lay. These hundred headings are usually placed either at the end of the first line of each entry or group of entries or in a space left at the end of the preceding entry. Although a number of hundred headings are

[1] Apart from works cited in individual articles in this series, documents and discussions concerning the hundredal system will be found in O. S. Anderson, *The English Hundred-Names* (Lund, 1934); *Inquisitions and Assessments Relating to Feudal Aids with other Analogous Documents, Preserved in the Public Records Office A.D. 1284–1431* (abbr. *Feudal Aids*), 6 vols. (HMSO, London, 1899–1920); F. Liebermann, *Die Gesetze der Angelsachsen*, 3 vols. (Halle, 1903–16); H. R. Loyn, *The Governance of Anglo-Saxon England, 500–1087* (London, 1984); A. J. Robertson (ed.), *The Laws of the Kings of England from Edmund to Henry I* (Cambridge, 1925); F. M. Stenton, *Anglo-Saxon England* (3rd edn., Oxford, 1971).

missing in such counties, especially from the *Terra Regis* section, it is only in the five south-western counties that hundredal rubrication is entirely absent. The Wiltshire folios mention two hundreds in passing when they record that the pleas of "Cicementone" and Startley (*Sutelesberg*) Hundreds were a part of the revenue of Malmesbury borough.[1] Another hundred-name finds its way into the text when Domesday notes that Edward of Salisbury holds six hides in the hundred of *Wrderusteselle*.[2] Here the hundred-name *Wrde* (Highworth) has been run into the place-name *Rusteselle* (Lus Hill) and has managed to survive from an earlier stage of the inquiry. There are not even any references to the work of the hundred courts in the checking of Domesday material, although there are several citations of the 'men of the shire'.

Nevertheless, for three of the south-western counties (Somerset, Cornwall and Devonshire) a reasonably secure picture of the hundreds as they existed around 1086 can be drawn from a comparison of the information contained in the Tax Returns (sometimes called the Geld Rolls) long associated with the Exeter text of Domesday (Exon), the immediate predecessor of Great Domesday;[3] from the order in which places are entered in each fief in Exon itself; and from pairs of plain lists of hundreds bound up with the same text.[4] Unfortunately there are no such Hundred Lists for Wiltshire, and only a single entry—that for William de Moyon's portion of Sutton Veny—remains from the Exon text. Had the complete text survived, it is likely that within each fief places would have been arranged in hundredal blocks and in a standard sequence, thus facilitating the reconstruction of hundreds. However, such blocks are not perceptible in the Exchequer text, in which inquest material has apparently been rearranged within the fief according to other criteria.[5] Thus, of all the south-western counties, it is Wiltshire whose eleventh-century hundreds are the most difficult to reconstruct.

None the less, Tax Returns survive for Wiltshire, and in three separate versions.[6] Although they are now bound up with Exon proper, and are probably close to it in date, they are not for that reason to be considered part of the same survey: there are so many discrepancies of detail that it is difficult to regard them as strictly contemporary, or as compiled from the same material.[7] Tax Returns exist for all five south-western counties and were probably based on lists of geld liability that are now lost but which perhaps also contributed to the substructure of the Domesday survey. They record the collection of geld at 6*s*. to the hide, and a typical hundredal return begins with the total hidage of that hundred and (in Cornwall, Devonshire and Somerset) the amount of geld paid;[8] it then names the holders of exempt land (usually the total of an individual fief-holder's demesne in that hundred), and finishes with a schedule of those by whom geld had not been paid; sometimes other details are added. Place-names are included sporadically, but the Wiltshire Tax Returns only duplicate a few names found in Domesday Book itself.[9] However, the principal contribution of the Tax Returns to a study of hundreds lies in the fact that a comparison of holders and hidage with Domesday entries often allows particular Domesday estates to be allotted to particular hundreds listed in the Tax Returns.

In all, the three Wiltshire versions of the Tax Returns supply the details of forty hundreds and one manor, Collingbourne Ducis, which seems to have been the nucleus of the later liberty of Everleigh.[10] These 'hundreds' vary in size between 'Selkley' Hundred at 196 hides and three and a half virgates and 'Frustfield' Hundred at eleven hides and half a virgate.[11] The hundreds appear in virtually the same order in all three versions of the Tax Returns, although Kinwardstone Hundred and Collingbourne Ducis manor are omitted from version A.[12] The three versions appear not to be independent of each other, but to relate to the same geld collection, version C being the earliest phase and version A the latest.[13] In addition, version A has excluded the hidage of a number

[1] GDB 64v. They were still attached to Malmesbury in the thirteenth century (*Rotuli Hundredorum*, ii (Record Commission, London, 1818), 230, 272), by which time the borough and its hundreds were in the hands of the Abbot of Malmesbury, by grant of King John. "Cicementone" is the eleventh-century name for the hundred later named Chedglow; *Sutelesberg* is an alternative name for Startley Hundred; see Table 1 below.

[2] GDB 69.

[3] The Liber Exoniensis (Exon) is preserved in Exeter Cathedral Library; the solitary printed edition is vol. iii (vol. iv in some bindings) of the Record Commission edition of DB, edited by Sir Henry Ellis and published in 1816. The surviving folios contain material for the whole of Somerset and Cornwall and for most of Devon., but for less than half of Dorset.

[4] There are no Hundred Lists for Dorset, for whose reconstruction, however, Exon material and the Tax Returns are available.

[5] Places are entered in hundred-blocks and these blocks have a standard sequence in many counties in DB; see the various 'Hundreds' articles in the present series, and P. H. Sawyer, 'The "Original Returns" and Domesday Book', *EHR* 70 (1955), 177–97.

[6] Version A: Exon ff. 1–3v; version B: ff. 7–9v; version C: ff. 13–16. The designation of the three versions is due to Jones, *Domesday for Wiltshire*.

[7] The problem of dating and of the relation of the material to DB is admirably reviewed by A. Williams in *VCH Dorset*, iii (1968), 115–23, and by R. R. Darlington in *VCH Wiltshire*, ii (1955), 174–6. For V. H. Galbraith's emphatic view that they date from 1086, see 'The Date of the Geld Rolls in Exon Domesday', *EHR* 65 (1950), 1–17, and the Appendix to his *The Making of Domesday Book* (Oxford, 1961), 223–30. The Exon survey of the Dorset boroughs is written in the same gathering of parchment as version B of the Wiltshire Tax Returns. This does not date the Returns, but shows that at least one version of them and Exon proper were kept together from the beginning.

[8] This detail is entered later in the Tax Returns for Wiltshire and Dorset.

[9] The place-name Winterbourne Stoke is supplied by the 'Dolesfield' Hundred Tax Return (versions B, C); East Knoyle by the Mere return (version A); and Bromham by that for Calne (version A).

[10] Collingbourne Ducis (*Colingeburna*), when used as a hundred-name, is called Collingbourne (Ducis) elsewhere in this article and in Box 1 of the accompanying map. For simplicity, however, the suffix is not enclosed in parentheses when used in the body of the text, even when the hundred-name is intended. For Everleigh, see Table 4, n.9 below.

[11] The names and hidages are given in Table 1.

[12] In version A Swanborough is entered in sixth instead of in ninth place and Stowford Hundred is entered after rather than before 'Cadworth'; in version C Blagrove is entered last rather than third to last.

[13] *VCH Wiltshire*, ii. 171–2.

of important royal manors—Compton Chamberlayne, Rushall, Corsham, Aldbourne, Coombe Bissett and Lydiard Millicent—which were probably accounted for separately at that stage of the proceedings: royal manors may in fact have been separately surveyed for Domesday Book, and the Somerset Hundred Lists are swollen by a number of royal manors, some of which are also accounted for in the solitary version of the Somerset Tax Returns.[1]

The Wiltshire Tax Returns have been studied by W. H. Jones, R. R. Darlington and R. Welldon Finn;[2] the first two have published reconstructions of all the hundreds, and Welldon Finn has tabulated the most straightforward quarter of them. Darlington's somewhat melancholy conclusion to his study is that: 'Owing to the nature of the evidence, several hundreds cannot be reconstructed, and it seems best to acknowledge that some of the problems created by the survival of the Geld Rolls are insoluble . . . On some matters it is unlikely that any two scholars would ever reach agreement.'[3] Nevertheless, because the Tax Returns remain the only contemporary evidence for the eleventh-century hundreds of Wiltshire, it is worth exploring the degree of uncertainty involved in their use.

Reconstruction of a Tax Return hundred proceeds in two stages: first it is necessary to identify with particular Domesday estates the extents of lands which are exempt from geld, or on which geld has not been paid. A single Tax Return exemption may account for several Domesday estates, as for example the sixty-six and a half hides allowed to the Abbot of Malmesbury in "Cicementone" Hundred, which must have embraced the demesne of the Domesday manors of Brokenborough, Kemble (now Glos.), Long Newnton (now Glos.), Charlton (near Malmesbury), Garsdon and Crudwell.[4] Sometimes the amount of geld not paid is smaller than the geldable hidage, presumably because part had been paid: this is so, for example, in the case of the tenant Warner who, in the return for Chippenham Hundred, is said to have held back the geld on one hide, no doubt part of his holding at Ditteridge of which the geldable extent was one hide and three virgates.[5] Occasionally, persons named as Tax Return holders do not appear in Domesday Book, perhaps because of a change of tenancy, or because the estate has been omitted in Domesday. Nevertheless, the land exempt from geld as well as that on which geld remains unpaid can be satisfactorily identified in most cases: fortunately the Wiltshire folios supply the demesne hidage for the majority of holdings, so a direct comparison with the Tax Returns is possible. One can even allocate some unnamed Domesday estates to their hundreds.[6]

The second stage, in theory much more uncertain, involves an attempt to increase the hidage already identified to the total of hides given in the Tax Return for that hundred. In effect, this means adding up the estates considered likely to have lain in that hundred in 1086, and adjusting this sum, by adding, deducting or re-allocating certain of them to neighbouring hundreds until the correct total is obtained. Even if the exact Tax Return totals for the whole county could be attained, or at least those for a group of contiguous hundreds, there would still be the danger that an estate or group of estates amounting to the same total hidage had been wrongly placed in one hundred and a compensating error made in the adjacent one. Moreover, some estates could have spanned hundred boundaries, but there is no means of establishing all those that did so or how many hides were involved. However, while some hundreds can be made to total exactly, wholesale agreement between Domesday Book estates and Tax Return hundreds is impossible, if only because the Tax Return total (3,956 hides, 2½ virgates) is short of the total hidage of estates listed in the Domesday folios for Wiltshire (4,050).[7] Part of the discrepancy may be due to the fact that a few estates are entered twice, once in their own name and once as the unnamed subdivision of some larger estate.[8] But just as the Tax Returns themselves announce the discovery of hides previously concealed,[9] so it is probable that the much more thorough Domesday survey had brought to light other hidden hides.

In practice, the percentage of error in the reconstruction of the Tax Returns is likely to be considerably less than these theoretical difficulties might suggest. A number of hundreds can be reconstructed either exactly or to within half a hide, and in those cases where Welldon Finn and Darlington have published their tabulations they are in agreement.[10] These hundreds are Bishops Cannings,[11] 'Cadworth',

[1] See Thorn, 'Hundreds and Wapentakes', *Somerset Domesday*, 34.

[2] Jones, *Domesday for Wiltshire*, 153–91; Darlington, *VCH Wiltshire*, ii. 178–217; Welldon Finn, 'Assessment of Wiltshire in 1083 and 1086'.

[3] *VCH Wiltshire*, ii. 177.

[4] The demesne hidage is respectively eight hides, twelve hides, fifteen hides, twelve hides, one and a half hides, eighteen hides, making the exact total of sixty-six and a half hides.

[5] GDB 71v.

[6] Ragnburh's unnamed five hides (f.74) probably lay in Heytesbury Hundred where the Tax Return allows him three and a half hides of demesne land. The demesne is, however, omitted from DB.

[7] The Tax Return total is taken from version B. If the additional forty-one carucates mentioned in the Tax Returns are counted as hides, the total becomes 3,997 hides, 2½ virgates. The Domesday figure is taken from F. W. Maitland, *Domesday Book and Beyond* (Cambridge, 1897), 400.

[8] The four and a half hides held by William Scudet as a subinfeudation of the king's manor of Westbury (f.65) appear to be duplicated on f.74v where he is said to hold in chief four and a half hides in Westbury. Similarly Hervey's one and a half hides of land in the royal manor of Netheravon (f.65) reappear on f.74v. An even larger problem of this nature affects Melksham Hundred; see p.36, n.9 below.

[9] In version A of the Tax Returns for both Warminster and Heytesbury Hundreds it is stated that a hide has been found which has not paid geld since 1066.

[10] Welldon Finn analysed the hundreds of Ramsbury, Bishops Cannings, Westbury, Downton, Damerham, 'Staple', Cricklade, 'Thornhill', Stowford and Dunworth.

[11] Bishops Cannings, when used as a hundred-name, is called (Bishops) Cannings elsewhere in this article and in Box 1 of the accompanying map. For simplicity, however, the prefix is not enclosed in parentheses when used in the body of the text, even when the hundred-name is intended.

"Cicementone", Cricklade, Damerham, Downton, Dunworth, 'Frustfield', Heytesbury, Highworth, Ramsbury, Rowbury, Startley, 'Studfold', 'Thornhill', Warminster and Westbury. To these can be added Collingbourne Ducis manor. Another group—Alderbury, Blagrove, Bradford, 'Branchbury', Calne, 'Cawdon', Chippenham, 'Dolesfield', 'Elstub', Melksham, Mere, "Scipa", Stowford, Swanborough, Thorngrove and 'Wonderditch'—can be brought to within five hides of a Tax Return total that is often well over a hundred hides in each case, the difference usually being an excess. This leaves only the hundreds of Amesbury, Dunley, 'Kingsbridge', Kinwardstone, 'Selkley', 'Staple' and 'Whorwellsdown' adrift by more than five hides.

Confidence that a reasonably accurate picture of the late eleventh-century hundreds can be drawn on this basis is increased by other factors. Those hundreds that can be reconstructed exactly do not form a single block, but are intermixed with others and thus define a good part of their boundaries. Moreover, those places that cannot be certainly identified from the individual hidages given in the Tax Returns do not always lie on the border of hundreds, so any uncertainty about them does not affect the perimeter of the hundred. Further, the difficulties are confined to particular areas: for example, the problems of 'Selkley' Hundred seem largely to lie within itself and not to involve adjacent hundreds. In other cases, such as the hundreds adjacent to Chippenham, Highworth and Malmesbury, the problems seem to involve the interrelation of the divisions of what was formerly a larger unit dependent on the royal manor or borough.[1]

It has to be admitted that, as with other aspects of Domesday Book, difficulties may well be created by a failure to identify a place or by the wrong identification of estates, some of which are less certainly identified in Wiltshire than in other Domesday counties.[2] Also there is the impossibility of allocating some unnamed holdings to their correct hundreds.[3] Moreover, in the present study a series of tentative adjustments has been made to Darlington's detailed and comprehensive reconstructions of the Tax Returns, resulting in a reduction in the size and number of the discrepancies between the Tax Return hidage and the reconstituted hundreds.[4] Thus the discrepancy of thirty hides he notes between "Cicementone" and Startley Hundreds can be resolved by assuming that thirty hides of the manor of Brokenborough (ten hides at Corston, ten at Sutton Benger and ten at Rodbourne near Malmesbury)[5] were in 1086 not included in "Cicementone" with Brokenborough itself, but in Startley. In the fourteenth century all three were in Chedglow Hundred, the successor of "Cicementone", the first two forming an awkward southwards projection, the third apparently a detached part of the hundred.[6] The shortage that Darlington notes in 'Wonderditch' Hundred and most of the excess in the adjacent Amesbury Hundred[7] can be accounted for by assuming that the manor of (Great and Little) Durnford lay in 'Wonderditch' Hundred in 1086 and was only transferred to Amesbury (where it lay in the fourteenth century) when 'Wonderditch' became a franchise of the Bishop of Salisbury.[8] Similarly, but less surely, the totals of Calne and Rowbury Hundreds depend on assuming that in 1086 Rowde was in the former hundred.[9] Rowbury and Highworth Hundreds can only be made nearly exact, and Swanborough can only be brought to within five hides of its total, if hides are allocated to a missing royal estate in each; in the case of the last two it is probable that there were royal estates at Highworth and Upavon, whose churches alone are mentioned in Domesday Book.[10] "Scipa" Hundred can only be given a total close to that in the Tax Returns at the expense of 'Staple' Hundred.[11]

Since most of the estates that can be positively identified in a particular hundred in the Tax Returns can be found in the same hundred (though it may have been renamed or occasionally amalgamated) in the thirteenth and fourteenth centuries, this fact can tip the balance of probability in difficult cases.[12] As with most

[1] See p.39 below.

[2] The absence of hundred heads and of a regular hundredal order within fiefs, the antiquity and restricted format of the English Place-Name Society volume (Gover *et al.*, *Place-Names of Wiltshire* (abbr. *PNWilts.*)), and the incompleteness of the series of magisterial *VCH* 'topographical' volumes, make some identifications less secure than in other counties. The differences between the present edition and that of Thorn and Thorn (eds.), *Domesday Book: Wiltshire*, are entered in Table 3.

[3] For example, the one-and-three-quarter-hide holding of Ælfric the Little (f.73v) cannot be allocated to a particular hundred.

[4] It is hoped to publish this revision separately at a later date.

[5] Six hides at Corston are mentioned in DB (f.67). Rodbourne near Malmesbury is at NGR ST 9383, and is not the same as the Rodbourne near Swindon named in DB (f.71). Sutton Benger lies at NGR ST 9478. All these places were among lands confirmed on Malmesbury Abbey by Edward the Confessor in 1065; see P. H. Sawyer (ed.), *Anglo-Saxon Charters: An Annotated List and Bibliography*, R. Hist. Soc. Guides and Handbooks, 8 (London, 1968) (henceforward cited by number preceded by S.), S.1038, and *VCH Wiltshire*, ii. 88.

[6] See R. E. Glasscock (ed.), *The Lay Subsidy of 1334*, Brit. Acad. Records of Social and Economic Hist. ns 2 (London, 1975), 337.

[7] *VCH Wiltshire*, ii. 180, 195.

[8] See *VCH Wiltshire*, vi (1962), 195; Glasscock (ed.), *Lay Subsidy of 1334*, 345. In 1086, (Great and Little) Durnford were divided between Wilton Abbey and William de Eu. In the thirteenth century they were in the hands of the Earls of Salisbury: *The Book of Fees*, ii (HMSO, London, 1923), 709, 744.

[9] Rowde was later drawn into the hundred of 'Rowbury Episcopi', a division of the eleventh-century hundred of Rowbury; *Feudal Aids*, v (1908), 205. It appears as a liberty in 1334: Glasscock (ed.), *Lay Subsidy of 1334*, 333.

[10] GDB 65v; see *VCH Wiltshire*, ii. 185, 192, 211.

[11] The royal manor of Lydiard Millicent could lie in either "Scipa" or 'Staple' Hundreds, but has here been assigned to "Scipa". Darlington (*VCH Wiltshire*, ii. 183, 210) hesitates between the two, but Lydiard Millicent, although it formed a geographically awkward projection from "Scipa" Hundred, was later in Highworth Hundred (Glasscock (ed.), *Lay Subsidy of 1334*, 343) with which "Scipa", but not 'Staple', had been merged (see Table 4 below). This leaves 'Staple' Hundred deficient in a royal manor of about ten hides, formerly held by Earl Harold. This could be Chilton Foliat (f.71) which later lay in Kinwardstone Hundred, but which cannot be included in its Tax Return total without creating an excess. But it is geographically remote from the known area of 'Staple' Hundred.

[12] The main sources for such a comparison are *The Book of Fees*, *Feudal Aids*, the *Lay Subsidy Rolls* and the *Rotuli Hundredorum*, all cited above.

other counties, the differences between the eleventh century and the later medieval hundreds are unlikely to have been very considerable, most transfers being caused by the creation of scattered 'franchisal' hundreds, usually for churches which preferred their dispersed estates to be in a single hundred.[1]

Even so, the hundred in which a few places lay in 1086 remains uncertain,[2] and two further difficulties lie in the way of reconstruction: the problems of unnamed estates and of detached parts of hundreds. Domesday Book does not set out to name every place that lay in the kingdom of England in 1086. It is evident that Chippenham, unhidated but with land for a hundred ploughs, and Wroughton with thirty hides, comprehended more than one settlement.[3] In the case of hundreds such as Bishops Cannings or Westbury, which contain but a single named place in Domesday Book, later evidence can often give a clearer idea of the extent of the estate: in the fourteenth century twelve distinct members of Westbury manor are named and eleven of Bishops Cannings.[4] In lârger hundreds, whole areas corresponding to later parishes are unnamed because they are subsumed in the details for some greater unit: these can only be included, and then only tentatively, in a particular hundred on the basis of later evidence—that of the hundred in which they are later named, or of the manor named in Domesday Book with which they can be shown to have a subsequent tenurial connection. Thus Martin (now Hants)[5] was no doubt a member of Damerham Hundred, and Whitsbury (now Hants)[6] of 'Cawdon'. Woodford (now represented by Upper, Middle and Lower Woodford) and Stratford sub Castle[7] would have been in 'Wonderditch' Hundred, and Berwick Bassett[8] probably in Calne Hundred. One can assume the inclusion of Lyneham in 'Kingsbridge' Hundred and of Box in that of Chippenham in 1086.[9] Sometimes the boundary of the hundred passed through the land of a later parish: Hinton Parva[10] and Earlscourt later lay in Bishopstone parish, but were in 'Thornhill' Hundred in 1086, while Bishopstone was part of the Bishop of Salisbury's manor of Ramsbury. Similarly, Bincknoll and Uffcott were later parts of Broad Hinton parish, but possibly lay in Blagrove Hundred in 1086, while Broad Hinton itself lay in 'Selkley' Hundred.[11]

As to detached parts of hundreds, reconstruction of the Tax Returns suggests that in 1086, as later, Dinton and Fisherton de la Mere were detached from Warminster Hundred; Bathampton and part of Orcheston[12] from Heytesbury Hundred; and Poulton (near Cirencester) both from Cricklade Hundred and from the county. Atworth, an unnamed member of Bradford on Avon in Domesday Book, will have been detached from Bradford Hundred by the intrusion of Great and Little Chalfield, which then belonged to Melksham Hundred.[13] Later evidence puts Higher Pertwood as a detachment of Warminster Hundred; 'Easton Bassett' (in Berwick St John)[14] of Donhead manor and Dunworth Hundred; Deptford of Heytesbury Hundred; part of West Wellow (now Hants) of Amesbury Hundred; Plaitford (now Hants) of Alderbury Hundred; and Bramshaw (now Hants) of 'Cawdon' Hundred; they may well all have been so detached in 1086. These last three form a cluster of detachments in the densely wooded Hampshire-Wiltshire border, and may have originated as 'denes'—detachments of the hundred for timber or pannage.[15] Kingswood,[16] unnamed in Domesday Book, but a detachment of Chippenham Hundred surrounded by Gloucestershire in later times, was probably a member of Chippenham manor in 1086, while it is probable or even definate that various detached parts of ecclesiastical manors were part of the original grants of the hundreds: Chittoe[17] of Bishops Cannings,

[1] The changes are itemized below, p.40, n.23, and summarized in Table 4.

[2] For example, Compton (in Enford) was divided between Amesbury Hundred and Everleigh Liberty in the fourteenth century: Glasscock (ed.), *Lay Subsidy of 1334*, 346. It might have been in 'Elstub' in 1086, being transferred away when 'Elstub' became an ecclesiastical hundred. Surrendell (f.72v), if correctly identified, lay at the junction of Startley, Thorngrove and Dunley Hundreds, but its five hides would form an excess in the reconstruction of each hundred's Tax Return. The next place entered in DB, Kington St Michael, was in Thorngrove Hundred. Surrendell, though in Hullavington parish (Startley Hundred), was in Chippenham Hundred in 1334 which could represent Thorngrove or Dunley Hundreds of DB (but not Startley); Glasscock (ed.), *Lay Subsidy of 1334*, 344.

[3] GDB 64v, 65v.

[4] Glasscock (ed.), *Lay Subsidy of 1334*, 348, 336, gives Bourton, Easton, Horton, Bishops Cannings, Coate, Roundway, Chittoe, 'Bedborough', Wick Green, Nursteed and Highway as constituents of Bishops Cannings, and Westbury, Brook, Westbury Leigh, Chapmanslade, Penleigh, Hawkeridge, Heywood, Bratton, Melbourne, Stoke, Dilton Marsh and Bremeridge as components of Westbury. Highway lay in 'Kingsbridge' Hundred in 1086, neither part of the vill being then held by the Bishop of Salisbury to whom it was later given.

[5] NGR SU 0619.

[6] NGR SU 1219.

[7] NGR SU 1237, 1136, 1235, 1332 respectively.

[8] NGR SU 0973. It was certainly part of Calne Hundred in the Middle Ages (Glasscock (ed.), *Lay Subsidy of 1334*, 337; *VCH Wiltshire*, xii (1983), 62), but it forms an awkward geographical projection into 'Selkley' Hundred.

[9] Glasscock (ed.), *Lay Subsidy of 1334*, 344.

[10] NGR SU 2383.

[11] *VCH Wiltshire*, ix (1970), 3, places Bincknoll and Uffcott possibly in 'Kingsbridge' Hundred in 1086; see *VCH Wiltshire*, ii. 198.

[12] The former separate parishes of 'Orcheston St George' and 'Orcheston St Mary' were in different hundreds (Heytesbury and 'Dolesfield' respectively). They were merged as civil parishes in 1934 and as ecclesiastical parishes in 1971 and are now known simply as Orcheston; see F. A. Youngs, Jun., *Guide to the Local Administrative Units of England: 1 Southern England*, R. Hist. Soc. Guides and Handbooks, 10 (London, 1979), 546.

[13] (Great and Little) Chalfield can be identified in the Tax Return for Melksham Hundred (see *VCH Wiltshire*, ii. 194; vii (1953), 1), but had probably once been in Bradford Hundred; see p.36, n.17 below.

[14] 'Easton Bassett' (in Berwick St John), now represented by Easton Farm (NGR ST 948221), was part of the grant or restoration of Donhead to Shaftesbury Abbey in 956 (Sawyer (ed.), S.630), and lay in an area otherwise occupied by the ecclesiastical hundred of Stowford; see p.36, n.11 below.

[15] These 'denes' are familiar from Kent, Surrey, Sussex and Hampshire; see H. C. Darby, *Domesday England* (Cambridge, 1977), 33–4. Bramshaw belonged to Britford manor (*Feudal Aids*, v. 201), a fact which explains the detachment.

[16] Near Wotton-under-Edge (Glos.); NGR ST 7492.

[17] NGR ST 9566. Bupton (NGR SU 0676) in Clyffe Pypard may also have been a part of Bishops Cannings in 1086, but has not been so mapped; *VCH Wiltshire*, ix. 30.

Compton Chamberlayne[1] of Damerham, Semley[2] of Stowford, and Bishopstone[3] of Downton.

All these matters have been borne in mind in the tentative reconstruction of the eleventh-century Wiltshire hundreds shown on the accompanying map.[4] Although it is inevitable that some uncertainties should remain, the importance to the historical geographer and to the local historian is such that a study of the likely boundaries seems worth while. For no county is Domesday evidence in itself sufficient for mapping; but there is enough other evidence for Wiltshire for an attempt to be made.

The picture that emerges is one of some complexity and one that has probably evolved some way from a simpler, earlier pattern: large hundreds jostle with small, and hundreds that contain the lands of several tenants-in-chief touch those that are in the hands of a single lord; while yet other hundreds, once in the hands of a single church, have lost some of their lands to lay landholders.

In 1086 Ramsbury Hundred was a ninety-hide manor-hundred of the Bishop of Salisbury,[5] who likewise held the seventy-hide manor-hundred of Bishops Cannings.[6] Westbury Hundred was a forty-hide manor formerly held by Queen Edith and treated, as are occasionally other smallish royal manors in other counties, as a hundred.[7] Collingbourne Ducis was also a royal manor, of twenty hides, but not called a hundred in the Tax Returns. It may have been the rump of a larger land-unit of Collingbourne left after the grant of Collingbourne Kingston to St Peter's Abbey, Winchester.[8] The large royal manor of Melksham (eighty-four hides in Domesday Book) seems to have been practically co-extensive with the hundred (eighty-six hides in the Tax Returns). Domesday, however, duplicates many of the eighty-four hides by specifying their separate tenure by other tenants-in-chief: the composite royal manor had thus, in effect, been broken up, but the taxation records were not abreast of the fact.[9]

Among the 1086 hundreds there were a number that had once been one-owner hundreds, but which before 1086 had lost parts by alienations. Downton Hundred had originally contained 100 hides and had been granted to the Bishop of Winchester, but its total is given as ninety-seven hides in the Tax Returns and of these several hides at Standlynch and Witherington were in other hands in 1086.[10] Likewise, Stowford Hundred had been granted as a hundred *mansiunculae* in 955 to Wilton Abbey and its extent had encompassed Tollard Royal and Ebbesborne Wake which were in lay hands in 1086.[11] In the Tax Returns it answered for 105 hides and seems as well to have included Trow and Fifield Bavant, also alienated from the Church. Damerham Hundred had also been a grant of a hundred hides, by King Edmund with reversion to the Church of Glastonbury.[12] At the time of the grant it was said to include Damerham and Martin (both now Hants) and Pentridge (Dorset), this last paying geld for six hides in the Dorset folios.[13] However, the Tax Returns allot to Damerham Hundred only sixty-three hides,[14] ten of which lay at Compton Chamberlayne which in 1086 was in King William's hands, having been held by Earl Harold in 1066. Whether Damerham had benefited from a special reduction in geld-liability or whether some of its lands had been taken into other hundreds is unclear.[15]

There had perhaps not been any other fully ecclesiastical hundreds in Wiltshire.[16] Although it is possible that the grant to Shaftesbury Abbey in 1001 of the manor of Bradford on Avon with its *conoebium*[17] also included the lordship of the hundred, as was later claimed, it is far from certain that the Abbey had ever actually held all hundred hides within the hundred.[18] Similarly, while the Abbess of Romsey held, in Edington and (Steeple and West) Ashton, seventy of the seventy-eight hides of 'Whorwellsdown' Hundred, and later claimed to hold the hundred itself by gift of King Edgar, it is probable that the lordship of the

[1] NGR SU 0230. [2] NGR ST 8926. [3] NGR SU 0726.

[4] Its boundaries, internal and external, have been checked against C. and J. Greenwood, *Map of the County of Wiltshire from an Actual Survey made in the years 1819 and 1820* (London, 1820). The hundreds in Thorn and Thorn (eds.), *Domesday Book: Wiltshire*, were mapped from those given in Gover *et al.*, *PNWilts.*, according to the policy established by the general editor of the former series, John Morris.

[5] Ramsbury was probably an ancient liberty of the Bishops of Ramsbury, predecessors of the Bishops of Salisbury; see *VCH Wiltshire*, xii. 1. [6] *VCH Wiltshire*, vii. 175.

[7] See *VCH Wiltshire*, viii (1965), 136–8.

[8] It probably included Everleigh (*VCH Wiltshire*, xi (1980), 105, 109) and part of Chute Wood (p.37 below).

[9] These members are Whitley, Poulshot, Whaddon (in Semington), Trowle, Trowbridge, Hilperton, (Great and Little) Chalfield and Staverton; see *VCH Wiltshire*, ii. 194.

[10] *VCH Wiltshire*, ii. 84; xi. 1. For grants and confirmations, see Sawyer (ed.), S.229, S.275, S.393, S.540, S.821, S.891, S.1515; and H. P. R. Finberg (ed.), *The Early Charters of Wessex* (Leicester, 1964), 235.

[11] See *VCH Wiltshire*, ii. 91; xiii (1987), 3; Sawyer (ed.), S.582. The bounds included both Broad Chalke and Bowerchalke, Ebbesborne Wake, Alvediston, Berwick St John, Tollard Royal and Semley, but excepted two enclaves: six hides belonging to Donhead (at 'Easton Bassett', see p.35, n.14 above) and six hides belonging to Ringwood (Hants). [12] Sawyer (ed.), S.513. [13] GDB 77v.

[14] The sixty-three hides of Damerham Hundred in versions B and C of the Tax Returns appear to have consisted of fifty-two hides held by Glastonbury Abbey and one hide held by the Church of Cranborne, both at Damerham, together with ten hides at Compton Chamberlayne. Version A of the Tax Returns gives a total of fifty-three hides and clearly excludes this last estate.

[15] See *VCH Wiltshire*, ii. 96.

[16] See the discussion in *VCH Wiltshire*, v (1957), 44–6.

[17] Sawyer (ed.), S.899. The bounds of the charter seem to correspond to the hundred of Bradford, including (Great and Little) Chalfield, which had been removed by 1086, and Limpley Stoke, lying west of the river Avon. If the abbey ever in fact held the whole hundred, considerable encroachments had been made by 1086 when a dozen estates were in other hands. The later members of the manor included Holt (NGR ST 8661), South Wraxall (NGR ST 8364), Atworth (NGR ST 8665), Limpley Stoke (NGR ST 7860) and Winsley (NGR ST 7960); see *Feudal Aids*, v. 210, and *VCH Wiltshire*, ii. 95; J. H. P. Pafford, 'Bradford-on-Avon: The Saxon Boundaries in Ethelred's Charter of 1001 A.D.', *Wiltshire Archaeol. and Nat. Hist. Mag.* (abbr. *WANHM*) 54 (1951), 210–18, 372; R. Harvey, 'The Saxon Charters of Bradford on Avon and Westwood', *WANHM* 79 (1985), 235–7.

[18] *Rotuli Hundredorum*, ii. 236; see *VCH Wiltshire*, vii. 1–3.

hundred rather than all the lands in it was meant, and even that more modest claim may have been untrue.[1] The early history of the Church of Malmesbury's holdings is obscure, but if it had ever once held all the lands around Malmesbury, it must have been subject to major encroachments before 1086; moreover, Malmesbury with its two appurtenant hundreds was a royal not an ecclesiastical borough in 1086. Later, however, the 'three hundreds of Malmesbury' were in the hands of its church.[2] Finally, 'Wonderditch' Hundred, though it might once have been an ecclesiastical hundred, in 1086 contained lands of the Bishop of Salisbury, Wilton Abbey and William de Eu.[3]

Two other areas might have been ecclesiastical hundreds, had their grants lasted: Calne had been granted to the Old Minster in Winchester *c.*950 by King Eadræd's will, yet was still royal demesne both in 1066 and 1086,[4] while nearly 100 hides, based on Bedwyn, were for a short time in the hands of Abingdon Abbey.[5]

While ecclesiastical hundreds often have 'artificial' boundaries because they have been carved out of some existing unit, many Wiltshire hundreds seem to have been delimited by topographical features. Thus Dunley Hundred was separated from Startley and Thorngrove Hundreds by the Fosse Way, and Chippenham Hundred from Bradford and Melksham Hundreds by another Roman road. On the northern and western edges of Salisbury Plain, the boundaries seem to have followed ancient hilltop roads. Demarcation was also provided by the hill ridges that lie between the valleys of the Wylye and Nadder, and of the Ebble and Nadder, while the rivers Ray and Avon themselves also formed boundaries. On the other hand, many of the 1086 boundaries must have been ill-defined: in the 'forests'[6] that Domesday does not name (Braydon, Chippenham, Clarendon, Melksham, Pewsham, Savernake, 'Selwood') and in those woods or forests that it does: Chute Wood, one-third of which belonged to Collingbourne Ducis, Melchet Wood in which the manors of South Newton and Washern had an interest for wood, fodder and pasture, and Grovely Forest where the king's foresters held one and a half hides. But it is unlikely that there was any virgin land in Wiltshire in 1086.[7]

The complicated combination of single-owner hundreds and hundreds of mixed tenure, of 'natural' and artificial boundaries, and of detachments, is made more complex by a number of other features. The Tax Returns make clear that the Abbess of Romsey had land in Heytesbury Hundred, and it is likely that part of her thirty-hide manor of Edington lay there, divided by the hundred boundary from the settlement of Edington which itself lay in 'Whorwellsdown' Hundred. Similarly, one part of Orcheston was in Heytesbury Hundred, while another part was in 'Dolesfield' Hundred.[8] Analysis of the Tax Return totals also suggests that both Burcombe and Ugford were divided between 'Branchbury' and 'Cadworth' Hundreds in 1086; Yatton Keynall between Chippenham and Thorngrove Hundreds; and Brokenborough between "Cicementone" and Startley Hundreds.[9] Later evidence suggests that other vills may have been similarly split.[10]

A number of vills were divided by the county boundary. Wulfric held West Winterslow (Wilts.) and with it one virgate of West Tytherley, most of which lay in Hampshire.[11] One hide of Idmiston lay in Hampshire,[12] and, on the same border, half of West Dean lay in Wiltshire, but the other half, 'West Dean All Saints', was in Hampshire until recent times and likewise held in 1086 by Waleran the huntsman.[13] Waleran had also put one and a half virgates of East Wellow (Hants) into Wiltshire.[14] Bramshaw seems to have been divided between Wiltshire and Hampshire in 1086, with only the Wiltshire portion named in Domesday Book,[15] although both parts are now in Hampshire. All these minor changes could have taken place between the Conquest and the date of Domesday

[1] *Rotuli Hundredorum*, ii. 235, 277; see *VCH Wiltshire*, ii. 93–4; viii. 193–4. On the attachment to a particular manor, see H. M. Cam, *Liberties and Communities in Medieval England: Collected Studies in Local Administration and Topography* (Cambridge, 1944; repr. London, 1963), 64–90.

[2] *VCH Wiltshire*, ii. 87–90; see p.32, n.1 above.

[3] Assuming that Great and Little Durnford were parts of the hundred in 1086 (see p.34, n.8 above). It is not certain that Wilsford (near Amesbury) was in it; see *VCH Wiltshire*, vi. 195–8.

[4] Sawyer (ed.), S.1515. The grant included Downton, which stayed with Winchester Church, and Damerham which remained a hundred but went to Glastonbury; see *VCH Wiltshire*, ii. 86.

[5] Sawyer (ed.), S.688, S.756; *VCH Wiltshire*, ii. 97. Bedwyn, which lay in Kinwardstone Hundred in 1086, presents a problem as it was both a manor and a borough at the time of the survey. Only the manor, which encompassed both Great and Little Bedwyn (NGR SU 2764, SU 2966) is named as such in DB, but the borough (mentioned indirectly on f.64v) is known from later evidence to have lain at Great Bedwyn alone. For simplicity, Bedwyn is used without affixes where it occurs in the body of this article.

[6] Medieval Latin *foresta* (from Classical Latin *foris*, 'outside') means land outside the manorial boundaries, not necessarily wooded and not assessed for geld.

[7] Savernake Forest was probably attached to Bedwyn (*Rotuli Hundredorum*, ii. 231, 259); Clarendon Forest, which incorporated Melchet Wood, to Alderbury Hundred (ibid. ii. 242). Grovely Forest was divided between 'Branchbury' and 'Cadworth' Hundreds (ibid. ii. 233, 244), and the manor of Wylye had *hedgebote* (repair of fences) within it, a fact not mentioned in DB; see Sawyer (ed.), S.469. 'Selwood' (near Mere) is no longer extant as a place-name but survives as an element in the name of Penselwood (Som.) at NGR ST 7531; it spanned the border of Wiltshire and Somerset.

[8] See p.35, n.12 above.

[9] See p.34, and 34, n.5 above.

[10] Listed in Table 2 below.

[11] GDB 48v, 50, 74. Part of West Tytherley continued to be taxed in Wiltshire, in Amesbury Hundred (Glasscock (ed.), *Lay Subsidy of 1334*, 345). It is not clear whether there was a medieval boundary change or whether the boundary left part of Tytherley in Wiltshire.

[12] GDB 66v.

[13] This portion of West Dean was added to West Tytherley in 1883 with a minor boundary change, leaving West Dean thereafter entirely in Wiltshire; *VCH Hampshire*, iv (1911), 499, 519; Youngs, *Local Administrative Units*, 225.

[14] GDB 50. If the one and a half virgates lay at Outwick, as seems to be implied by f.48, the transfer will have been short-lived, since Outwick is there included in Fordingbridge Hundred (Hants) where it remained.

[15] The Hampshire portion of Bramshaw will have lain in Fordingbridge Hundred. In the nineteenth century, as probably before, the boundary that divided Wiltshire from Hampshire followed the main road (the B3079) through the centre of the vill; see Youngs, *Local Administrative Units*, 200, 532.

Book, but the division between Hampshire and Wiltshire of the land units comprising East and West Dean, East and West Wellow, North and South Tidworth and Cholderton and East Cholderton appears to have been long established.[1]

On the border with Dorset, Aiulf the sheriff held the adjacent estates of Tollard Royal (Wilts.) and Farnham (Dorset). Farnham included a portion called Tollard Farnham, and it may be that the 1086 boundary incorporated this in Wiltshire.[2] At least in recent times a tithing of Bradford on Avon ancient parish, incorporating Limpley Stoke,[3] projected into Bath Hundred (Som.) west of the river Avon, which otherwise at this point formed the boundary between the two counties. This land belonged to Shaftesbury Abbey (the holder of Bradford on Avon) and the arrangement was certainly medieval, but it is not quite clear how the county boundary lay in 1086.[4] Part of Latton (if *Lechetone* of the Gloucestershire folios is correctly identified) lay in Gloucestershire,[5] while one of the twenty-five hides that before 1066 comprised Coleshill (Berks.) lay in Wiltshire, being apparently inscribed in this county as an afterthought.[6] Shalbourne was more equally divided, with six and a half hides in Berkshire and five hides and one virgate in Wiltshire.[7]

The ties of tenure were sometimes more powerful than proximity or county administration and this led to a number of counties having outlying portions separated from their main body. The most complex interlacing, yet the easiest to date, is at the junction of Worcestershire, Gloucestershire, Oxfordshire and Warwickshire. The Wiltshire detachments are simpler yet more obscure. Kingswood, near Wotton-under-Edge, was an outlying portion of Chippenham manor in the later Middle Ages, and remained in Wiltshire until 1844,[8] and it can be assumed, though not yet proved, that it was in Wiltshire in 1086. On the other hand, Poulton (near Cirencester) was certainly part of the county in 1086.[9] At the time of the compilation of Domesday Book, Woodchester (Glos.) was effectively in the county (although it did not stay there), because Edward had put it 'in the farm of Wiltshire'.[10] Other cases are less clear: Inglesham, which lay in Wiltshire but at the meeting-point of Berkshire, Wiltshire and Gloucestershire, was probably one of the unnamed members of the royal manor of Faringdon (Berks.), and was soon itself to become, if not already regarded as, a part of Berkshire.[11] The later medieval map of Berkshire also shows that eleven vills, not mentioned in Domesday Book and now involved with the Berkshire parishes of Hurst, Shinfield, Swallowfield and Wokingham, were regarded as forming the small outlying hundred of Ashridge appurtenant to the Wiltshire hundred of Amesbury.[12] In 1086, most of these places were members of the manor of Sonning (Berks.), held by the Church of Salisbury. At some stage they came into the hands of the Earls of Salisbury, were alienated from the church and removed from the county. No subdivisions or subtenancies of the sixty hides that lay in Sonning before 1086 are given in Domesday Book, and since two of the places concerned were regarded as parts of Berkshire in 1166–7,[13] it is unlikely that any was in Wiltshire in 1086, although the matter requires further investigation.[14] So does the case of Minety (Wilts.), part of which was purchased, with Cirencester (Glos.), from Richard I by the Abbot and Convent of Cirencester and, from that time at least, lay in Gloucestershire; it is not certain if it was an outlying part of Cirencester Hundred, and so in Gloucestershire, in 1086.[15] Concerning Gussage St Michael and part of Gillingham (both now in Dorset), one can be more certain. Although both places appear as main holdings in the Wiltshire folios, their presence can be detected in the Tax Returns for the Dorset hundreds of Badbury and Gillingham respectively. They seem to have found their way into Wiltshire when the inquest material was arranged (as in much of the surviving parts of Exon) by county within each fief, rather than by fief within each county, and the material was wrongly abstracted and allocated.[16]

[1] Part of Conholt (now all in Wiltshire) at NGR SU 3355 lay in Hampshire in 1334 (Glasscock (ed.), *Lay Subsidy of 1334*, 112, 119, 348; *VCH Hampshire*, iv. 1, 329) and probably earlier.

[2] *VCH Wiltshire*, xiii. 83.

[3] NGR ST 7860.

[4] *VCH Wiltshire*, vii. 5, 9; see p.36, n.17 above. The 1086 county boundary could have followed the course of the river Avon and cut through Shaftesbury Abbey's manor, being re-aligned later.

[5] GDB 170. Latton may have been included in Gloucestershire by a misdivision of inquest material at an earlier stage, since the holder, Humphrey the cook, does not appear as a separate landholder in Wiltshire, although he is joint holder of (Lower and Upper) Widhill with Theobald. On the identification of Latton, see J. S. Moore (ed.), *Domesday Book: Gloucestershire* (Chichester, 1982), note to 71,1; J. S. Moore, 'The Gloucestershire Section of Domesday Book: Geographical Problems of the Text, Part I', *Trans. of the Bristol and Gloucestershire Archaeol. Soc.* 105 (1987), 126–7.

[6] GDB 72v. For the Berkshire portions, see GDB 59v, 61, 63.

[7] GDB 57v, 73, 74(x2), 74v.

[8] Youngs, *Local Administrative Units*, 178; see p.35, n.16 above.

[9] GDB 68v. Only a slight change of boundary is needed, however, to connect this Poulton with the county.

[10] GDB 164.

[11] See Thorn, 'Hundreds and Wapentakes', *Berkshire Domesday*, 31. Inglesham (NGR SU 2098, here mapped in Berkshire) returned to Wiltshire in 1844 (Youngs, *Local Administrative Units*, 20, 541), rejoining another portion (Upper Inglesham, also unnamed in DB) that had always stayed in Wiltshire.

[12] In Glasscock (ed.), *Lay Subsidy of 1334*, 346, the eleven are given as Diddenham, Farley Hill, Twyford, Great and Little Sheepbridge, Beaches, Buckhurst, Odes, Hinton, Hinton Pipard and Hinton Hatch. Ashridge Hundred is named from a place in Wokingham (Berks.) at NGR SU 8170.

[13] The Hintons and Farley Hill are in Berkshire in *Pipe Roll 13 Henry II*, Pipe Roll Society 11 (London, 1889), 10; *VCH Wiltshire*, v. 1.

[14] *VCH Berkshire*, i (1906), 320; iii (1923), 198, 228, 237, 247, 253, 261, 263, 267, 271; and Youngs, *Local Administrative Units, passim*.

[15] *VCH Gloucestershire*, ii (1907), 80, n.12. Five hides at Minety had been granted in the mid ninth century to Malmesbury Abbey by Æthelwulf, King of the West Saxons (Sawyer (ed.), S.320, S.322). This suggests that the land lay in Wessex, not Mercia, at that stage, but it is not certain whether the five hides then included the portion later in Gloucestershire. The Gloucestershire part is marked with a broken boundary on the accompanying map.

[16] The clearest examples of such misallocation of material are found in the Northamptonshire folios; see Thorn, 'Hundreds and Wapentakes', *Northamptonshire and Rutland Domesday*, 38.

Nevertheless, land in one county sometimes depended on a manor situated in another: the Hampshire folios record that Lyndhurst (Hants) had once belonged to Amesbury;[1] while the Wiltshire folios state that land in Amesbury had been given in exchange for the loan of Bowcombe (I.o.W., Hants). An addition to the latter entry expands on this by saying that Earl William fitzOsbern gave "Quintone", Swindon and (?Great) Cheverell, which were thegnlands, in exchange for land on the Isle of Wight which belonged to the farm of Amesbury.[2]

Many of the Wiltshire hundreds are named after their principal manors.[3] Of the ecclesiastical hundreds, Bishops Cannings, Damerham, Downton, and Ramsbury all have the name of their tenurial *caput*. Bradford on Avon manor may have had the lordship of the hundred attached to it.[4] In addition, many hundreds, as in other counties, are named from royal manors. In Wiltshire such are Amesbury, Calne, Chippenham, Melksham, Warminster and Westbury, and to this list of royal dominance should be added Collingbourne Ducis manor, Cricklade Hundred (which depended on a borough of which the king received the third penny), Alderbury, Heytesbury and Highworth Hundreds whose royal manors are represented only by their churches and their lands,[5] and Mere Hundred.[6] Only one of the remaining hundreds, 'Frustfield', is actually named from a Domesday vill, an unimportant one, but some of the other hundreds are named from a moot site which lay in a major manor that may well have controlled the hundred. Thus the place which gave its name to Kinwardstone Hundred lay in Burbage, whose church belonged to the king[7] and which was itself probably a member of Bedwyn, an important royal manor, and one of the seven Wiltshire places (Ashton Keynes, Amesbury, Bedwyn, Chippenham, Chiseldon, Edington and Pewsey) mentioned in King Alfred's will.[8] The site of 'Whorwellsdown' lay in Steeple Ashton, part of a forty-hide manor held by the Abbess of Romsey who later claimed the hundred.[9] 'Elstub' itself lay in the thirty-hide manor of Enford held by the Bishop of Winchester which was the nucleus of the later ecclesiastical hundred. Blagrove lay in the vill of Wroughton in which the major manor was a thirty-hide holding of the same bishop. 'Wonderditch' lay in its dominant manor, the fifty hides of Salisbury (based on Old Sarum), while Startley lay in the Abbot of Malmesbury's manor of Great Somerford, 'Cawdon' lay in the royal manor of Coombe Bissett, and Stowford lay in the centre of its single-franchise hundred. The other places which named hundreds and whose sites are known[10] seem not to have lain in manors that were important in 1086; on the other hand it is quite possible that some of the unlocated sites[11] were in major manors. Certainly some of the hundreds named from lost places had a royal manor that may have been pre-eminent: Tilshead in 'Dolesfield' and Lydiard Millicent in "Scipa", for example.[12] On the Hampshire pattern,[13] it may be that those hundreds, some of them small, whose names are not connected with important manors, were severances from larger units. Thus, just as "Cicementone" and Startley Hundreds both depended on the royal borough of Malmesbury, so Dunley and Thorngrove Hundreds may have been appurtenant to the king's manor of Chippenham, with whose hundred they are later combined, and 'Staple' and "Scipa" Hundreds to the royal holding of Highworth, "Scipa" being later absorbed by Highworth Hundred.

Behind the complexity of names, sizes, shapes and interlacement, there ought to lie a simpler, earlier arrangement, although one is difficult to perceive. If one turns to figures, then at first sight the coincidence of forty-one Tax Return hundreds (with Collingbourne Ducis manor accounting for the odd one) totalling 3,956 hides, two and a half virgates, forty-one carucates, and 4,050 or so hides in Domesday Book, might suggest that Wiltshire had once been laid out in a pattern of forty hundreds each containing a hundred hides—a pattern familiar at a later stage in the shiring of England from a Mercian county such as Worcestershire.[14] But the early eleventh-century County Hidage allocates 4,800 hides to the county,[15] a total that is also suggested by the early tenth-century Burghal Hidage, if the constituents of Wiltshire are taken as Wilton (1,400 hides), Chisbury (700 hides), Malmesbury (1,200 hides) and Cricklade (1,500 hides).[16] The discrepancy between the 4,050 hides of Domesday Book and the 4,800 hides of the County Hidage might

[1] GDB 39.
[2] GDB 64v.
[3] Listed in Table 4 below.
[4] See p.36, nn.17–18 above.
[5] For Heytesbury and Highworth, see f.65v; for Alderbury, see f.68v. Although they name hundreds, these royal lands, represented only by churches in DB, may not be large unsurveyed estates, but offshoots of more important royal manors—Alderbury perhaps of Amesbury, Heytesbury of Warminster (see p.40, n.10 below), Highworth of Cricklade.
[6] *Rotuli Hundredorum*, ii. 230; see N. A. Hooper, 'An Introduction to the Wiltshire Domesday', p.7, n.4 above.
[7] GDB 65v.
[8] Sawyer (ed.), S.1507; the identification of some other places mentioned in this will is uncertain and a few may have been in Wiltshire. Eadræd's will (ibid. S.1515) bequeaths the royal manors of Amesbury, Bradford on Avon, Calne, Damerham (now Hants), Downton and Shalbourne.
[9] See p.37, n.1 above.
[10] 'Cadworth', "Cicementone", Dunley, Dunworth, Rowbury, 'Selkley', 'Staple', Swanborough, Thorngrove; see Table 4. 'Selkley' may have depended on Marlborough (*Rotuli Hundredorum*, ii. 234; *VCH Wiltshire*, xii. 63) or possibly on Upavon where there was a royal church (f.65v).
[11] 'Branchbury', 'Dolesfield', 'Kingsbridge', "Scipa", 'Studfold' and 'Thornhill'.
[12] On Lydiard Millicent, see p.34, n.11 above.
[13] This is discussed in P. H. Hase, 'The Development of the Parish in Hampshire, particularly in the Eleventh and Twelfth Centuries' (unpubl. Ph.D. dissertation, Cambridge Univ., 1975); also Thorn, 'Hundreds and Wapentakes', *Hampshire Domesday*, 36.
[14] Worcestershire had twelve hundreds and 1,200 hides in 1086, Herefordshire probably twelve hundreds and 1,200 hides before its extension south and west of the river Wye; Thorn, 'Hundreds and Wapentakes', *Worcestershire Domesday*, 32–3; *idem*, 'Hundreds and Wapentakes', *Herefordshire Domesday*, 23.
[15] Maitland, *Domesday Book and Beyond*, 456.
[16] There are variant readings for Chisbury (500 hides), Malmesbury (1,500, 2,200 hides), and Cricklade (1,300, 1,400 hides). See Maitland, *Domesday Book and Beyond*, 502–3; D. Hill, 'The Burghal Hidage: the Establishment of a Text', *MA* 13 (1969), 84–92; S. Keynes and M. Lapidge (eds. and trans.), *Alfred the Great* (Harmondsworth, 1983), 193–4, 339–41.

be accounted for by the six royal estates (Calne, Bedwyn, Amesbury, Warminster, Chippenham, Tilshead),[1] clearly large holdings but not assessed for geld in Domesday Book, by other estates omitted and by the assessment of boroughs in hides, a practice sporadically found elsewhere in Domesday Book.[2] It is difficult to see how Wiltshire could ever have consisted of forty-eight separate hundreds. The forty-one hundreds of the Tax Returns, including Collingbourne Ducis manor, might be increased to forty-two by the inclusion of a hundred of Malmesbury, co-extensive with the lands of the borough, for one certainly existed in later times, just as a hundred of Cambridge borough existed in 1086 in Cambridgeshire.[3] On the other hand, some of the late eleventh-century 'hundreds', for example 'Cawdon', Dunley, 'Frustfield' and Westbury, were very small and look like fragments of larger units. But even if the number of hundreds is reduced by deducting these, it can be again increased by accepting some hundreds as double-hundreds or hundreds and a half: Kinwardstone at $196\frac{1}{4}$ hides and 'Selkley' at $196\frac{7}{8}$ hides could be 'double-hundreds', Startley at $152\frac{1}{4}$ hides a 'hundred and a half'. But the Tax Return figures are so varied, with no hundred at an exact fifty hides or a multiple thereof, that it is likely that an original, tidier pattern has been disrupted by the transfer of individual estates, by the creation of single-owner hundreds and by the division of larger units. In fact, it is probably a mistake to look for forty-eight separate hundreds. Rather, in Wiltshire it is likely that, as in Oxfordshire in 1086, and in Gloucestershire and Somerset at an earlier stage, several hundreds of hides had depended on a series of royal manors.[4] The core of these manors is likely to have consisted of those that were held in 1066 by King Edward, were unhidated and were responsible for one night's farm: Calne, Bedwyn, Amesbury, Warminster, Chippenham and Tilshead.[5] It may be that these royal *tunas*, together with others formerly royal that were later granted to churches, had once between them administered the territory of Wiltshire as a number of *regiones*,[6] perhaps even before hidation took place. Calne possibly dominated the 200 hides that were later divided into 'Kingsbridge' and Calne Hundreds,[7] and Bedwyn perhaps controlled Kinwardstone, $196\frac{1}{4}$ hides in the Tax Return.[8] Amesbury could have been responsible for the territory of Amesbury, Alderbury and 'Frustfield' Hundreds;[9] Warminster for that of Heytesbury and Warminster Hundreds; Tilshead for that of 'Branchbury' and 'Dolesfield' Hundreds;[10] Chippenham for the hundreds of Dunley, Thorngrove and Chippenham.[11] Cricklade at forty-nine hides was perhaps a half-hundred, and one might extend the list by adding the hundreds dependent on Malmesbury ("Cicementone" and Startley),[12] and assuming that there were hundreds dependent on Highworth ("Scipa", 'Staple', Highworth),[13] on Marlborough ('Selkley'),[14] and on Salisbury ('Wonderditch').[15] Bradford, Melksham, 'Whorwellsdown' and Westbury Hundreds roughly make a 300-hide unit, perhaps one dependent on Melksham or Bradford on Avon;[16] Mere and Dunworth perhaps were once based on Mere;[17] and those that became an intricate fretwork, in which the ecclesiastical hundreds of Stowford and Damerham intrude into 'Cawdon' and 'Cadworth', might once have been 300 hides dependent on Britford or Coombe Bissett.[18] It is not so easy to see the relationship of Blagrove and 'Thornhill' Hundreds,[19] or of Rowbury and 'Studfold',[20] or of Swanborough, 'Elstub' and Collingbourne Ducis,[21] or find a manor on which they might have depended.[22]

The 1086 hundreds are largely recognizable in the thirteenth and fourteenth centuries.[23] Most continue in

[1] Britford had twenty ploughlands, but was assessed at a single hide.

[2] Bedford (f.209), though not assessed in hides, counted as a half-hundred TRE; Chester and Huntingdon paid geld for fifty hides (ff.262v, 203); Shrewsbury and Cambridge both had hundreds of their own (ff.252, 189).

[3] GDB 189. *The Book of Fees* says: *Abbas de Malmesbur' habet tria hundreda, scilicet Malmesbur', Sterkel', Cheggeslawe*, 'The Abbot of Malmesbury has three hundreds, Malmesbury, Startley, Chedglow'. Brokenborough, when granted to the abbey in 956, was 100 *mansae* (Sawyer (ed.), S.629). It is just possible that the fifty hides that are later not accounted for (*VCH Wiltshire*, ii. 88) are represented by Malmesbury 'Hundred'.

[4] See Cam, *Liberties and Communities*, 64–90 and 91–106.

[5] Britford should perhaps be included: it falls in the *Terra Regis* section between Chippenham and Tilshead and was assessed at a single hide, though supporting twenty ploughs; however it paid £30, far short of the commuted figure found elsewhere for one night's farm. Bradford on Avon may have had a similar status in the tenth century.

[6] See Stenton, *Anglo-Saxon England*, 300–1.

[7] A total of $201\frac{1}{2}$ hides in the Tax Return. This figure and those given below are taken from version B of the Tax Returns.

[8] See Cam, *Liberties and Communities*, 68; *Rotuli Hundredorum*, ii. 231.

[9] 204 hides together in the Tax Returns. The addition of the ninety-seven hides of Downton would make a 300–hide unit.

[10] These four hundreds are interlaced: Heytesbury and Warminster total 227 hides in the Tax Returns, 'Dolesfield' and 'Branchbury' $178\frac{3}{8}$ hides; perhaps, before the growth of detachments, each pair was of 200 hides. In later times at least, Heytesbury and Warminster Hundreds had a joint moot site (Table 4, n.29 below); this arrangement may have looked back to a time when there was a single 'hundred'.

[11] 283 hides in the Tax Returns.

[12] $321\frac{3}{4}$ hides in the Tax Returns. Perhaps fifty hides should be added for Malmesbury itself; see n.3 above.

[13] 192 hides together according to the Tax Returns.

[14] $196\frac{7}{8}$ hides in the Tax Return. For the dependency on Marlborough, see p.39, n.10 above.

[15] Seventy hides in the Tax Return.

[16] 303 hides and 13 carucates in the Tax Returns. The *Rotuli Hundredorum*, ii. 232, state that Bradford Hundred had been part of Melksham.

[17] $207\frac{3}{4}$ hides in the Tax Return.

[18] $272\frac{1}{2}$ hides and 3 carucates in the Tax Returns. This grouping might have once depended on Wilton rather than on Britford or Coombe Bissett.

[19] 335 hides in the Tax Returns.

[20] $191\frac{1}{8}$ hides in the Tax Returns. Perhaps Bishops Cannings (70 hides) was once part of the unit.

[21] $270\frac{3}{8}$ hides and 18 carucates in the Tax Returns.

[22] There were royal churches at Upavon and Avebury; the hundreds of Swanborough and 'Selkley' could have depended on a royal manor there; see p.39, n.10 above.

[23] See Table 4. Major individual changes after 1086 involved the transfer of Aldbourne from 'Thornhill' to 'Selkley' Hundred; Great and Little Chalfield from Melksham to Bradford Hundred; Compton (in Enford) from 'Elstub' to Amesbury Hundred/Everleigh Liberty; Great and Little Durnford from 'Wonderditch' to Amesbury Hundred; Highway from 'Kingsbridge' to Bishops Cannings Hundred; Rowde from Calne to 'Rowbury Episcopi' Hundred; Stitchcombe from Kinwardstone to 'Selkley' Hundred; Tockenham and Wootton Bassett from Blagrove to 'Kingsbridge' Hundred.

both name and extent; a few such as Stowford retain their shape and size, but are renamed. Highworth and Chippenham are amalgamated, or perhaps re-amalgamated, with two adjacent hundreds apiece. Rowbury Hundred, on the other hand, was divided, while 'Elstub' grew into a scattered ecclesiastical hundred.[1]

A Note on the Wiltshire Place-names

Many of the estates recorded in Domesday Book are fragments of larger units and share a common name which was perhaps that under which a large tract of territory was granted by charter in earlier centuries. Thus the holdings at Langford (Little Langford, Hanging Langford, Steeple Langford) amount to twenty-six hides; at Manningford (Manningford Bruce, Manningford Bohune and Manningford Abbots) to twenty hides; at Somerford (Great Somerford and Little Somerford) to fourteen hides, one virgate and forty-eight acres; and at Orcheston (formerly 'Orcheston St Mary' and 'Orcheston St George')[2] to fifteen hides. The separate components of these vills are rarely given separate names in Domesday Book, although the later history of the manor can usually identify the particular estate involved. Sometimes it is likely that the Domesday estate actually had a more exact name in 1086, or later acquired one, such as Bushton (Bishop's *tun*) for the Bishop of Winchester's holding of *Clive*, or Clevancy, the later name of Alvred of Marlborough's *Clive*. In Domesday Book both are undifferentiated parts of a large unit of over seventy hides named from the escarpment that runs from Wroughton to Compton Bassett.[3]

[1] See Table 4, n.4 below.

[2] See p.35, n.12 above.

[3] The exact size of *Clive* is unclear, because not all the places named *Clive* in DB necessarily referred to this 'Cliff'. Clyffe Pypard parish probably accounts for many of the settlements, but those of Miles Crispin (f.71) were at Broad Town (NGR SU 0977).

Such specific names are not noticed in this edition, apart from when they derive from the name or the occupation of the 1066 or 1086 holder,[4] but an exception is made for river-names which are particularly prone to differentiation in this way, even though the settlements had originally (at least for documentary purposes) been called simply after the river. Thus, in Wiltshire Domesday, the name Deverill occurs nine times; the name Winterbourne (referring to three separate rivers, now the Bourne, the Till and the Upper Kennet) is found twenty-one times;[5] and the rivers Og and Wylye also name estates. While the settlements on the banks of a river may share its name in Domesday Book, it is likely that by 1086 or soon after many settlements had their own names, or prefixed or suffixed names: thus Deverill refers to Brixton Deverill, Hill Deverill, Longbridge Deverill, Monkton Deverill and Kingston Deverill. On the Upper Kennet lie Winterbourne Monkton, Winterbourne Bassett and Rabson; on the river Bourne lie Winterbourne Dauntsey, Winterbourne Earls, Winterbourne Gunner and Gomeldon; while on the Till are Addestone, Berwick St James, Elston, Maddington, Rollestone and Shrewton. The exact spread of the eleventh-century settlement could not be mapped along these rivers without adopting these differentiating names, only some of which derive from the holder's occupation.[6]

[4] Alderstone, for example, represents the holdings of Ealdræd at 'Frustfield' (f.73v).

[5] This figure includes one *Wintreburne* held by the king (f.65), which by a comparison with an entry in the fief of Edward of Salisbury (f.69) can be shown to lie at *Wintreburnestoch* (Winterbourne Stoke) on the river Till.

[6] Rabson is from Middle English *at ther Abbedeston*, 'at the Abbess' farm', referring to the holding of the Abbess of Amesbury. Addestone is 'Abbot's *tun*', referring to the holding of the Abbey of St Peter, Winchester. Maddington is *Maydenes Winterburn* in 1249, alluding to the holding of the nuns of Amesbury. Shrewton is *Winterburn Shyreveton* in 1236, meaning 'sheriff's *tun*', the holder in 1086 being Edward of Salisbury, Sheriff of Wiltshire. See Gover *et al.*, *PNWilts.*, 309, 233, 236.

For Tables 1–4 see overleaf

TABLE 1: The Hundreds of Wiltshire

Modern Name	The three Exon Tax Returns A: ff.1–3v; B: ff.7–9v; C: ff.13–16[1]	Administrative status and assessment in Tax Returns[2]: h = hide; c = carucate	Number on map
Alderbury	*Aluuartberia/Alwartberia/Alwareberia*	hundred: $65\frac{3}{8}$ h	33
Amesbury	*Ammresberia/Amresberia/Ambresberia*	hundred: $127\frac{1}{2}$ h	30
(Bishops) Cannings	*Canenga/Chalenga/Caninga*	manor (Bishop of Salisbury): 70 h	18
Blagrove	*Blachegrava/Blachegra/Blachegrava*	hundred: A/B 165 h; C $165\frac{1}{8}$ h	8
Bradford	*Bradefort/Bradefort/Bradeford*	hundred: 99 h	16
'Branchbury'	*Brencesberga/Brencesberga/Brencesberga*	hundred: $108\frac{1}{2}$ h	31
'Cadworth'	*Cadeuuorda/Cadeuurda/Cadeworda*	hundred: $45\frac{1}{2}$ h	36
Calne	*Calna/Calna/Calna*	hundred: 91 h	13
'Cawdon'	*Cauuadona/Cauuadona/Cauduna*	hundred: A $35\frac{1}{2}$ h; B/C 59 h 3c	38
Chippenham	*Cepeham/Cepeham/Cepeham*	hundred: A 120 h; B/C 142 h	12
"Cicementone"	*Cicimethorna/Chechemetorn/Cicemethorn* (*Cicementone*, GDB 64v)	hundred: $169\frac{1}{2}$ h	1
*Collingbourne (Ducis)	–/*Colingeburna/Colingeburna*	manor (royal): A missing; B/C 14 h 10 c	26
Cricklade	*Crichalada/Crichelada/Crechelade*	hundred: 49 h	2
†Damerham	*Damreham/Damraham/Domerham*	manor (Abbey of Glastonbury): A 53 h; B/C 63 h	39
'Dolesfield'	*Dolesfelt/Dolefelt/Dolesfeld*	hundred: A $67\frac{5}{8}$ h; B/C $69\frac{7}{8}$ h 3 c	29
†Downton	*Dontona/Duntona/Duntona*	ecclesiastical hundred (Bishop of Winchester): 97 h	40
Dunley	*Duneslawi/Denelau/Denelau*	hundred: 28 h	6
Dunworth	*Donouuorda/Duneworda/Doneworda*	hundred: 121 h	35
'Elstub'	*Alestaba/Eilestebba/Ailestebba*	hundred: A 68 h; B/C 73 h 8 c	25
'Frustfield'	*Ferstesfelt/Fersteffelt/Ferstesfeld*	hundred: $11\frac{1}{8}$ h	41
Heytesbury	*Extredeberia/Hestredeberia/Hechtredeberia*	hundred: $137\frac{1}{2}$ h	28
Highworth	*Wrda/Worda/Worda* (*Wrde*, GDB 69)	hundred: A 51 h; B/C 60 h	5
'Kingsbridge'	*Chinbriga/Chinbrige/Chingbrigge*	hundred: $110\frac{1}{2}$ h	11
Kinwardstone	–/*Cheneuuarestan/Chenewarestan*	hundred: A missing; B/C $196\frac{1}{4}$ h	19
Melksham	*Melchesam/Methesham/Melchessam*	hundred: A 39 h; B/C 86 h 13 c	17
Mere	*Mera/Mere/Mera*	hundred: A $85\frac{5}{8}$ h; B/C $86\frac{3}{4}$ h	34
Ramsbury	*Ramesberia/Ramesberia/Ramesberia*	manor (Bishop of Salisbury): 90 h	15
Rowbury	*Rueberga/Rugeberga/Rugeberga*	hundred: A $82\frac{3}{4}$ h; B/C $96\frac{7}{8}$ h	21
"Scipa"	*Scipa/Scipa/Scipa*	hundred: 80 h	4
'Selkley'	*Selchelai/Selchelaium*[3]*/Selchelaia*	hundred: $196\frac{7}{8}$ h	14
'Staple'	*Stapla/Stapla/Stapla*	hundred: A 42 h; B/C 52 h	3
Startley	*Sterchelea/Starcheleia/Sterchelea* (*Sutelesberg*, GDB 64v)	hundred: $152\frac{1}{4}$ h	7
†Stowford	*Stanforda/Stafort/Staford*	ecclesiastical hundred (Abbey of Wilton): 105 h	37
'Studfold'	*Stotfalda/Stophalde/Stotfalda*	hundred: $94\frac{1}{4}$ h	22
Swanborough	*Suaneberga/Suaneberga/Suaneberga*	hundred: A $128\frac{1}{4}$ h; B/C $183\frac{3}{8}$ h	23
Thorngrove	*Thornegrava/Thornegrava/Thorngrava*	hundred: 113 h	10
'Thornhill'	*Thornehella/Tornhylla/Torenhella*	hundred: A 128 h; B/C 170 h	9
Warminster	*Warministra/Warministrum*[3]*/Warminister*	hundred: A $88\frac{1}{2}$ h; B/C $89\frac{1}{2}$ h	27
Westbury	*Westberia/Westberia/Westberia*	manor (royal): A 40 h; B/C 40 h 7 c	24
'Whorwellsdown'	*Vueruesdona/Weruedesdona/Weruedesdona*	hundred: 78 h	20
'Wonderditch'	*Windredic/Windredic/Windredic*	hundred: 70 h	32

Hundred-names have been given in the nominative case. Where a hundred-name ends in an *-e*, but without the diphthong mark generally used to denote the genitive (*-ae*), it has been assumed to be in the genitive case if it succeeds the words '*In Hundredo*'. However, where the phrase is '*In Hundredo de*' and the hundred-name ends in an *-e*, as in *Mere*, it is very probable that the name is in its Anglo-Saxon form and so is indeclinable: the correct case-ending in Latin would be the ablative *-a*.

*Not stated to be a hundred in the Tax Returns.

†Parts of these former ecclesiastical units were alienated in 1086.

[1] For the Tax Returns, see p.32, n.6 above.

[2] The hidages given in the three Wiltshire Tax Returns do not always agree. Where they differ, variant totals are given, labelled A, B and C respectively. A/B and B/C indicate that in this case the relevant Tax Returns do agree. Where virgates occur they are expressed as fractions of a hide.

[3] Reading *(de) Selcheleio* and *(de) Warministro* as the ablatives of a Latin second-declension neuter noun, here restored to their respective nominatives.

TABLE 2: Places in Wiltshire divided between Hundreds in 1086

Vill or land-unit	Hundreds between which divided, including number on map
Brokenborough	"Cicementone" and Startley Hundreds, 1 and 7
Burcombe	'Branchbury' and 'Cadworth' Hundreds, 31 and 36
*Cannings	Bishops Cannings Hundred (co-extensive with Bishops Cannings manor), 18, and 'Studfold' Hundred, 22 (All Cannings)
*Collingbourne	Kinwardstone Hundred, 19 (Collingbourne Kingston), and the manor of Collingbourne Ducis, 26
*Deverill	Heytesbury Hundred, 28 (Brixton Deverill, Hill Deverill, Longbridge Deverill), and Mere Hundred, 34 (Kingston Deverill, Monkton Deverill)
Edington	'Whorwellsdown' and Heytesbury Hundreds, 20 and 28
*Lydiard	"Scipa" Hundred, 4 (Lydiard Millicent), and Blagrove Hundred, 8 (Lydiard Tregoze)
*Orcheston	Heytesbury Hundred, 28 ('Orcheston St George'), and 'Dolesfield' Hundred, 29 ('Orcheston St Mary')[1]
*Tockenham	Blagrove Hundred, 8 (Tockenham), and 'Kingsbridge' Hundred, 11 (Tockenham Court)
Ugford	'Branchbury' and 'Cadworth' Hundreds, 31 and 36
*Winterslow	Amesbury Hundred, 30 (East Winterslow), and Alderbury Hundred, 33 (West Winterslow)
Yatton Keynell	Thorngrove and Chippenham Hundreds, 10 and 12
	Places probably divided in 1086, but one part is not named in Domesday Book
Trowle	Bradford Hundred, 16,† and Melksham Hundred, 17
*Wraxall	Chippenham Hundred, 12 (North Wraxall), and Bradford Hundred, 16 (†South Wraxall)
	Four other places named by Domesday Book were divided between hundreds in the fourteenth century, and may have been so divided in 1086
Imber	Rowbury and Heytesbury Hundreds, 21 and 28
Milford	'Wonderditch' and Alderbury Hundreds, 32 and 33
Swindon	The fourteenth-century hundred of Highworth,[2] and Blagrove Hundred, 8
Tilshead	'Whorwellsdown' and 'Dolesfield' Hundreds, 20 and 29

*Domesday vill now represented by two or more separate modern settlements, lying in adjacent hundreds.
†Implied but not named in Domesday Book.

[1] See p.35, n.12 above.
[2] The fourteenth-century hundred of Highworth included the areas of two Domesday hundreds (see Table 4 below). Swindon lay in that part of the hundred which would have corresponded to the Domesday hundred of "Scipa", 4.

TABLE 3: Variant place-name identifications

This table shows new place-name identifications made, or old ones reconsidered, since the publication of Thorn and Thorn (eds.), *Domesday Book: Wiltshire* in 1979. Differences of spelling are ignored, as are cases where preference has been given to a more localized identification, most of which are found in the notes to the above edition.

GDB	Name-form	*Domesday Book: Wiltshire*	This edition
65v	*Elendune*	Wroughton	'Elingdon' (in Wroughton)
66	*Scepeleia*	Shipley	"Scepeleia"
66	*Wintreburne*	Winterbourne	Winterbourne (?Dauntsey)
66v	*Wintreburne*	Winterbourne	(?)Gomeldon
70	*Standone*	Standen (in Chute)	North Standen (Berks.)
71	*Hantone*	Hampton (in Highworth)	Broad Hinton
72	*Bereford*	Barford (in Downton)	Barford St Martin
72v	*Scage*	Shaw (in Chute)	Shaw (in Overton)
72v	*Hantone*	Hampton (in Highworth)	Broad Hinton
73	*Estone*	Easton	Easton (Easton Piercy and Lower Easton Piercy)
73	*Laventone*	(West) Lavington	Market Lavington
73	*Laventone*	(?Market) Lavington	West Lavington
73	*Etone*	Castle Eaton	"Etone"
73v	*Wintreburne*	'Winterbourne'	(?)Rollestone

TABLE 4: The Domesday hundreds of Wiltshire showing the places from which they were named, and their relationship to the hundreds of the fourteenth century

Modern name and number on map	Place from which named with NGR if known and if not indexed below	Approximate relationship to the hundreds of the fourteenth century[1]
Alderbury, 33	Domesday manor, divided between four holders in 1086, one of them holding church-land in alms of the king	Continued as Alderbury
Amesbury, 30	Domesday manor (the king/Edward of Salisbury)	Continued as Amesbury
(Bishops) Cannings, 18	Domesday manor (Bishop of Salisbury)[2]	Continued as Bishops Cannings
Blagrove, 8	Blagrove in Wroughton parish (SU 1183)	Continued as Blagrove, with the loss of part of one manor[3]
Bradford, 16	Domesday manor and borough of Bradford on Avon (Abbey of Shaftesbury)	Continued as Bradford, with the loss of Westwood to 'Elstub', 25[4]
'Branchbury', 31	Name lost, site unknown[5]	Continued as 'Branchbury',[4] with the loss of Stockton to 'Elstub', 25[4]
'Cadworth', 36	Name lost; the site was probably in Barford St Martin or Baverstock parishes[6]	Continued as 'Cadworth'
Calne, 13	Domesday manor and borough (royal)	Continued as Calne
'Cawdon', 38	Name lost, but lay in the north of Coombe Bisset parish (SU *c*.109271)[7]	Continued as 'Cawdon'
Chippenham, 12	Domesday manor (royal)	Continued as Chippenham, having absorbed Dunley, 6, and Thorngrove, 10
"Cicementone", 1	Name lost; site probably in Chedglow parish (ST 9493)[8]	Renamed Chedglow
Collingbourne (Ducis), 26	Domesday manor (royal)	Absorbed into Everleigh Liberty[9]
Cricklade, 2	Domesday borough (royal)	Continued as Cricklade
Damerham, 39	Domesday manor (Abbey of Glastonbury); now in Hampshire	Continued as Damerham[10]
'Dolesfield', 29	Name lost, site unknown[11]	Continued as 'Dolesfield'
Downton, 40	Domesday manor (Bishop of Winchester)	Continued as Downton
Dunley, 6	East and West Dunley Farms and Dunley Wood, in Hullavington, Littleton Drew and Grittleton parishes respectively (ST 8581, ST 8481, ST 8581)[12]	Absorbed by Chippenham, 12
Dunworth, 35	Dunworth Copse and Dunworth Cottage in Wardour parish (ST 952279)[13]	Continued as Dunworth, with the loss of Fonthill Bishop to the new hundred of 'Knoyle Episcopi'[14]
'Elstub', 25	'Elstub', a field-name in Enford parish[15]	Continued as 'Elstub', with substantial additions from other holdings of the Bishop of Salisbury[4]
'Frustfield', 41	Domesday manor, divided between four lay landholders in 1086. Site lost, but probably in the parish of Whiteparish (SU 2423)[16]	Continued as 'Frustfield'
Heytesbury, 28	Vill of Heytesbury, represented in DB only by a royal church	Continued as Heytesbury
Highworth, 5	Vill of Highworth, represented in DB only by a royal church	Continued as Highworth, having absorbed "Scipa", 4
'Kingsbridge', 11	Name lost, site unknown[17]	Continued as 'Kingsbridge'
Kinwardstone, 19	Kinwardstone Farm in Burbage parish (SU 2360)	Continued as Kinwardstone, with the loss of Ham to 'Elstub', 25[4]
Melksham, 17	Domesday manor (royal)	Continued as Melksham
Mere, 34	Domesday manor, divided between three thegns of the king in 1086[18]	Continued as Mere, with the loss of two manors[19]
Ramsbury, 15	Domesday manor (Bishop of Salisbury)	Continued as Ramsbury
Rowbury, 21	Rowbury Lane (ST 999563) on the boundary of Market Lavington and Potterne parishes[20]	Divided into the hundreds of 'Rowbury Episcopi' and 'Rowbury Regis'[21]
"Scipa", 4	Name lost, site unknown[22]	Absorbed by Highworth Hundred, 5
'Selkley', 14	A lost wood-name near Marlborough; it appears to have lain between West Overton and Fyfield (SU 1368, SU 1468 respectively)[23]	Continued as 'Selkley', with the loss of Fyfield and 'East Overton' to 'Elstub', 25[4]
'Staple', 3	Name lost, but the site was in Purton parish[24]	Continued as 'Staple'
Startley, 7	Startley in Great Somerford parish (ST 9482)[25]	Continued as Startley
Stowford, 37	Stowford Bridge in Ebbesbourne Wake parish (SU 007247)	Renamed Chalke from Broad Chalke and Bowerchalke, its two principal manors
'Studfold', 22	Name lost, site unknown[26]	Continued as 'Studfold'
Swanborough, 23	Swanborough Tump at the meeting-point of Wilcot, Manningford Bruce and Manningford Abbots parishes (SU 1360)[27]	Continued as Swanborough with the loss of Alton Priors to 'Elstub', 25[4]
Thorngrove, 10	Thorngrove Cottage in Castle Combe parish (ST 843789)	Absorbed by Chippenham, 12
'Thornhill', 9	Name lost, site unknown[28]	Continued as 'Thornhill'
Warminster, 27	Domesday manor and borough (royal)[29]	Continued as Warminster
Westbury, 24	Domesday manor (royal)	Continued as Westbury
'Whorwellsdown', 20	Probably the name of a hill near Cresswell Down (ST 9054) at the junction of Steeple Ashton, Edington, and Bratton parishes[30]	Continued as 'Whorwellsdown'
'Wonderditch', 32	The name, now lost, of a ditch or dyke in the Avon valley, running near Little Durnford (SU 1234) and Stratford sub Castle (SU 1332)[31]	Continued as 'Wonderditch'

WILTSHIRE

Notes to Table 4

[1] Information is taken from *Feudal Aids*, and Glasscock (ed.), *Lay Subsidy of 1334*.

[2] The moot of the hundred was probably at 'Spilsbury' (OE *spell*, 'speech', and *beorg*, see n.13 below), NGR SU *c*.0360. At SU 025599 nearby is Tinkersfield (formerly Tinkfield) Farm (OE *thing*, 'assembly'). See Gover *et al.*, *PNWilts.*, 249, 313.

[3] Blagrove Hundred lost part of Wroughton to 'Elstub' Hundred, 25.

[4] 'Elstub' Hundred was enlarged by the addition of Wroughton (from Blagrove Hundred, 8), Westwood (from Bradford Hundred, 16), Stockton (from 'Branchbury' Hundred, 31), Ham (from Kinwardstone Hundred, 19), Fyfield and 'East Overton' (from 'Selkley' Hundred, 14), Alton Priors (from Swanborough Hundred, 23), Hinton Parva (SU 2383, an unnamed part of Wanborough in 1086, from 'Thornhill' Hundred, 9), and Patney (SU 0758, an unnamed part of Alton Priors in 1086, from 'Studfold' Hundred, 22). For Hinton Parva and Patney, see *VCH Wiltshire*, xi. 159–60, 105–7 respectively.

[5] O. S. Anderson, *The English Hundred-Names: The South-Western Counties* (abbr. *EHNSW*) (Lund, Leipzig, 1939), 147; Gover *et al.*, *PNWilts.*, 225.

[6] Anderson, *EHNSW*, 145; Gover *et al.*, *PNWilts.*, 211.

[7] The name survived in that of some fields called 'Cawdon Dean' in the 1840 Tithe Apportionment for Coombe Bisset parish; see Gover *et al.*, *PNWilts.*, 220; Anderson, *EHNSW*, 145.

[8] "Cicementone" is conjecturally *Checghæmathorn*, the 'thorn-tree of the dwellers at Chedglow' (Gover *et al.*, *PNWilts.*, 53; Anderson, *EHNSW*, 159), the first element being shared with Chedglow, the later name of the hundred.

[9] In 1334 (Glasscock (ed.), *Lay Subsidy of 1334*, 346), the liberty of Everleigh included Collingbourne Ducis, Everleigh (SU 1954), part of Compton (in Enford) and Haxton (SU 1449). The last two places were probably in 'Elstub' Hundred, 25, in 1086; see p.35, n.2 above. Collingbourne Ducis is, however, included in Kinwardstone Hundred, 19, in *Feudal Aids*, v. 203, 221, and Everleigh is included in 'Elstub', ibid. 202; see *VCH Wiltshire*, xi. 106.

[10] In the fourteenth century a number of other Glastonbury manors began to be annexed to Damerham, although the *Lay Subsidy Rolls* and *Feudal Aids* do not record them. Longbridge Deverill was a liberty from the late twelfth century, then joined Christian Malford, Kington Langley, Kington St Michael, Grittleton and Nettleton to form an enlarged Damerham Hundred, called Damerham and North Damerham from the sixteenth century.

[11] Anderson, *EHNSW*, 147; Gover *et al.*, *PNWilts.*, 232.

[12] The *hlaw* that formed the moot of Dunley Hundred was probably west of the Fosse Way (also Foss Way on some maps), which no doubt formed its eastern boundary; Anderson, *EHNSW*, 155; Gover *et al.*, *PNWilts.*, 75–6.

[13] Gover *et al.*, *PNWilts.*, 197–8. Adjacent at ST 954276 are Spelsbury Cottage and Farm (OE *spell*, 'speech', and probably *beorg*).

[14] Fonthill Bishop (from Dunworth Hundred, 35) with East Knoyle (from Mere Hundred, 34), together with Upton (ST 8732) and Hindon (ST 9133), both not named in DB, formed 'Knoyle Episcopi' Hundred; see *VCH Wiltshire*, xi. 1.

[15] On 'Elstub', see Gover *et al.*, *PNWilts.*, 327; Anderson, *EHNSW*, 168. The field lay at SU *c*.144506.

[16] Gover *et al.*, *PNWilts.*, 386; Anderson, *EHNSW*, 170. An approximate location is provided by Alderstone (SU 2424) which was one of the Domesday manors of 'Frustfield'; see p.41, n.4 above; Taylor, 'Whiteparish'; Taylor, 'Three Deserted Medieval Settlements'.

[17] Anderson, *EHNSW*, 163; Gover *et al.*, *PNWilts.*, 265. The traditional moot was in Clyffe Pypard, half a mile north-west of Woodhill Park (SU 0677); *VCH Wiltshire*, ix. 5.

[18] See p.39, n.6 above. On f.74 in the entry for Godric's one virgate, the Latin is ambiguous and it is not certain whether this land actually lay in Mere or only paid its geld there.

[19] Mere lost East Knoyle to the new hundred of 'Knoyle Episcopi' (n.14 above) and Kingston Deverill to Amesbury, 30.

[20] Anderson, *EHNSW*, 166; Gover *et al.*, *PNWilts.*, 238, 242.

[21] Potterne and West Lavington, together with Rowde (which in 1086 was probably in Calne Hundred, 13), became members of the hundred of 'Rowbury Episcopi'.

[22] Anderson, *EHNSW*, 160; Gover *et al.*, *PNWilts.*, 30.

[23] Anderson, *EHNSW*, 163; Gover *et al.*, *PNWilts.*, 291 and p.xl.

[24] 'Steeple Piece', a field-name just north of Purton Church in the 1840 Tithe Apportionment, may be the last trace of the name; Gover *et al.*, *PNWilts.*, 34; see Anderson, *EHNSW*, 160.

[25] Gover *et al.*, *PNWilts.*, 65, 73. *Sutelesberg*, the name used for its one incidental mention in GDB, has a different origin, and refers to a lost place near Malmesbury; Anderson, *EHNSW*, 158.

[26] Gover *et al.*, *PNWilts.*, 311, 316–7; Anderson, *EHNSW*, 167. The traditional moot site was at Foxley Corner (SU 0557).

[27] Gover *et al.*, *PNWilts.*, 317, 320; Anderson, *EHNSW*, 167; *VCH Wiltshire*, x (1975), 5.

[28] It probably lay in the parish of Liddington and is not the same place as the extant Thornhill in Clyffe Pypard parish (SU 0778, in 'Kingsbridge' Hundred, 11); see Gover *et al.*, *PNWilts.*, 281; Anderson, *EHNSW*, 162; *VCH Wiltshire*, ix. 5.

[29] Fields called 'Moothill' are found both in Warminster and Bishopstrow parishes (1840 Tithe Apportionment). The hundreds of Warminster and Heytesbury met jointly at 'Iley Oak' in Sutton Veny, near Southleigh Wood: Gover *et al.*, *PNWilts.*, 151, 154; Anderson, *EHNSW*, 150; *VCH Wiltshire*, viii. 5.

[30] Gover *et al.*, *PNWilts.*, 135, 138; Anderson, *EHNSW*, 152.

[31] Gover *et al.*, *PNWilts.*, 371; Anderson, *EHNSW*, 147; *VCH Wiltshire*, vi. 198.

BIBLIOGRAPHY

INDICES

TO THE DOMESDAY FOLIOS

BIBLIOGRAPHY

The following bibliography, arranged in date order, is derived by kind permission from D. Bates, *A Bibliography of Domesday Book*, published by Boydell and Brewer Ltd for the Royal Historical Society, 1986. Dr Bates has added certain entries to this county list in order to update it, and to include appropriate references which are cited in the 'General Studies' section of his original work.

WILTSHIRE

1. H. P. Wyndham, *Wiltshire extracted from Domesday Book: to which is added a Translation of the Original Latin into English* (Salisbury, 1788). Some attempt made to identify place-names.
2. G. P. Scrope, 'History of the Wiltshire Manors subordinate to the Barony of Castle Combe', *Wiltshire Archaeol. and Nat. Hist. Mag.* 2 (1855), 261–89. A little on the DB fee of Humphrey de l'Isle.
3. W. H. Jones, 'Bradford-upon-Avon: General History of the Parish', *Wiltshire Archaeol. and Nat. Hist. Mag.* 5 (1859), 1–88, 210–55, 342–90. See pp.23–6 for the DB entry.
4. J. Wilkinson, 'History of Broughton Gifford', ibid. 5. 267–341; 6 (1860), 11–72. See 5. 267–80 for the DB entries.
5. H. James (director), *Domesday Book: or the Great Survey of England of William the Conqueror, A.D. MLXXXVI. Facsimile of the Part Relating to Wiltshire.* Photozincographed by Her Majesty's Command at the Ordnance Survey Office, Southampton (Southampton, 1862).
6. W. H. Jones, *Domesday for Wiltshire* (London, Bath, 1865). An extended text, translation and notes, with a long introduction. Generally regarded as being of high quality.
7. W. H. Jones, 'Gleanings from the Wiltshire Domesday', *Wiltshire Archaeol. and Nat. Hist. Mag.* 10 (1866–7), 165–73; 13 (1871–2), 42–58. For the boundaries of DB Wiltshire and DB personal names preserved in modern place-names.
8. W. H. Jones, 'The History of the Parish of All Cannings', *Wiltshire Archaeol. and Nat. Hist. Mag.* 11 (1867–9), 1–40, 175–203. See pp.5–6, 176–8.
9. W. H. Jones, 'The Names of Places in Wiltshire', *Wiltshire Archaeol. and Nat. Hist. Mag.* 14 (1873–4), 156–80, 253–79; 15 (1875), 71–98.
10. W. H. Jones, 'Potterne', *Wiltshire Archaeol. and Nat. Hist. Mag.* 16 (1876), 245–86. See pp.250–4.
11. J. Tait, 'Large Hides and Small Hides', *EHR* 17 (1902), 280–2. Evidence is mainly drawn from Cambs. and Wilts. See 35.
12. M. Bateson, 'The Burgesses of Domesday and the Malmesbury Wall', *EHR* 21 (1906), 709–22.
13. J. Beddoe, 'A Contribution to the Anthropology of Wiltshire', *Wiltshire Archaeol. and Nat. Hist. Mag.* 34 (1906), 15–41. Includes a table of DB population and a discussion of Norman immigration into Wilts.
14. W. H. Jones and J. E. Jackson (annotated and brought up to date by J. Beddoe), *Bradford-on-Avon: A History and Description* (Bradford-on-Avon, 1907).
15. E. Ekblom, *The Place-Names of Wiltshire: their Origin and History* (Uppsala, 1917). Superseded by 25.
16. J. A. Rutter, 'Domesday: Villeins on Comital Manors', *Devon and Cornwall Notes and Queries*, 11 (1920–1), 310–15. For a shorter version, see *N&Q* 12th ser., 11 (1921), 65, with a reply by O. J. Reichel at p.152 and a rejoinder by Rutter at p.192.
17. G. B. Grundy, 'The Place-Names of Wiltshire', *Wiltshire Archaeol. and Nat. Hist. Mag.* 41 (1920–2), 335–53. Identifies some DB place-names. See 25.
18. H. C. Maxwell Lyte, 'Fitzurse', *Somerset Archaeol. and Nat. Hist. Soc. Proc.* 68 (1922), 93–104. Identifies Urse who held half a hide in Corby with the Urse who held of the Abbey of Glastonbury in Wilts.
19. H. B. Walters, 'The Wiltshire Hundreds', *Wiltshire Archaeol. and Nat. Hist. Mag.* 46 (1932–4), 301–11.
20. G. Kidston, 'Notes on the Early History of Box', ibid. 568–78.
21. F. W. Morgan, 'Woodland in Wiltshire at the Time of Domesday Book', *Wiltshire Archaeol. and Nat. Hist. Mag.* 47 (1935–7), 25–33.
22. F. W. Morgan, 'Domesday Woodland in South-West England', *Antiquity*, 10 (1936), 306–24.
23. F. W. Morgan, 'The Domesday Geography of Wiltshire', *Wiltshire Archaeol. and Nat. Hist. Mag.* 48 (1937–9), 68–81.
24. G. B. Grundy, 'The Ancient Woodland of Wiltshire', ibid. 530–98. Some of his calculations are questionable.
25. J. E. B. Gover, A. Mawer and F. M. Stenton, *The Place-Names of Wiltshire*, EPNS 16 (Cambridge, 1939).
26. W. J. Arkell, 'Some Topographical Names in Wiltshire', *Wiltshire Archaeol. and Nat. Hist. Mag.* 49 (1940–2), 221–4.
27. H. C. Brentnall, 'The Hundreds of Wiltshire', *Wiltshire Archaeol. and Nat. Hist. Mag.* 50 (1942–4), 219–29.
28. R. Welldon Finn, 'The Assessment of Wiltshire in 1083 and 1086', ibid. 382–401.
29. R. B. Pugh, 'The Early History of the Manors in Amesbury', *Wiltshire Archaeol. and Nat. Hist. Mag.* 52 (1947–8), 70–110.
30. R. Welldon Finn, 'The Making of the Wiltshire Domesday', ibid. 318–27.
31. G. J. Kidston, 'Cumberwell near Bradford-on-Avon', *Wiltshire Archaeol. and Nat. Hist. Mag.* 53 (1949–50), 471–85. Identified *Cumbrewelle*.
32. M. W. Hughes, 'The Domesday Boroughs of Wiltshire, with Special Reference to Marlborough', *Wiltshire Archaeol. and Nat. Hist. Mag.* 54 (1951–2), 257–78.
33. M. M. Postan, 'Glastonbury Estates in the Twelfth Century', *EconHR* 2nd ser., 5 (1952–3), 358–67. Reprinted in M. M. Postan, *Essays on Medieval Agriculture and General Problems of the Medieval Economy* (Cambridge, 1973), 249–61.
34. R. R. Darlington, 'Anglo-Saxon Wiltshire', *VCH Wiltshire*, eds. R. B. Pugh and E. Crittall, ii (London, 1955), 1–34.
35. R. R. Darlington, 'Introduction to the Wiltshire Domesday', ibid. 42–112, 169–77. A good discussion of many matters of both general and local significance. For a correction, see 43.
36. R. R. Darlington, 'Translation of the Text of the Wiltshire Domesday', ibid. 113–68.
37. R. R. Darlington, 'Text and Translation of the Wiltshire Geld Rolls', ibid. 178–217.
38. R. R. Darlington, 'Summaries of Fiefs in the Exon Domesday', ibid. 218–21.

39. R. LENNARD, 'The Demesnes of Glastonbury Abbey in the Eleventh and Twelfth Centuries', *EconHR* 2nd ser., 8 (1955–6), 355–63.

40. T. R. THOMSON, 'The Bounds of Ellandune *c.*956', *Wiltshire Archaeol. and Nat. Hist. Mag.* 56 (1955–6), 265–70. For the DB manors of Salthorpe, Elcumbe, Ellandun, Nether Wroughton, Over Wroughton and Westlecott.

41. M. M. POSTAN, 'Glastonbury Estates in the Twelfth Century: A Reply', *EconHR* 2nd ser., 9 (1956–7), 106–18. Reprinted in Postan, *Essays on Medieval Agriculture*, 261–77.

42. G. A. J. HODGETT, 'Feudal Wiltshire', *VCH Wiltshire*, v (1957), 44–71.

43. T. H. ASTON, 'The Origins of the Manor in England', *TRHS* 5th ser., 8 (1958), 59–83. Reprinted with 'a postscript' in T. H. Aston *et al.* (eds.), *Social Relations and Ideas: Essays in Honour of* R. H. *Hilton* (Cambridge, 1983), 1–43.

44. T. R. THOMSON (ed.), *Materials for the History of Cricklade* (Oxford, 1958–61).

45. D. WALKER, 'The "Honours" of the Earls of Hereford in the Twelfth Century', *Trans. of the Bristol and Gloucestershire Archaeol. Soc.* 79 (1960), 174–211. For the DB holdings of Durand, Sheriff of Gloucester, and his nephew Walter fitzRoger.

46. H. R. LOYN, 'The Origin and Early Development of the Saxon Borough with Special Reference to Cricklade', *Wiltshire Archaeol. and Nat. Hist. Mag.* 58 (1961–3), 7–15.

47. T. R. THOMSON, 'English Place Name Society, Volume xvi (Wiltshire)', ibid. 228–9. Identifies *Sevamentone* with Sevington in Leigh Delamere.

48. R. WELLDON FINN, *Domesday Studies: The Liber Exoniensis* (London, 1964). An important and valuable study.

49. H. C. DARBY and R. WELLDON FINN (eds.), *The Domesday Geography of South-West England* (Cambridge, 1967; repr. 1979).

50. C. C. TAYLOR, 'Whiteparish: a Study of the Development of a Forest-Edge Parish', *Wiltshire Archaeol. and Nat. Hist. Mag.* 62 (1967), 79–102. For settlement pattern of DB entries for Cowesfield and Frustfield.

51. C. C. TAYLOR, 'Three Deserted Medieval Settlements in Whiteparish', *Wiltshire Archaeol. and Nat. Hist. Mag.* 63 (1968), 39–45. For deserted DB settlements in Cowesfield and Frustfield.

52. S. C. MORLAND, 'Hidation on the Glastonbury Estates: A Study in Tax Evasion', *Somerset Archaeol. and Nat. Hist. Soc. Proc.* 114 (1970), 74–90.

53. J. MUSTY, 'A Preliminary Account of a Medieval Pottery Industry at Minety, North Wiltshire', *Wiltshire Archaeol. and Nat. Hist. Mag.* 68 (1973), 79–88. An omission from DB (Minety).

54. R. LENNARD, with an introduction by B. F. Harvey and E. Stone, 'The Glastonbury Estates: a Rejoinder', *EconHR* 2nd ser., 28 (1975), 517–23.

55. M. M. POSTAN, 'The Glastonbury Estates: a Restatement', ibid. 524–7.

56. B. HARVEY, *Westminster Abbey and its Estates in the Middle Ages* (Oxford, 1977).

57. C. and F. THORN (eds.), *Domesday Book: Wiltshire* (Chichester, 1979). Text, translation and valuable notes. Includes some new place-name identifications and notes on the hundreds and the county boundary. For additions and corrections, see F. and C. Thorn (eds.), *Domesday Book: Worcestershire* (Chichester, 1982).

58. B. J. WHITEHEAD, 'The Topography and History of North Meadow, Cricklade', *Wiltshire Archaeol. and Nat. Hist. Mag.* 76 (1981), 129–40. For DB entries for Cricklade and surrounds.

59. J. M. MCDONALD and C. D. SNOOKS, *Domesday Economy: A New Approach to Anglo-Norman History* (Oxford, 1986).

60. D. STROUD, 'The Site of the Borough of Old Sarum 1066–1226: An Examination of Some Documentary Evidence', *Wiltshire Archaeol. and Nat. Hist. Mag.* 80 (1986), 120–6.

61. J. MUSTY *et al.*, 'Excavations at the Deserted Medieval Village of Gomeldon, near Salisbury', ibid. 127–69. For DB Wintreburne.

The following volumes are those of the Alecto County Edition of Domesday Book which have been published to date. Included for convenience are the names of the authors of the 'Introductions' to each volume. All the articles on 'Hundreds and Wapentakes' are by F. R. Thorn.

1. A. WILLIAMS and R. W. H. ERSKINE (eds.), *The Northamptonshire and Rutland Domesday* (London, 1987).
   D. N. HALL, 'An Introduction to the Northamptonshire Domesday', ibid.
   T. D. CAIN, 'An Introduction to the Rutland Domesday', ibid.

2. A. WILLIAMS and R. W. H. ERSKINE (eds.), *The Berkshire Domesday* (London, 1988).
   N. A. HOOPER, 'An Introduction to the Berkshire Domesday', ibid.

3. A. WILLIAMS and R. W. H. ERSKINE (eds.), *The Buckinghamshire Domesday* (London, 1988).
   J. BRADBURY, 'An Introduction to the Buckinghamshire Domesday', ibid.

4. A. WILLIAMS and R. W. H. ERSKINE (eds.), *The Cornwall Domesday* (London, 1988).
   I. N. SOULSBY, 'An Introduction to the Cornwall Domesday', ibid.

5. A. WILLIAMS and R. W. H. ERSKINE (eds.), *The Herefordshire Domesday* (London, 1988).
   C. P. LEWIS, 'An Introduction to the Herefordshire Domesday', ibid.

6. A. WILLIAMS and R. W. H. ERSKINE (eds.), *The Worcestershire Domesday* (London, 1988).
   A. WILLIAMS, 'An Introduction to the Worcestershire Domesday', ibid.

7. A. WILLIAMS and R. W. H. ERSKINE (eds.), *The Gloucestershire Domesday* (London, 1989).
   A. WILLIAMS, 'An Introduction to the Gloucestershire Domesday', ibid.

8. A. WILLIAMS and R. W. H. ERSKINE (eds.), *The Hampshire Domesday* (London, 1989).
   B. J. GOLDING, 'An Introduction to the Hampshire Domesday', ibid.

9. A. WILLIAMS and R. W. H. ERSKINE (eds.), *The Somerset Domesday* (London, 1989).
   G. A. LOUD, 'An Introduction to the Somerset Domesday', ibid.

INDEX OF PLACES

NOTES

In this edition, the place-names found in the translation, on the county map, and in the following Index of Places are all interrelated and have been established according to strict editorial policy. The central source for each of these three elements has been a specially compiled card-index containing a card for every mention of a place-name in Domesday Book: this index itself has been adjusted as research progressed. Thus the separate disciplines of identification, map-making, indexing, and rendering the Latin into readable English have all contributed to this compendium of Domesday place-names and to the manner of the presentation of each category. However, a word of caution is appropriate here, because the reader should be aware that the simple exchange of a Domesday name for even the most obvious modern equivalent does not necessarily mean that the original settlement lay precisely at that location, nor that it had a similar territorial form.

It is important to realize that the place-names of Domesday Book do not represent modern religious, social, administrative or agricultural units such as parishes, townships, villages, hamlets or farms, except by coincidence. They stand for estates or taxable units that may not in reality have been either independent or self-supporting. No bounds are given and these estates, depending on their size, may well have extended over more than one modern parish, be interlaced with other holdings, or possess a number of widely scattered members. Most Domesday estates will have contained several settlements, all of which had names in 1086, but which the survey leaves unnamed and whose statistics it engrosses with others. Frustratingly, Domesday says nothing that allows us to determine the centre, the extent, or the form of the estate.

Many Domesday estate-names will doubtless have been those actually current in the locality concerned; but others are 'book-names'—administrators' designations and often very general in scope—such as the name of a valley, hill, river or tract of land. These were probably known by more specific names on the ground, but Domesday Book does not record them. Especially where a vill is shown to have been in divided ownership in 1086, or where the Domesday unit is the fragment of some great multiple estate of pre-Conquest times, Domesday may well retain the 'charter' or 'book' name of its more extensive predecessor even though other evidence may indicate that a more precise appellation was almost certainly in use at the time.

The Domesday name may now be represented by a parish name, or by that of a township, hamlet or isolated farm. It may no longer survive as a settlement-name at all, but only as that of a river, wood, hill, road or bridge. The name may even have become lost before it appeared on any map; and finally it may have escaped identification altogether, either because the place designated scarcely survived the eleventh century or because the form in which Domesday transmits the place-name is corrupt and so far unintelligible.

A Domesday place can only be considered to be satisfactorily identified when the proposed name has passed a number of tests. Is the evolution of the 1086 name-form to the suggested modern equivalent philologically acceptable? Does it lie in the hundred indicated or implied by the text, or reconstructed from it? Do the details of land, equipment, resources and industry given by the entry in Domesday Book accord with what could have been practicable within the proposed area? Can the estate be identified among the possessions of the 1086 holder's heirs or successors in later centuries? In practice, by no means all published identifications satisfy these requirements and the accuracy and reliability of identifications varies considerably from county to county. Much depends on the quality of the work of the eighteenth- and nineteenth-century 'antiquarian' pioneers and of the sections on Domesday in the relevant volume of the *Victoria County Histories*. The standard of more recent work, the existence of a county volume among the publications of the English Place-Name Society, or of 'topographical' volumes from the *Victoria County History* make the identifications of some counties more secure than those of others. The evidence so gathered will have been reviewed for H.C. Darby's monumental series on Domesday Geography (1952–77) and for the Phillimore edition of Domesday Book (1975–86), but with varying thoroughness. For the present publication, it has been impractical to re-examine every item of this complex and widely scattered evidence afresh, but in cases where modern published identifications conflict or where there are other obvious reasons for doubt, the evidence has been rescrutinized.

In the following Index of Places, a system of square-bracketed editorial additions and of single or double inverted commas imply varying degrees of certainty in identification, and are set out in the key below. A further key precedes the translation in this volume and contains the related conventions employed there. Among the symbols on the county map, of which this index is also the gazetteer, will be found a system of circles, complete, broken, or interlinked, which serves the same function, besides a full treatment of the county- and hundred-boundaries in 1086.

By far the greater part of the evidence for the identification of place-names is derived from Great Domesday Book itself. However, occasionally a holding was entered without its eleventh-century name, or the name given has been replaced by a later one, and where possible these have been supplied from the testimony of certain other documents that are directly related to the making of Domesday Book or to its use. Such documents deemed admissible as evidence in this context are, for example, the Exon Book for the south-western counties, Evesham A for Worcestershire, and the Herefordshire Domesday. In this volume the only source accepted for identifications other than the Domesday folios is Exon.

F. R. Thorn

GENERAL

1. Scope of Index

The index refers to all place-names found in the text written at the time of the compilation of Great Domesday Book, 1086–7, including all contemporary corrections, notes and additions in the margins. Insertions added to the MS in medieval and later times are not indexed, but identifications are incorporated which have been assisted by the evidence of any secondary documents that might exist as indicated in the introduction to these notes above.

Only references to the folios and translation supplied with this volume are indexed. A section listing any named holdings in this county which are recorded in the folios of other shires will be found on the associated county map.

2. Use of suprascript numbers

Where a place-name occurs more than once on a folio, its incidence is indicated by a suprascript number.

Note that occasionally a named entry can be followed immediately by further reference(s) to the same vill, usually designated by terms such as *ibi*, 'there'; *ibidem*, 'in the same place'; *in eadem villa*, 'in the same vill'. Such entries are not indexed as the place-name itself is absent.

3. Use of "..."

Double inverted commas indicate a name found only in Domesday Book and for which there is no known later equivalent, or of which the form may be corrupt. The name so enclosed is printed in Roman type.

4. Use of '...'

Single inverted commas indicate the latest or most typical known form of a name which remained in use beyond the eleventh century, but which either has not survived into modern times at all, or which only appears on twentieth-century maps as the name of a feature such as a river, hill, wood etc., rather than as a place of habitation. This also applies to names without a continuous history and which have only recently been revived for antiquarian reasons.

MODERN PLACE-NAMES (ROMAN TYPE)

5. Authority

The modern place-names are consistent with those marked on the particular 1:100,000 Ordnance Survey grey base-map employed as the background for each associated county map. Note that place-names can vary from edition to edition of OS maps and their absence from this particular map does not mean that they are necessarily lost.

6. Modern counties

Throughout this edition the county-boundaries are regarded as those that existed prior to the restructuring of the counties in 1974.

7. National Grid Reference

Four-figure National Grid References are given for modern place-names which represent settlements recorded in Domesday Book. Note that these NGRs do not necessarily pin-point the precise location of such settlements in 1086 for the reasons set out in the introduction to these notes above.

8. Common prefixes and suffixes: Great, Little, etc.

Modern places which are distinguished by common prefixes such as Old, Great and Little, Upper, Middle and Lower, Nether and Over, East and West, North and South have their main entry indexed under the relevant place-names, in the same way as those with distinguishing suffixes such as All Saints, St Andrew and Abbots.

9. Use of 'or', 'and'

Where a place is designated by two or more prefixes or suffixes and linked by 'or', e.g. Great or Little, All Saints or St Andrew, it is uncertain which of these two modern places represents the holding in question or whether both did so. Where the prefixes are linked by 'and', e.g. East and West, St Peter and St Martin, the inference is that both modern places lie within the territory of a single estate of 1086.

10. Use of 'in', 'near'

In the event of two or more places in one county having the same name, they are distinguished by the addition of the parish-names in square brackets, e.g. [in Compton]. The only exception is when the parish- and place-name are the same, or where the place-name forms part of the parish-name. In these cases one will be followed by the parish-name, [in Compton], while the other will be related to a prominent nearby town or feature, [near Wallingford].

11. Choice of representative names distinguished by affixes

In a given locality a single place-name in Domesday Book may now be represented by a number of variant names distinguished by different prefixes or suffixes. Where a major derivative name signifying a village or hamlet still exists, such as Great, Little, Higher, Lower, St Mary, St Peter, this is preferred to minor or dependent variant names, such as Park, Moor, Gate, Green, Manor. Similarly minor settlement-names, where only they survive, are preferred to non-settement names such as those of fields, hills, woods, streams, marshes.

Where the name in Domesday Book is represented on modern maps only by the name of a minor feature, the principal element alone is used in the index and in the translation, so that Weston Farm, Lodge, Hall, Bridge, Wood etc., appear only as Weston.

12. Places now 'lost'

A number of places named in Domesday Book either no longer exist as distinct settlements or have disappeared altogether due to urban development, inundation by reservoirs, coastal erosion, rural depopulation, and other causes. These 'lost' places are treated variously, both in the translation and in this index, according to the circumstances that have caused them to disappear.

a. Places which have been absorbed into an area of urban development, but have given their name to a distinct suburb or district. These are designated as 'in' the relevant town or city which is enclosed in square brackets, e.g. Knowle [in Bristol].

b. Places absorbed into urban development, as above, but of which the name has not survived as that of a distinct suburb or district. These are designated as 'in' the relevant town or city in square brackets, also as above, but the place-name is enclosed within single inverted commas, e.g. 'Tessall' [in Birmingham].

c. Places now lost under water have their names enclosed in single inverted commas and are followed by an indication of their former whereabouts in square brackets if known, e.g. 'Syndercombe' [in Clatworthy Reservoir].

d. Names of places lost in rural areas are enclosed in single or double inverted commas as set out in 3 and 4 above. However, they may also be designated as being 'in' the parish to which they belonged when this is known, e.g. "Sortelai" [in Quainton], 'Ashden' [in Compton].

e. Those lost places which can be reliably located have been plotted on the accompanying county map. Those which can only be approximately located are included in the Index and the translation but are not mapped.

13. Use of names other than Domesday derivatives

All modern names used in this edition are derived from those of 1086 with only the following exceptions:

a. Where the name of the Domesday Book estate has been entirely superseded by a more recent name that covers the same extent, e.g. Reigate (Surrey) for 'Churchfield'; Padstow (Corn.) for *Lanwenehoc*.

b. Where the later name of the Domesday Book estate is derived from the TRE or TRW holder or his title, e.g. Dodington (Som.) for 'Stowey'; Bishopstone (Herefs.) for 'Mansell'.

c. Where it is now possible to identify places which were sited along the banks of a river and which bear only the river name in Domesday Book, as with many settlements on the Ottery (Devon) and the Piddle (Dorset).

d. Where the holding is un-named in Domesday Book, but its name can be reliably established from any other contemporary documents, such as those mentioned in the introduction to these notes above.

PLACE-NAMES IN DOMESDAY BOOK (*ITALIC TYPE*)

14. Variant forms

All variant forms found in these county folios of Domesday Book are indexed.

15. Abbreviations

Place-names that are specifically shortened in the MS with abbreviation-marks are given in their extended form.

16. Use of *u*, *v*, *w*

Since *u* and *v* are used indiscriminately in this MS, as in others of the period, they are here transposed to be closest to the modern spelling of the place-names. Double-*u* (*uu*) is always transposed as *w*, except in names enclosed in double inverted commas (see 3 above) where the scribe's original orthography is maintained.

17. Use of hyphenated endings

Where the spelling of a name varies only by the addition of a final letter or letters, the shorter version is given followed by the variant ending after a hyphen. Thus *Evelai*, *Evelaia* appears as *Evelai-a*; *Heiford*, *Heiforde* as *Heiford-e*; *Winewic*, *Winewiche* as *Winewic-he*.

OTHER

18. Page and folio references

References to the pages of editorial matter in this volume are printed in **bold**, and are followed by the references to the folio numbers of the facsimile and the translation, which are identical for both.

19. Recto and Verso

Folio numbers without suffix indicate the *recto* of the folio, while suffix 'v' indicates the *verso*.

20. Use of ‡

A double-dagger ‡ before a main entry refers to the errata section printed at the end of this index, if such is required.

WILTSHIRE

A

B

C

D

T

U

V

W

EDITOR'S NOTE

In the continuous-tone process of reproduction employed for the facsimile, certain problems of definition arise where the red of the rubrication is either contiguous with or superimposed over the dark browns of the lettering. Very occasionally this association of colours causes slight distortions to the capitals of the place-names which are normally through-lined in red, and can result in an apparent misreading. Accordingly, in order to resolve any doubt, every place-name has been checked against the manuscript itself and the following readings are thereby confirmed:

Modern name, folio number, column and ● counted from top	in the facsimile could be read as	confirmed from the manuscript as
ALDERBURY, 68v left, 12th ●	ALWARSERIE	ALWARBERIE
BADBURY, 66v left, 6th ●	BADERERIE	BADEBERIE
BIDDESDEN, 72v left, 8th ●	BEDRSDENE	BEDESDENE
EISEY, 68v left, 10th ●	AISE	AISI
LUCKINGTON, 72v left, 4th ●	LOOHINTONE	LOCHINTONE
SHREWTON, 69 right, 7th ●	WINTRERVRNE	WINTREBVRNE
STAPLEFORD, 74 right, 26th ●	STÆPLEFORD	STAPLEFORD
THORNHILL, 74v left, bottom ●	TORNVCLE	TORNVELE
WOLFHALL, 74v left, 12th ●	VLFCLA	VLFELA

INDEX OF PERSONS AND ECCLESIASTICAL BODIES

NOTES

1. TRE, TRW

Most of the entries in Domesday Book record two distinct categories of landholder: those English or Anglo-Scandinavian owners who held land before the Conquest (TRE, *tempore regis Edwardi*, 'in the time of King Edward'), and those who dispossessed them after 1066 (TRW, *tempore regis Willelmi*, 'in the time of King William') – or more particularly twenty years later at the time of the Conqueror's survey. It is usual for the Church to maintain continuity of ownership throughout both periods, but it is rare for an individual to do so. Since Domesday Book is a description of the situation at the time of its compilation in 1086–87, the circumstances obtaining TRE are invariably entered in the past tense, TRW in the present.

2. Use of * †

Prefixed asterisks * indicate references to the names of English or Anglo-Scandinavian landholders or churches mentioned only in a TRE context. Daggers † signify those which are stated to have continued their tenancy from the TRE to the TRW period. Names found only TRW have no prefixed symbol.

3. The Kings

The references to King Edward and to King William are divided for convenience into categories which encompass various aspects of kingship. The references to King Edward implied by the abbreviation TRE are not indexed. Where the text shows that someone in the TRE period *tenuit de rege Edwardo*, 'held of King Edward', the references are indexed under the category of King Edward 'as lord'.

References to the equivalent TRW phrase *tenet de rege*, 'holds of the king', are not indexed as it was not used systematically and was anyway superfluous because in feudal theory current after the Conquest all land was technically held of the king.

4. Abbeys and Churches

The terms *Abbatia*, 'Abbey', and *Æcclesia*, 'Church' are sometimes used interchangeably in Domesday Book for large monastic institutions. In this index, 'Abbey' is always used for the Benedictine houses, both in England and on the continent, while 'Church' is reserved for secular houses, i.e. colleges of priests, non-monastic bishoprics, minsters, etc. Only churches recorded as owning land are indexed here.

5. Personal Names TRE

All TRE names are standardized in accordance with O. von Feilitzen, *The Pre-Conquest Personal Names of Domesday Book* (Uppsala, 1937) with the following exceptions: Alfred, Edgar, Edith, Edmund, Edward, Edwin, Harold, Morcar, Siward, Stigand, Swein and Waltheof.

Old English forms are used in preference to Scandinavian variants. When no Old English form is attested, names are standardized first to their Anglo-Scandinavian, then to their Old Danish, Old Swedish, and finally Old Norse forms.

6. Personal Names TRW

There is no authority equivalent to von Feilitzen for TRW names, and their transposition into modern forms by individual historians has seldom been consistent. For this edition the editors have retained what they perceive to have become the 'accepted' forms of certain names despite inconsistencies. Thus, for example, *Albertus Lotharingensis* becomes Albert of Lorraine, not the Lotharingian, whilst *Walterius Flandrensis* remains Walter the Fleming, not of Flanders, in the style used for most non-Norman continentals. However, a policy of standardization has been established for the aspects of nomenclature which follow.

Modern anglicized forms of Christian names are preferred, e.g. Gilbert for *Giselbertus*, Geoffrey for *Goisfridus*, Hugh for *Hugo*, Ralph for *Radulfus*.

Continental and English toponymics appear in the modern form of the place-name e.g. Robert d'Oilly not *Robert de Oilgi*, Roger of Westerham not *Roger de Oisteram*. As in these examples, 'de' is used for continental places of origin, 'of' for English names.

Continental patronymics are expressed with the prefix 'fitz', e.g. Hugh fitzBaldric. The equivalent English or Anglo-Scandinavian names are expressed as 'son of', e.g. Swein son of Azur. This rule is also applied to patronymics in TRE names.

Ambiguous TRW personal names which are attested in both Anglo-Scandinavian and Continental sources are given their Continental forms unless the manuscript specifically identifies any person so named as English.

TRW names with obscure Latin forms or with no modern equivalent appear in the Index as they do in the manuscript, but without the *-us* ending, e.g. Otbert for *Otbertus*, Winemar for *Winemarus*.

7. Titles

Main entries are indexed under the toponymic, and the personal name(s), where known, are supplied in square brackets, e.g. Mortain, [Robert], Count of; Coutances, [Geoffrey de Mowbray], Bishop of. If these name(s) occur explicitly in the folios of this county, the square brackets are left off.

8. Occupational Names

Examples: Alwine the huntsman, Gilbert the cook, Regenbald the priest. Although Domesday Book describes many of these persons with other descriptive suffixes—for instance Regenbald occurs variously in different counties as 'the priest', 'the chaplain', 'the king's chaplain', and 'of Cirencester'—only that or those which occur in the folios of this particular county are listed here.

9. Cross-indexing

All patronymics, non-titular toponymics, rank-names, by-names and occupational names are cross-indexed with the main entry under the Christian name. Examples:

Main Entry	Cross-reference
Eudo fitzHubert	Hubert, *see* Eudo fitzHubert
Alvred of Lincoln	Lincoln, *see* Alvred of Lincoln
Leofwine Cild	Cild, *see* Leofwine Cild
Alwine Cobbold	Cobbold, *see* Alwine Cobbold
Gilbert the cook	cook, *see* Gilbert the cook

In the case of Abbeys, main entries will be found under the place-name with the dedication cross-indexed: Ramsey, Abbey of St Benedict (main entry); St Benedict, Ramsey, Abbey of.

Secular churches are indexed under Church with a cross-reference to the dedication, and also to the place-name: Church of Saint-Remy of Rheims (main entry); Saint-Remy of Rheims, Church of; Rheims, Church of Saint-Remy of.

10. Folio References

Only one reference to a name is indexed per folio. The frequent use of *idem*, 'the same man', is not indexed as the name itself is not present. References are linked by a hyphen when the consecutive entries for a holder's fief cover more than one folio.

Folio numbers without suffix indicate the *recto* of the folio, while suffix 'v' indicates the *verso*.

WILTSHIRE

ERRATA

For Eadnoth the steward read Eadnoth the staller, f.69 in the translation.

For Thorold read Thorald, f.74 in the translation.

TRANSLATION

TRANSLATION

NOTES TO THE TRANSLATION

SOURCE AND STANDARDIZATION

THE translations in the County Edition of Domesday Book are based in the main upon those that appear in the *Victoria Histories of the Counties of England*, of which publication commenced in 1900 and is still in progress. The translator of the relevant county folios of Domesday Book in volume two of *VCH Wiltshire* (1955) was R. R. Darlington. Alecto Historical Editions are grateful to the publishers of *VCH* for permission to make use of this translation.

In order that the translations contained in each of the county volumes can be served by a common system of indices, the text of all sources has been standardized so that place- and personal names as well as technical terms and certain common phrases are consistent throughout. The opportunity has also been taken to correct such errors as may have become apparent as a result of subsequent research.

For a detailed statement of the policies governing the treatment of names, see the notes which precede the 'Index of Places' and the 'Index of Persons and Ecclesiastical Bodies' above.

METHODS OF RELATING THE TRANSLATION TO THE FACSIMILE

Throughout the folios of Great Domesday Book there is considerable variation in the number of lines written per page, in the depth and width of the columns, and in the spaces that separate the numbered chapters. In order to assist the use of the facsimile and this translation together, the type-size and the lay-out of the pages of the translation have been designed to match the configuration of the MS text as closely as possible.

The MS was foliated in the seventeenth century on only the *recto* side of each page. In the translation the *verso* is also foliated with the number followed by v.

● to the left, within the column, signifies the presence of one of the larger rubricated initial letters that commonly begin each entry. This device is provided to enable the reader more easily to relate passages in the translation to those in the facsimile by counting the spots on the former against the more prominent initials in the latter.

TYPOGRAPHY

Roman type is reserved for the original text of Great Domesday, including all corrections and marginal additions made to the MS at the time of its compilation in the late eleventh century.

Italic type is used for all matter added subsequently during the Middle Ages and up to recent times.

The use of upper and lower case is the same as in the MS:

FULL CAPITALS represent the large rustic capitals used for county- and chapter-headings, which are all written in red.

LARGE AND SMALL CAPITALS represent matter written in black rustic capitals within the text and usually through-lined in red. Those not written in capitals, whether intentionally or in error, are here transposed in lower case.

MARGINALIA

The translations of those passages entirely written in the margin are printed as close as is possible to the position they occupy in the MS, in smaller type where necessary. A complete key to the system of symbols employed here for the marginal notes and signs found in the MS, such as § for the transposition signs, M, B, S, etc. preceding ● in certain counties, and [1], [2], [3], □, ⬚, ☒, etc., is given in Appendix I, 'The Marginalia of Great Domesday Book', in the associated *Domesday Book Studies* volume, pp. 160–2.

EDITORIAL CONVENTIONS

Square brackets are reserved for editorial insertions.

[*sic*]	indicates a scribal error in the MS, here reproduced in the translation. The only exception is incorrect chapter numbering.
[. . .]	signifies a gap in the MS text, either left blank by the scribe for an insertion to be added later, or as a result of erasure. Three full points within the brackets are the standard length in the translations regardless of the actual extent of the gap in the MS.
† 7 hides †	Daggers enclose the tentative translation of a passage, phrase or numeral which is obscure in the MS, owing either to slips of the pen, to unclear alteration by the scribe, or to the worn condition of the parchment.
7 hides	Underlining indicated words or passages marked for deletion in the MS: the same convention is followed in the translation where no correction has been added suprascript. In the latter case, only the corrected text is given.
| it is worth 12*s.* |	Bars within the text enclose the full extent of a passage of which part is written in the margin, where a note will be found to that effect in square brackets.
[?] WESTON	The modern equivalent given for a Domesday place-name which is probable, but not certain.
[? Weston]	A place left un-named in Domesday Book, but which can be tentatively identified from internal evidence or from the evidence of other related documents.
WESTON [in Parishbrook]	Where a county contains two or more modern places with the same name, they are differentiated by indicating the parish 'in' which each of them lies.
WESTON [near Oldborough]	In the above instance, when one of the place-names is the same or partially the same as the name of the parish in which it lies, giving the awkward WESTON [in Weston], its situation is instead indicated as being 'near' a prominent town or feature.
[Great or Little] WESTON	The use of 'or' indicates that it is uncertain which of two or more modern places now represent the Domesday place-name, or whether all did so.
[Great and Little] WESTON	The use of 'and' indicates that two or more modern places lie within the territory of the same Domesday estate.
WESTON [Oxon.]	County abbreviations indicate that a locality recorded in the folios of this county lies within the boundaries of another in modern times. Throughout this edition the modern county boundaries are taken to be those that obtained prior to the restructuring of the counties in 1974.

Use of Inverted Commas

"CELVERDESCOTE" Double inverted commas indicate a place-name found only in Domesday Book and for which there is no known later equivalent, or of which the form may be corrupt.

Hundred- and wapentake-names are similarly treated, but a typical form is used if there are variants.

'SCULTHORP' Single inverted commas indicate the latest or most typical known form of a name which remained in use beyond the eleventh century, but which either has not survived into modern times at all, or which only appears on twentieth-century maps as the name of a feature such as a river, hill, wood etc., rather than as a place of habitation. This also applies to names without a continuous history and which have only recently been revived for antiquarian reasons.

Hundred- and wapentake-names which are antiquarian revivals are similarly treated. Single inverted commas also indicate such names derived from places which had disappeared before the compilation of the first OS 1-inch maps in the early nineteenth century, either because they never were the names of inhabited communities, or because they had fallen into disuse by that time. In such cases the name-form adopted is the latest, most typical or a regularized form.

[Blank in MS]

● In the borough of MALMESBURY the king has 26 inhabited messuages and 25 messuages in which are houses which pay no more geld than waste land. Each one of these messuages renders 10*d.* as rent; this is all together 43*s.* 6*d.*

There is half a waste messuage, [part] of the fief of the Bishop of Bayeux, which renders no service.

The Abbot of Malmesbury has 4½ messuages and outside the borough 9 cotsets who pay geld with the burgesses. The Abbot of Glastonbury has 2 messuages; Edward the sheriff, 3 messuages; Ralph de Mortimer, 1½; Durand of Gloucester, 1½; William de Eu 1; Humphrey de l'Isle, 1; Osbern Giffard, 1; Alvred of Marlborough, half a waste messuage; Geoffrey Marshal, the same; Tovi, 1, and the fourth part of 1 message; Drogo fitzPons, half [a messuage]; the wife of Eadric, 1; Roger of Berkeley, 1 messuage belonging to the king's farm; and Ernulf de Hesdin, 1 [messuage] likewise belonging to the king's farm of which he
2 incautiously took possession. These 2 render no service.

The king has 1 waste messuage of the land which Azur held.

HERE ARE NOTED THE LANDHOLDERS IN WILTSHIRE

● I KING WILLIAM
II The Bishop of Winchester
III The Bishop of Salisbury
IIII The Bishop of Bayeux
V The Bishop of Coutances
VI The Bishop of Lisieux
VII The Abbey of Glastonbury
VIII The Abbey of Malmesbury
IX The Abbey of Westminster
X The Abbey of Winchester
XI The Abbey of Cranborne
XII The Abbess of Shaftesbury
XIII The Abbess of Wilton
XIIII The Abbess of Winchester
XV The Abbess of Romsey
XVI The Abbess of Amesbury
XVII The Church of Bec
XVIII Gerald the priest of Wilton
XIX The canons of Lisieux
XX The Count of Mortain
XXI Earl Roger
XXII Earl Hugh
XXIII Earl Aubrey
XXIIII Edward of Salisbury
XXV Ernulf de Hesdin
XXVI Alvred of Marlborough
XXVII Humphrey de l'Isle
XXVIII Miles Crispin
XXIX Gilbert de Breteuil
XXX Durand of Gloucester
XXXI Walter Giffard
XXXII William de Eu
XXXIII William de Braose
XXXIIII William de Moyon
XXXV William de Falaise
XXXVI Walter de Douai
XXXVII Waleran the huntsman
XXXVIII William fitzGuy
XXXIX Henry de Ferrers
XL Richard son of Count Gilbert
XLI Ralph de Mortimer
XLII Robert fitzGerald
XLIII Robert fitzRolf
XLIIII Roger de Courseulles
XLV Roger of Berkeley
XLVI Bernard Pauncevolt
XLVII Berengar Giffard
XLVIII Osbern Giffard
XLIX Drogo fitzPons
L Hugh l'Asne
LI Hugh fitzBaldric
LII Humphrey the chamberlain
LIII Gunfrid Mauduit
LIIII Alvred d'Epaignes
LV Aiulf the sheriff
LVI Nigel the physician
LVII Osbern the priest
LVIII Richard Puignant
LIX Robert Marshal
LX Robert the Fair
LXI Richard Sturmy
LXII Reginald Canute
LXIII Matthew de Mortagne
LXIIII Joscelin [. . .] Riviere
LXV Godescal
LXVI Herman and other king's sergeants
LXVII Oda and other king's thegns
LXVIII Hervey and other king's servants

● THE KING has from the borough of WILTON £50. When Hervey received it in custody, it rendered £22.

From WILTSHIRE the king has £10 for a hawk and 20*s.* for a sumpter-horse, and 100*s.* and 5 orae for fodder.

From half a mill at SALISBURY the king has 20*s.* by weight.

From the third penny of SALISBURY the king has £6. From the third penny of MARLBOROUGH, £4. From the third penny of CRICKLADE, †£5†. From the third penny of BATH [Som.], £11. From the third penny of MALMESBURY, £6.

As increment £60 by weight [is due]; EDWARD the sheriff pays this.

● WALTER Hosed, from 2 parts of the borough of Malmesbury, pays £8 to the king;

the borough itself rendered as much TRE, and in this farm were the pleas of the hundreds of "Cicementone" and Startley, which belonged to the king. From the mint the borough itself renders 100*s.* In the same borough Earl Harold had an acre of land, in which are 4 messuages, and 6 others [which are] waste, and 1 mill rendering 10*s.* All this rendered 100*s.* TRE. When the king was going on an expedition, whether by land or sea, he had from this borough either 20*s.* for the support of his butsecarls or took with him 1 man for [each] honour of 5 hides.

THE LAND OF THE KING

● THE KING holds CALNE. King Edward held it, and it has never paid geld; hence it is not known how many hides are there. There is land for 29 ploughs. In demesne are 8 ploughs, and 8 slaves. There are 37 villans and 78 bordars and 10 coliberts having 21 ploughs. There are 45 burgesses, and 7 mills rendering £4. 12*s.* 6*d.*, and 50 acres of meadow, and pasture 2 leagues long and 1 league broad. This vill renders a farm of 1 night with all customary dues.

Nigel holds the church of this manor of the king, with 6 hides of land. There is land for 5 ploughs. In demesne are 2 [ploughs], and 6 slaves. There are 7 villans and 2 bordars and 11 cotsets with 3 ploughs. There are 2 mills rendering 20*s.*, and 25 burgesses paying
2 20*s.*, woodland 2 furlongs long and 1 furlong and 24 acres broad, [and] pasture 4 furlongs long and 2 furlongs broad. The whole is worth £8.

Alvred d'Epaignes holds 5 hides of land which Nigel claims. This land, according to the testimony of the shire, belonged to the church TRE.

● THE KING holds [Great and Little] BEDWYN. King Edward held it. It has never paid geld, nor has it been assessed in hides. There is land for 80 ploughs less 1. In demesne are 12 ploughs, and 18 slaves. There are 80 villans and 60 cotsets and 14 coliberts [with 67 ploughs]. There are 8 mills rendering 100*s.*, [and] 2 woods having 2 leagues in length and 1 league in breadth. There are 200 acres of meadow, and pasture 12 furlongs long and 6 furlongs wide. To this manor belong 25 burgesses. This vill renders a farm of 1 night with all customary dues. In this manor there was TRE a grove, having half a league [in] length and 3 furlongs in breadth, and it was in the demesne of the king. Now Henry de Ferrers holds it.

● THE KING holds AMESBURY. King Edward held it. It has never paid geld, nor has it been assessed in hides. There is land for 40 ploughs. In demesne are 16 ploughs, and 55 slaves and 2 coliberts. There are 85 villans and 56 bordars having 23 ploughs. There are 8 mills rendering £4. 10*s.*, and 70 acres of meadow, pasture 4 leagues long and 3 leagues broad, [and] woodland 6 leagues long and 4 leagues broad.

This manor, [. . .] with its appendages, renders a farm of 1 night with all customary dues.

In this manor are included the lands of 3 thegns, which they themselves held TRE. These [lands] in Amesbury Earl William gave in return for the loan of BOWCOMBE [I.o.W., Hants]. §

● Of the land of this manor, King Edward, in his infirmity, gave 2 hides to the Abbess of Wilton, which she never had previously; afterwards, however, she held them. § Earl William gave "Quintone" and Swindon and [? Great] Cheverell, which were thegnlands, for land in the Isle of Wight, which belonged to the farm of Amesbury.

THE KING holds WARMINSTER. King Edward held it. It has paid no geld, nor has it been assessed in hides. There is land for 40 ploughs. In demesne are 6 ploughs, and 24 slaves and 13 swineherds. There are 15 villans and 8 cotsets and 14 coliberts with 36 ploughs. There are 7 mills rendering £4, and 80 acres of meadow, pasture 1 league long and half a league broad, [and] woodland 2 leagues long and 2 broad. There are 30 burgesses.

This manor renders a farm of 1 night with all its customary dues.

● THE KING holds CHIPPENHAM. King Edward held it. It has paid no geld, nor has it been assessed in hides. There is land for 100 ploughs. In demesne are 16 ploughs, and 28 slaves. There are 48 villans and 45 bordars and 20 cottars and 23 swineherds. Among them all they have 66 ploughs. There are 12 mills rendering £6, and 100 acres of meadow, woodland 4 leagues in length and breadth, [and] pasture 2 leagues long and 1 league broad. This manor, with its appendages, renders a farm of 1 night with all customary dues, and it is worth £110 by tale.

Bishop Osbern holds the church of this manor, with 2 hides, from TRE. One of these hides is thegnland, the other belongs to the church. The whole is worth 55*s.*

To this manor belongs one [piece of] land which King Edward had given to Wulfgeat, his huntsman, and it was [part] of his demesne. This now belongs to the king's farm and it is reckoned as 1 hide. There is land for 2 ploughs, and these are there, and 3 slaves; and 4 villans and 4 cotsets with 1 plough. [There is] pasture 4 furlongs long and 1 furlong broad. It is worth £3. To the farm of this manor belongs half a virgate of land, which was thegnland. Eadric held it TRE.

● The king holds Britford. King Edward held it, and it paid geld for 1 hide. There is land for 20 ploughs. In demesne are 2 ploughs, and 6 slaves and 10 coliberts. There are 12 villans and 6 bordars and 14 cotsets with 17 ploughs. There are 2 mills rendering 20*s*., and 100 acres of meadow, [and] pasture 1 league long and half a league broad. This manor renders £30 by weight. The woodland is in the hand of the king, and he has 40*s*. from it in his farm. Osbern the priest holds the church of this manor, with 1 hide of land belonging to the church. It is worth 40*s*.

● The king holds Tilshead. King Edward held it. It has paid no geld, nor has it been assessed in hides. There is land for 40 ploughs. In demesne are 9 ploughs, and 22 slaves and 10 coliberts. There are 34 villans and 32 cotsets with 18 ploughs. There are 9 mills rendering 100*s*. and 30*d*., and 66 burgesses paying 50*s*. There is meadow 1 league in length and a half broad, pasture $1\frac{1}{2}$ leagues long and 1 league broad, [and] woodland 2 leagues long and 1 league broad. This manor renders the farm of 1 night with its customary dues, and it is worth £100 by tale.

● The king holds Compton Chamberlayne. Earl Harold held it, and it paid geld for 10 hides. There is land for 10 ploughs. In demesne are 2 ploughs, and 2 slaves; and 28 villans and 2 bordars with 8 ploughs. There is a mill rendering 12*s*. 6*d*., and 20 acres of meadow, and 8 acres of pasture and 15 acres of woodland. This manor renders £12 by weight.

● The king holds Rushall. Gytha held it TRE, and it paid geld with its appendages for 37 hides. [. . .] There is land for $27\frac{1}{2}$ ploughs. In demesne are 19 hides, and there are 12 ploughs, and 37 slaves. There are 28 villans and 40 bordars with 14 ploughs. There are 5 mills rendering 72*s*., and 112 acres of meadow, pasture $3\frac{1}{2}$ leagues long and $1\frac{1}{2}$ leagues in breadth, [and] woodland 1 league long and half a league broad. It was and is worth £32. 10*s*. [The Abbey of] Saint-Wandrille has the church of this manor, with 2 hides of land, and there are $1\frac{1}{2}$ ploughs. It is worth 40*s*.

● The king holds Aldbourne. Gytha held it TRE, and it paid geld for 40 hides. There is land for 45 ploughs. In demesne are 18 hides, and there are 10 ploughs, and 25 slaves and 14 coliberts. There are 73 villans and 38 cotsets with 26 ploughs. There are 4 mills rendering 16*s*. 8*d*, meadow 1 league long and 5 furlongs broad, pasture 1 league long and half a league broad, [and] woodland 2 leagues long and half a league broad. To this manor belong 6 burgesses in Cricklade, paying 64*d*. This manor renders £70 by weight, but by the English it is only valued at £60 by tale. To the church of this manor belong 2 hides. There is land for 2 ploughs. These the priest of the same church has, and it is worth 40*s*.

● The king holds Corsham. Earl Tosti held it TRE. There are 34 hides, but it renders geld for 18 hides. There is land for 50 ploughs. In demesne are 11 hides, and there are 7 ploughs, and 10 slaves. There are 65 villans and 48 cotsets and 9 cottars with 38 ploughs. There are 2 mills rendering 8*s*. 6*d*., and 32 acres of meadow, and 1 hide of pasture, and woodland 2 leagues in length and breadth. This manor with its appendages renders £30 by weight. The English, however, value it at £31 by tale. [The Abbey of] Saint-Etienne of Caen has the church of this manor with 3 hides of land. There is land for 5 ploughs. These 3 villans with 6 cotsets have there. It is worth £7. Edgar holds the church of Poulshot, which belongs to this manor, and his father held it. It is worth 5*s*.

● The king holds Melksham. Earl Harold held it, and, with its appendages, it paid geld for 84 hides. There is land for 60 ploughs. In demesne are 34 hides, and there are 19 ploughs, and 35 slaves and 31 coliberts. There are 100 villans less 8 and 66 bordars having 39 ploughs. There are 8 mills rendering £7. 6*s*., and 130 acres of meadow, and 8 leagues of pasture in length and breadth, [and] woodland 4 leagues in both length and breadth. This manor renders £111. 11*s*. by weight. The English, however, value it at as many pounds by tale.

Rumold the priest has the church of this manor with 1 hide of land, and it is worth 40*s*.

● The king holds Coombe Bissett. Gytha held it TRE, and it paid geld for $23\frac{1}{2}$ hides. There is land for 20 ploughs. In demesne are 11 hides, and there are 3 ploughs, and 7 slaves. There are 28 villans and 7 bordars and 43 cotsets having 17 ploughs. There are 2 mills rendering 25*s*., and 60 acres of meadow, and pasture 1 league long and another wide, and 10 acres of scrubland. This manor renders £24 by weight; TRE as much by tale. Leofric the priest holds the church of this manor with half a hide of land, and it is worth 20*s*.

● The king holds Bromham. Earl Harold held it, and it paid geld for 20 hides. There is land for 10 ploughs. In demesne are 10 hides, and there are 2 ploughs, and 4 slaves. There are 14 villans and 6 bordars and 30 cotsets with 8 ploughs. There are 2 mills rendering 5*s*., and 40 acres of meadow, and 12 acres of pasture, [and] woodland 5 furlongs long and 3 furlongs broad. It was worth £20; now £24. Of the land of the villans a priest holds of the king 1 hide and 1 virgate of land. It is 2
worth 15*s*.

● The king holds Wootton Rivers. Queen Edith held it, and it paid geld for 30 hides less 1 virgate. There is land for 30 ploughs. In demesne are 13 hides and 1 virgate of land, and there are 2 ploughs, and 12 slaves. There are 40 villans and 17 cotsets with 14 ploughs. There are 6 acres of meadow, and pasture 6 furlongs long and 3 furlongs broad, [and] woodland 6 furlongs long and as much broad. It was worth £26; now £30. [The Abbey of] Mont-Saint-Michel holds 2 churches of this manor with 1 hide of land. It is worth 20*s*.

● The king holds Westbury. Queen Edith held it, and it paid geld for 40 hides. There is land for 47 ploughs. In demesne are 17 hides, and there are 7 ploughs, and 28 slaves and 16 coliberts. There are 38 villans and 23 bordars and 9 bee-keepers. Among them all they have 40 ploughs. The potters there pay 20*s*. a year, and 6 mills render 70*s*. 6*d*., and [there are] 80 acres of meadow, pasture 3 leagues long and 3 leagues broad, [and] woodland 3 leagues long and half a league broad. There are 29 swineherds. This manor renders £100 by tale. Of the same land of this manor the church has $1\frac{1}{2}$ hides. § William Scudet [holds] $4\frac{1}{2}$ hides and has there 7 ploughs.

§ A certain young clerk holds them. The church is worth 50*s*.

● The king holds Winterbourne Stoke. Queen Edith held it, and it paid geld for 2 hides and 1 virgate of land. There is land for 12 ploughs. In demesne is half a virgate of land, and there are 3 ploughs, and 11 slaves and 5 coliberts. There are 15 villans and 15 bordars with 8 ploughs. There is a mill rendering 10*s*., and 8 acres of meadow, [and] pasture 2 leagues long and as much broad. It was and is worth £33. The church of the same manor has 1 hide of this land. The Abbot of Jumieges holds this church with the land, and it is worth 60*s*.

● The king holds Netheravon. Earl Harold held it, and it paid geld for 20 hides. There is land for 22 ploughs. In demesne are 2 hides, and there are 6 ploughs, and 46 slaves and 8 coliberts. There are 30 villans and 40 bordars with 16 ploughs. To this manor belong 5 burgesses in Wilton; they pay 6*s*. There are 3 mills rendering 30*s*., and 70 acres of meadow, [and] pasture 3 leagues long and half a league broad. It was worth £40; now £57. Of this land of this manor Hervey holds $1\frac{1}{2}$ hides, and there he has 1 plough. A thegn has $2\frac{1}{2}$ hides, and he has there 1 plough. Nigel the physician holds the church of this manor with 1 hide. This with all its appendages is worth £32. [The church] itself, however, is waste, and the roof so damaged, that it is almost tumbling down.

● The king holds Collingbourne Ducis. Earl Harold held it, and it paid geld for 20 hides. There is land for 45 ploughs. In demesne are 5 hides, and there are 5 ploughs, and 12 slaves. There are 49 ploughs [*sic*] and 26 bordars with 15 ploughs, and 20 acres of meadow. [There is] pasture 2 leagues long and 1 league broad, [and] woodland 1 league long and as much broad, and a third part of the woodland which is called Chute. It was worth £40; now £60. To the church belongs half a hide. Gerald, the priest of Wilton [Church], holds the tithe of this church, and it is worth 10*s*. The church itself is waste and dismantled.

● The king holds East Knoyle. Æthelgifu held it TRE, and it paid geld for 30 hides. [There is] land for 15 ploughs. In demesne are $17\frac{1}{2}$ hides, and there are 5 ploughs, and 10 slaves. There are 16 villans and 10 bordars and 18 cotsets with 10 ploughs. There are 15 acres of meadow, and pasture 1 league long and half a league wide, [and] woodland half a league long and as much wide. It was worth £28; now £30. Of this land Gilbert has 1 hide. There are 3 bordars. It is worth 7*s*. 6*d*.

● The king holds Lydiard Millicent. Godric held it TRE, and it paid geld for 10 hides. There is land for 8 ploughs. In demesne [are] 6 hides less 1 virgate, and there are 4 ploughs, and 9 slaves. There 10 villans and 6 bordars have 6 ploughs. There is a mill rendering 32*d*., and 20 acres of meadow, [and] woodland 1 league long and half a league broad. It was worth £10; now £12.

● These 2 vills belonged to Earl William.

● The king holds Ogbourne St George. [. . .] TRE it paid geld for 30 hides. There is land for 25 ploughs. In demesne are 18 hides, and there are 4 ploughs, and 6 slaves. There 24 villans and 14 bordars have 10 ploughs. There are 6 acres of meadow, and pasture half a league long and 4 furlongs broad, and as much woodland. It is worth £25.

Ralph the priest holds the church of Highworth, and to it belong 3 hides which did not pay geld TRE. There is land for 2 ploughs. These the priest has there, with 6 bordars, and 10 acres of meadow. It is worth 100*s*.

Vitalis the priest holds the church of Burbage with 1 virgate of land. It is worth 20*s*.

Regenbald the priest [. . .] holds the church of Pewsey with 1 carucate of land. It is worth 20*s*.

Regenbald the priest holds the church of Avebury, to which belong 2 hides. It is worth 40*s*.

Alweard the priest holds the church of Heytesbury, to which belong 3 hides. There is land for 2 ploughs. These are there, with 2 villans and 6 cottars, and 6 acres of meadow. It is worth 60*s*.

● Bishop Osbern has the church of Hazelbury with half a virgate of land. It is worth 10*s*.

[The Abbey of] Saint-Wandrille holds the church of Sherston, to which belong 3 virgates of land. It is worth 28*s*. It also holds the church of Upavon, to which belong 2½ hides. There is land for 2 ploughs. It is worth £10. 15*s*.

● Bishop Osmund holds of the king half a church in alms, to which belongs half a hide. There is 1 plough, with 5 bordars, and a mill rendering 6*s*. It is worth 25*s*.

William de Beaufour has 1 hide with a church in Marlborough. It is worth 30*s*.

Beorhtweard the priest holds the church of [Great and Little] Bedwyn. His father held it TRE. To it belong 1½ hides. There is land for 1 plough, which [plough] is there. It was and is worth 60*s*.

II. THE LAND OF THE BISHOP OF WINCHESTER

● The Bishop of Winchester holds Downton. [. . .] TRE it paid geld for 100 hides less 3. 2 of these [hides] are not the bishop's, because they were taken away, with 3 others, from the church and out of the hand of the bishop in the time of King Cnut. There is land for 46½ ploughs. Of this land 30 hides are in demesne, and there are 13 ploughs, and 40 slaves. There are 64 villans and 27 bordars having 17 ploughs. There are 7 mills rendering 60*s*., and 60 acres of meadow, pasture 2 leagues long and 1 league broad, [and] woodland 1½ leagues long and half a league broad.

Of the same land of this manor William de Braose holds 14 hides; Waleran 5 hides; Ralph 5 hides; Ansgot 3½ hides; and the king has, in his forest, 4 hides. The church of the same manor has 4 hides; and all these hold of the bishop. Those who held these lands TRE could not separate themselves from the church. When Bishop Walkelin received this manor, it was worth £60; now what he has in demesne is worth £80; what the knights [hold] £23; what the church [holds] £3.

● The same bishop holds Fonthill Bishop. TRE it paid geld for 10 hides. There is land for 7 ploughs. In demesne are 5 hides of this land, and there are 2 ploughs, and 5 slaves. There are 8 villans and 5 bordars with 3 ploughs. There is a mill rendering 5*s*., and 8 acres of meadow, pasture half a league long and 3 furlongs broad, and as much woodland. It was worth £10; now £14.

● The same bishop holds Fyfield, and Edward [holds] of him, and it paid geld for 5 hides TRE. This land belonged to the sacrist of the church; Alsige, a monk, held it of the bishop. There is land for 3 ploughs. Of this land 3 hides are in demesne, and there are 2 ploughs, with 1 slave. There are 3 villans and 9 bordars with 2 ploughs. There are 3 acres of meadow, and 30 acres of pasture, [and] woodland 3 furlongs long and 1 furlong broad. It was and is worth 100*s*.

These [Lands] are for the Sustenance of the Monks

● The same bishop holds Alton Priors, and it paid geld for 20 hides TRE. There is land for 14 ploughs. Of this land 6 hides and 1 virgate of land are in demesne, and there are 4 ploughs, and 8 slaves. There are 27 villans and 15 cotsets with 8 ploughs. There are 2 mills rendering 12½*s*., and 100 acres of meadow, pasture 6 furlongs long and 4 furlongs broad, [and] woodland 7 furlongs long and 2 furlongs broad. Of the same land William Scudet holds 3 hides of the bishop, and he has there 2 ploughs. What the monks have is worth £24; what William [has] 100*s*.

● The same bishop holds Ham. TRE it paid geld for 10½ hides and half a virgate of land. There is land for 7 ploughs. Of this land 5½ hides are in demesne, and there are 3 ploughs, with 1 slave. There are 9 villans and 10 cotsets with 3 ploughs. There are 8 acres of meadow, pasture 3 furlongs long and 1 furlong broad, [and] woodland 6 furlongs long and 3 furlongs broad. Of the same land William holds 2 hides of the bishop. He who held them before him could not withdraw from the church. This manor was worth £6 when the bishop received it; now the demesne is worth £9; what William holds [is worth] £3.

● The same bishop holds Westwood. TRE it paid geld for 3 hides. [There is] land for 5 ploughs. Of this land 2 hides [are] in demesne, and there are 3 ploughs, and 3 slaves. There are 6 villans and 4 bordars with 1 plough. There is a mill rendering 10*s*., and 6 acres of meadow, [and] woodland 2 furlongs long and 1 furlong broad. When the bishop received it, it was worth £6; now £4.

● The same bishop holds 'Elingdon' [in Wroughton]. TRE it paid geld for 30 hides. There is land for 12 ploughs. Of this land 15 hides are in demesne, and there are 4 ploughs, and 3 slaves. There 25 villans and 14 bordars have 7 ploughs. There 6 mills render 42*s*. 6*d*., and [there are] 60 acres of meadow, pasture half a league long and 3 furlongs broad, and 20 acres of woodland.

Of this land 1 knight has 1½ hides, and he has there 1 plough. Godric, who held it TRE, could not be separated from the church. When the bishop received it, it was worth £14; now it is worth £18.

● The bishop himself holds Bushton. TRE it paid geld for 10 hides. There is land for 5 ploughs. Of the same land 6½ hides are in demesne, and there are 2 ploughs, and 3 slaves. There are 7 villans and 3 cotsets with 2 ploughs. There are 30 acres of meadow, [and] woodland 2 furlongs long and 1 furlong broad. When the bishop received it, it was worth £3; now £6.

● The same bishop holds Wanborough. TRE it paid geld for 19 hides. There is land for 10 ploughs. Of the same land 9 hides are in demesne, and there are 3 ploughs, and 6 slaves. There are 19 villans and 13 bordars with 5 ploughs. There is a mill rendering 5*s*., and 40 acres of meadow, [and] pasture half a league long and 15 furlongs broad. Of this land Richer holds 1 hide. When the bishop received it, it was worth £15; now £18.

● The same bishop holds Enford. TRE it paid geld for 30 hides. There is land for 24 ploughs. Of the same land 10 hides are in demesne, and there are 3 ploughs, and 6 slaves. There are 12 villans and 15 bordars with 10 ploughs. There are 2 mills rendering 25*s*., and 17 acres of meadow, [and] pasture 2½ leagues long and 1½ leagues broad. Of the same land William holds 5 hides and Harold 2 hides, an Englishman 3 hides. They have there 10 ploughs. A priest has 1 hide. Those who held [these lands] TRE could not be separated from the church. When the bishop received it, it was worth £34; now the demesne is worth £20; what the priest and the knights hold [is worth] £19.

● The same bishop holds 'East Overton' [near Marlborough]. TRE it paid geld for 15 hides. There is land for 7 ploughs. Of this
1 land 8½ hides are in demesne, and there are 2 ploughs. There [. . .] villans have 5 ploughs. There are 15 acres of meadow, pasture 8 furlongs long and 4 furlongs broad, [and] woodland 5 furlongs long and 2 furlongs broad.

Of the same land Durand holds 2 hides less half a virgate. He who held them TRE could not be separated from the church. It was and is worth 20*s*. The demesne is worth £8; when the bishop received it, it was worth £6.

● The same bishop holds Stockton. TRE it paid geld for 10 hides. There is land for 6 ploughs. Of this land 3½ hides are in demesne, and there are 2 ploughs, and 3 slaves. There are 4 villans and 6 bordars with 2 ploughs. There is a mill rendering 10*s*., and 10 acres of meadow, pasture 5 furlongs long and 2 furlongs broad, and 40 acres of woodland.

Of the same land Richer holds 2 hides, and Ansketil 2½ hides. They have there 2 ploughs. This manor when the bishop received it was worth £8; now the demesne is worth 100*s*. and 10*s*.; what the men hold is worth £4. The land which they hold could not be separated from the church TRE.

III. THE LAND OF THE BISHOP OF SALISBURY [2]

• THE BISHOP OF SALISBURY holds POTTERNE. TRE it paid geld for 52 hides. There is land for 40 ploughs. Of this land 10 hides are in demesne, and there are 6 ploughs, and 4 slaves and 5 coliberts. There are 29 villans and 40 bordars with 30 ploughs. There 6 mills render 43*s.* 4*d.*, and [there are] 40 acres of meadow, pasture 2½ leagues long and 1 league and 3 furlongs broad, [and] woodland 1 league long and 10 furlongs broad. The demesne of the bishop is and was worth £60.

Of the same land of this manor 2 Englishmen hold 6 hides and 1 virgate of land. 1 of them is a knight by the command of the king, and was the nephew of Bishop Herman. And Alweard holds 3 hides which Wulfweard White, TRE, bought from Bishop Herman, for his lifetime only, so that they should afterwards revert to the bishop's farm, because they were [part] of the demesne of the bishop. These thegns have there 4 ploughs, with 2 slaves and 9 bordars. It is worth £7; what the priest of this manor holds is worth 40*s.*

Of the land of the same manor Ernulf de Hesdin holds 3 hides and 1 virgate of the king. The bishop, however, claims them, since he who held them TRE could not be separated from the bishop.

• The same bishop holds BISHOPS CANNINGS. TRE it paid geld for 70 hides. There is land for 45 ploughs. Of this, 10 hides are in demesne, and there are 5 ploughs, and 6 slaves. There are 48 villans and 40 bordars with 28 ploughs. There are 6 mills rendering 7*s.* 6*d.*, and 30 acres of meadow, pasture 1 league long and 8 furlongs broad, [and] woodland 1 league long and 10 furlongs broad. In the borough of CALNE a house belonging to this manor renders 20*d.* a year.

Of the same land of this manor a priest holds 2 hides; Everard 10 hides; Herman 4 hides; Quintin 3 hides; Walter 2 hides; Beorhtweard 5 hides; Alweard 1 hide; the wife of the reeve 1 hide. These have 8 ploughs, with 3 villans and 30 bordars having 4 ploughs. The demesne of the bishop is worth £60; what the others hold is worth £35.

• The same bishop holds RAMSBURY. TRE it paid geld for 90 hides. There is land for 54 ploughs. Of this land 30 hides are in demesne, and there are 8 ploughs, and 9 slaves. There are 68 villans and 43 bordars having 29 ploughs. There are 80 acres of meadow, and 10 mills render £6 and 30*d.* [There is] pasture 14 furlongs long and 5 furlongs broad, [and] woodland 16 furlongs long and 4 furlongs broad.

Of the same land of this manor the priests hold 4 hides; Otbold 12 hides; Herbert 5 hides; Quintin 5 hides; the wife of the reeve 1 hide. These have in demesne 11 ploughs; and 31 bordars with 6 ploughs. In Cricklade 5 burgesses belonging to this manor pay 5*s.* The demesne of the bishop is worth £52. 15*s.*; what the others hold, £17. 5*s.*

• The same bishop holds SALISBURY. TRE it paid geld for 50 hides. There is land for 32 ploughs. Of this land 10 hides are in demesne, and there are 8 ploughs. There are 25 villans and 50 bordars with 17 ploughs. 7 burgesses in Wilton belonging to this manor pay 65*d.* In the manor [are] 4 mills rendering 47*s.* 7*d.*, and half a mill rendering 30*s.*, and 142 acres of meadow. [There is] pasture 20 furlongs long and 10 furlongs broad, and elsewhere pasture 5 furlongs long and 1 furlong broad. [There is] woodland 4 furlongs long and 2 furlongs broad.

Of the same land of this manor Edward holds 5 hides; Odo 5 hides; Hugh 3 hides less 1 virgate. Those who held them TRE could not be separated from the bishop. There are in demesne 5 ploughs; and 3 villans and 17 bordars with 2 ploughs.

The demesne of the bishop is worth £47; what the men hold is worth £17. 10*s.*

• The same bishop holds CHARNAGE. Algar held it TRE, and it paid geld for 5 hides. There is land for 3 ploughs. Of this land 4 hides are in demesne, and there are 2 ploughs; and 3 villans and 6 bordars and 2 cotsets with 1½ ploughs. There are 10½ acres of meadow, pasture 3 furlongs long and 2 furlongs broad, [and] woodland 2 furlongs long and 1 furlong broad. It was worth 40*s.*; now £4. This is in exchange for "SCEPELEIA". Hugh holds it of the bishop.

IIII. THE LAND OF THE BISHOP OF BAYEUX

• THE BISHOP OF BAYEUX holds NORTH TIDWORTH, and Odo [holds] of him. Eadwulf held it TRE, and it paid geld for 5 hides. There is land for 3 ploughs. Of this land 4 hides less 1 virgate are in demesne, and there are 2 ploughs, and 2 slaves. There is 1 villan and 6 bordars with 1 plough. [There is] pasture 3 furlongs long and 2 furlongs broad. It is worth £4. 10*s.*

• The same bishop holds WOODHILL, and Odo [holds] of him. Eadwulf held it TRE, and it paid geld for 6 hides. There is land for 3 ploughs. Of this land 5 hides are in demesne, and there are 2 ploughs, and 6 slaves. There is 1 villan and 4 bordars with 1 plough. There are 12 acres of meadow, and pasture 1 furlong long and as much broad, [and] woodland, 1 furlong long and 3 acres broad. It is worth £4.

• The same bishop holds SWINDON, and Wadard [holds] of him. Leofgeat held it TRE, and it paid geld for 5 hides. Of these, 1 is in demesne, and there is 1 plough, and 4 slaves. There are 5 villans and 2 bordars with 2 ploughs. There is a mill rendering 4*s.*, and 30 acres of meadow and as much pasture. |It was worth 40*s.*; now £4.| |[partly in margin]|

• The same bishop holds DITCHAMPTON, and Robert [holds] of him. Azur held it TRE, and it paid geld for 2 hides. There is land for 2 ploughs. 18 cottars have these there; and there are 4 mills rendering 27*s.*, and 4 acres of meadow and 10 acres of pasture. It was worth 100*s.*; now £8.

V. THE LAND OF THE BISHOP OF COUTANCES

• THE BISHOP OF COUTANCES holds DRAYCOT FITZ PAYNE, and Roger [holds] of him. Alweard and Alnoth held it as 2 manors TRE, and it paid geld for 5 hides. There is land for 2½ ploughs. Of this land 4 hides less 1 virgate are in demesne, and there are 2 ploughs, and 3 slaves. There 4 bordars and 7 cotsets have half a plough. There are 60 acres of pasture. It was worth 30*s.*; now 60*s.*

• The same bishop holds 'WITTENHAM' [in Wingfield], and Roger [holds] of him. Ælfgeat held it TRE, and it paid geld for 5 hides. There is land for 5 ploughs. Of this land 3 hides are in demesne, and there is 1 plough, and 3 slaves. There are 5 villans and 5 bordars with 4 ploughs. There is a mill rendering 12*s.* 6*d.*, and 10 acres of meadow, and 16 acres of woodland, [and] pasture 2 furlongs long and 1 furlong broad. It was and is worth £4. 10*s.*

• The same bishop holds WINGFIELD, and Roger [holds] of him. Azur held it TRE, and it paid geld for 3½ hides. There is land for 3 ploughs. Of this land 2 hides are in demesne, and there is 1 plough. There are 3 villans and 9 bordars with †1† plough. There is a mill rendering 20*s.*, and 7 acres of meadow, and 20 acres of woodland, [and] pasture 3 furlongs long and 2 furlongs broad. It was and is worth 70*s.*

• The same bishop holds MALMESBURY. Gilbert held it TRE, and it paid geld for 1 hide. There is land for half a plough. Of this land 3 virgates of land are in demesne, and there is half a plough, with 3 bordars. There are 4 acres of meadow, and pasture 2 furlongs long and 1 furlong broad. It is worth 13*s.*

• The same bishop holds HIGHER PERTWOOD, and Osbert [holds] of him. Wulfweard held it TRE, and it paid geld for 2 hides. There is land for 2 ploughs. Of this land [. . .] ½ hides are in demesne, and there is 1 plough. There are 2 villans and 3 bordars with 1 plough. There are 20 acres of pasture and 4 acres of woodland. It was and is worth 40*s.*

• The same bishop holds LITTLETON DREW, and Robert [holds] of him. Alweard held it TRE of the Abbot of Glastonbury, and he could not be separated from that church, and it paid geld for 5 hides. There is land for 8 ploughs. Of this land 2 hides are in demesne, and there are 2 ploughs, and 4 slaves. There are 6 villans and 6 bordars with 5 ploughs. There is a mill rendering 7*s.* 6*d.*, and 15 acres of meadow. It was and is worth £7.

• The same bishop holds WINTERBOURNE [? Dauntsey]. Leofsidu held it TRE, and it paid geld for 2½ hides. There is land for 2 ploughs. Of this land 1½ hides are in demesne, and there is 1 plough, and 2 slaves. There are 5 villans and 1 cottar and 4 bordars with 1 plough. There is a mill rendering 12*s.* 6*d.*, and 20 acres of pasture. It was worth 30*s.* when the bishop received it; now £4.

VI. THE LAND OF THE BISHOP OF LISIEUX

• THE BISHOP OF LISIEUX holds [?]YATTON KEYNELL. Leofnoth held it TRE, and it paid geld for 2 hides and 3 virgates. There is land for 3 ploughs. Of this 2 hides are in demesne, and there is 1 plough; and 2 bordars and 6 cotsets with 1 plough. There is a mill rendering 10*s.*, and 3 acres of meadow, [and] woodland 2 furlongs long and as much broad. It was and is worth 40*s.* Turstin holds it of the bishop.

• The same bishop holds SOMERFORD KEYNES [Glos.]. Alweard held it TRE, and it paid geld for 10 hides. There is land for 7 ploughs. Of this 5 hides are in demesne, and there are 3 ploughs, and 5 slaves; and 14 villans and 8 bordars with 4 ploughs. There is a mill rendering 10*s.*, and 100 acres of meadow, [and] woodland 3 furlongs long and 2 furlongs broad. It is worth £7.

VII. THE LAND OF THE CHURCH OF GLASTONBURY

● THE CHURCH OF ST MARY OF GLASTONBURY holds DAMERHAM [Hants], and TRE it paid geld for 52 hides. There is land for 30 ploughs. Of this land 16 hides are in demesne, and there are 4 ploughs, and 6 slaves and 38 coliberts. There are 14 villans and 17 bordars with 19 ploughs. There 4 mills render 20*s*., and [there are] 26 acres of meadow, pasture 3 leagues long and 1 league broad, [and] woodland 5 furlongs long and 4 furlongs broad.

● Of the same land Serlo holds 5 hides; the wife of Hugh 3 hides; Roger 1 hide and 8 acres. Those who held [these lands] TRE could not be separated from the church. There are 3½ ploughs.

The whole manor TRE was worth £36. It now renders £61, but by the men [the lands] are not valued at more than £45, on account of the confusion of the land, and on account of the farm, which is too high. The land of the thegns is worth £7. 15*s*.

● The same church holds HANNINGTON, and Robert [holds] of the abbot. There are 15 hides. There is land for 10 ploughs. In demesne are 3 ploughs, and 7 slaves; and 18 villans and 10 cotsets with 6 ploughs. There are 2 mills rendering 8*s*., and 1 house rendering 5*d*., meadow 3 furlongs long and 3 furlongs broad, [and] pasture 4 furlongs long and 3 furlongs broad. In all it is worth £15. Of this same land the abbot had sold 3 hides to a certain thegn TRE for the lives of 3 men, and the abbot himself had the service from them, and afterwards they were to return to the demesne, and so now they are with the other 12 hides.

● The same church holds [? Monkton] DEVERILL. TRE it paid geld for 10 hides. There is land for 8 ploughs. Of this land 5 hides are in demesne, and there are 2 ploughs, and 2 slaves. There are 10 villans and 8 cotsets with 5 ploughs. There is a mill rendering 5*s*., and 1 acre of meadow, [and] pasture half a league long and as much broad.

Of the same land a thegn holds 1½ hides; and this land neither could nor can be separated from the church. The manor, when Abbot Turstin received it, was worth £8; now £10.

● The same church holds CHRISTIAN MALFORD. TRE it paid geld for 20 hides. There is land for 10 ploughs. Of this land 14 hides are in demesne, and there are 3 ploughs, and 2 slaves. There are 11 villans and 12 bordars and 12 cotsets with 6 ploughs. There 2 mills render 40*s*., and [there are] 36 acres of meadow, [and] woodland 1 league long and half a league broad. Of the same land Robert holds half a hide, and Edward 1 virgate. This land [being] thegnland could not be separated from the church TRE. The whole manor is worth £10. 10*s*.

The Abbot of Glastonbury leased 6 acres of meadow to Beorhtric TRE in Stanton [Stanton St Quintin and Lower Stanton St Quintin]. Osbern Giffard holds them now. In like manner he leased 4 acres of meadow in Littleton Drew to Alweard. Bishop Geoffrey holds them now. These 10 acres of meadow ought to belong to Christian Malford.

● The church itself holds BADBURY. TRE it paid geld for 20 hides. There is land for 10 ploughs. Of this land 13½ hides are in demesne, and there are 3 ploughs, and 4 slaves. There are 11 villans and 10 bordars with 3 ploughs. There is a mill rendering 40*d*., and 100 acres of meadow, [and] pasture 1 league long and 3 furlongs broad. In Cricklade 1 burgess pays 5*d*. It was worth £8; now £10.

● The church itself holds MILDENHALL, and Edward [holds] of it. Hugolin had held it previously. It was in the hand of the abbot TRE, and it paid geld for 10 hides. There is land for 10 ploughs. Of this land 4 hides are in demesne, and there are 2 ploughs. There are 15 villans and 5 bordars with 4 ploughs. There is a mill rendering 30*s*., and 10 acres of meadow, and pasture half a league long and 3 furlongs broad, and as much woodland. It was worth £12; now £18.

● The church itself holds WINTERBOURNE MONKTON. TRE it paid geld for 25 hides. There is land for 15 ploughs. Of this land 10 hides are in demesne, and there are 4 ploughs, and 7 slaves. There are 17 villans and 8 bordars with 7 ploughs. There are 6 acres of meadow and 100 acres of pasture. Of the same land Gilbert holds 3½ hides. Ordgar held them TRE, and he could not be separated from the church. The whole manor was worth £12; now £20.

● The church itself holds NETTLETON. TRE it paid geld for 20 hides. There is land for 12 ploughs. Of this land 10 hides are in demesne, and there are 4 ploughs, and 2 slaves. There are 10 villans and 12 bordars with 6 ploughs. There are 3 mills rendering 22*s*. 6*d*., and 4 acres of meadow, [and] woodland half a league long and 2 furlongs broad. It was worth £8; now £13.

● The church itself holds GRITTLETON. TRE it paid geld for 30 hides. There is land for 20 ploughs. Of this land 10 hides are in demesne, and there are 13 ploughs, and 2 slaves. There are 10 villans and 11 bordars with 7 ploughs. There are 10 acres of meadow and 8 acres of pasture.

Of the same land the Bishop of Coutances holds 5 hides, and Urse 4½ hides. Those who held them TRE could not be separated from the church. There are 10 ploughs.

The demesne of the abbot is worth £12; the bishop's [land] £7; Urse's [land] 40*s*.

● The church itself holds KINGTON LANGLEY. TRE it paid geld for 29 hides. There is land for 16 ploughs. Of this land 11 hides are in demesne, and there are 4 ploughs, and 4 slaves. There are 15 villans and 5 bordars with 8 ploughs. There are 15 acres of meadow, and 10 acres of pasture, [and] woodland 1½ leagues long and half a league broad. In Malmesbury, 1 burgess, paying 15*d*., belongs to this manor.

Of the same land Urse holds 2½ hides; Roger 2 hides less 1 virgate; Ralph 1½ hides. They have there 3 ploughs. Those who held these lands TRE could not be separated from the church. The demesne of the abbot is worth £14. 10*s*.; the men's [land] 100*s*.; when the abbot received it, it was worth £8.

● In LITTLE LANGFORD the abbot of the same church holds 2 hides, and Edward [holds] of him. 2 thegns held them of the abbot TRE, and it paid geld for 2 hides. There is land for 1½ ploughs. Of this land 1 hide and 3 virgates are in demesne, and there is 1 plough, and 2 slaves, and 7 bordars, and 17 acres of meadow and 20 acres of pasture. It was and is worth 60*s*.

In the same vill Edward holds 1 hide of the king, which by right belongs to the thegnland of the abbey.

● The church itself holds [?]IDMISTON. TRE it paid geld for 10 hides. 1 of these lies in Hampshire. There is land for 7 ploughs. Of this land 3 hides are in demesne, and there is 1 plough, and 2 slaves. There are 8 villans and 5 bordars with 2 ploughs. There are 6 acres of meadow, and 10 acres of woodland, [and] pasture 1 league long and 3 furlongs broad.

Of the same land Humphrey holds 2½ hides, and has there 1 plough, and 4 acres of meadow and 20 acres of pasture. He who held them TRE could not be separated from the church. It is worth 40*s*.

The demesne of the abbot is worth £6; when received, it was worth 100*s*.

● The church itself holds [?]GOMELDON. TRE it paid geld for 5 hides. There is land for 3 ploughs. Of this land 2½ hides are in demesne, and there is 1 plough, and 2 slaves. There are 6 villans and 3 bordars with 1½ ploughs. There is a mill rendering 15*s*., and 6 acres of meadow and 60 acres of pasture. It was and is worth £4.

Of these 5 hides Waleran holds 1 virgate of land and the abbot claims it, which the thegns testify should belong to the church.

● The church itself holds [? Longbridge] DEVERILL. TRE it paid geld for 10 hides. There is land for 9 ploughs. Of this land 5 hides are in demesne, and there are 3 ploughs, and 2 slaves. There are 14 villans and 24 bordars and 12 cottars with 6 ploughs. There are 3 mills rendering 14*s*. 10*d*., and 6 acres of meadow, pasture half a league long and 2 furlongs broad, [and] woodland 2 leagues long and half a league broad.

Of the same land a knight holds 1 hide and 1 virgate of land of the abbot. Æthelsige, who held it TRE, could not be separated from the church. The whole manor is worth £12.

VIII. THE LAND OF THE CHURCH OF MALMESBURY

● THE CHURCH OF ST MARY OF MALMESBURY holds HIGHWAY. TRE it paid geld for 11 hides. There is land for 6 ploughs. In demesne are 3 ploughs. There 3 villans and 6 bordars and 4 cottars with 1 slave have 3 ploughs. There are 15 acres of meadow and as many acres of pasture. It was worth 100*s*.; now £8.

● The church itself holds DAUNTSEY. TRE it paid geld for 10 hides. There is land for 6 ploughs. Robert holds it of the abbot. Alweard, who held it of the abbot TRE, could not be separated from the church. In demesne are 2 ploughs and 2 slaves; and 10 villans and 11 cotsets and 3 cottars with 4 ploughs. There is a mill rendering 20*s*., and 12 acres of meadow, [and] woodland half a league long and as much broad. It was and is worth £6.

● The church itself holds Little Somerford, and Gunfrid [holds] of the abbot. TRE it paid geld for 5 hides. Alweard, who held it TRE, could not be separated from the church. There is land for 6 ploughs. Of this land 2 hides are in demesne, and there are 3 ploughs. There are 7 villans and 5 bordars and 12 cotsets and 3 slaves having 4 ploughs. There is a mill rendering 20*s.*, and 40 acres of meadow, and 8 acres of woodland. At Malmesbury a burgess pays 12*d.* It was worth 60*s.*; now 100*s.*

● The church itself holds Brinkworth. TRE it paid geld for 5 hides. There is land for 8 ploughs. Of this land 1 hide is in demesne, and there are 2 ploughs, and 3 slaves. There are 9 villans and 13 cotsets and 18 cottars with 6 ploughs. There are 12 acres of meadow, [and] woodland 2 furlongs long and 1 furlong broad. Of the same land 1 knight holds 1 hide. It was and is worth £4; the land of the knight, 15*s.*

● The church itself holds Norton [near Malmesbury]. TRE it paid geld for 5 hides. There is land for 8 ploughs. Of this land 2½ hides are in demesne, and there are 2 ploughs, and 5 slaves. There are 7 villans and 3 cotsets with 3 ploughs. There is a mill rendering 15*s.*, and 6 acres of meadow, [and] pasture 2 furlongs long and 1 furlong broad. It was worth £6; now £4.

● The church itself holds Brokenborough. TRE it paid geld for 50 hides. There is land for 60 ploughs. Of this land 8 hides are in demesne, and there are 5 ploughs, and 16 slaves. There are 64 villans and 7 cottars and 15 cotsets having 59 ploughs. There are 8 mills rendering £6. 12*s.* 6*d.*, and 50 acres of meadow, and 30 acres of pasture, [and] woodland 3 leagues long and 2 leagues broad.

● Of the same land Ranulph Flambard holds in Corston 6 hides. [There is] land for 5 ploughs. He has there 2 ploughs, and 2 villans and 2 cotsets and 2 slaves with 1 plough, and a mill rendering 12*s.* 6*d.*, and 10 acres of meadow, and 15 acres of pasture, and woodland 3 furlongs long and 1 furlong broad.

● Of the same land, also, Robert holds 3½ hides; William 2 hides; an Englishwoman 1 hide. Those who held these lands TRE could not be separated from the church.

Of the demesne of the monks, [and] of the land of the villans, 2 knights hold 3½ hides. The demesne of the abbot, when received, was worth £26; now £30; what Ranulph [. . .] and the others hold is worth £11. 4*s.*

● The church itself holds Kemble [Glos.]. TRE it paid geld for 30 hides. There is land for 30 ploughs. Of this land 12 hides are in demesne, and there are 2 ploughs, and 6 slaves. There are 30 villans and 15 cotsets with 18 ploughs. There are 2 mills rendering 15*s.*, and 40 acres of meadow, [and] woodland 1 league long and 3 furlongs broad.

● Of the same land Tovi holds 2 hides and 1 virgate of land, and William 4 hides, in Chelworth [in Crudwell]. Those who held them TRE could not be separated from the church. There are 2 ploughs, and 6 slaves, and 6 bordars, and a mill rendering 10*s.*, and 8 acres of meadow. Of the land of the villans Ansketil holds 1 hide.

The demesne of the abbot is worth £13; when received, it was worth £10; what the men hold is worth £8.

● The church itself holds Long Newnton [Glos.]. TRE it paid geld for 30 hides. There is land for 23 ploughs. Of this land 15 hides are in demesne, and there are 4 ploughs, and 4 slaves. There are 19 villans and 5 cottars and 2 cotsets with 9 ploughs. There are 2 mills rendering 30*s.*, and 18 acres of meadow and 80 acres of pasture.

Of the same land Osbern holds 3 hides, and William 2 hides. They have there 6 ploughs. Of the land of the villans the abbot gave 1 hide to a certain knight of his. When the abbot received it, it was worth £10; now his demesne is worth £12; what the men hold is worth £6.

● The church itself holds Charlton [near Malmesbury]. TRE it paid geld for 20 hides. There is land for 13 ploughs. Of this land 12 hides are in demesne, and there are 2 ploughs, and 7 slaves. There are 23 villans and 13 cottars and 2 cotsets with 5 ploughs. There is a mill rendering 15*s.*, and 12 acres of meadow, and 15 acres of pasture, [and] woodland 2 furlongs long and 1 furlong broad. Of the same land Ranulph Flambard holds 1½ hides, and has there 1½ ploughs. Of the land of the villans Ralph holds 1½ hides, and has there 1 plough. When the abbot received the manor, it was worth £8; now his demesne is worth as much; what the men hold is worth 40*s.*

● The church itself holds Garsdon. Wulfgifu held it TRE, and it paid geld for 3 hides. There is land for 6 ploughs. Of this land 1½ hides are in demesne, and there are 2 ploughs, and 6 slaves. There are 5 villans and 5 cotsets with 3 ploughs. There are 2 mills rendering 25*s.*, and 10 acres of meadow, and 10 acres of pasture, [and] woodland half a league long and 2 furlongs broad; and 1 burgess pays 3*s.* It was worth 60*s.*; now 100*s.*

● The church itself holds Crudwell. TRE it paid geld for 40 hides. There is land for 25 ploughs. Of this land 18 hides are in demesne, and there are 4 ploughs, and 5 slaves. There are 48 villans and 24 bordars and 10 cottars and 7 coliberts with 18 ploughs. There are 24 acres of meadow, [and] woodland 2 leagues long and as much broad. It was and is worth £16. Of the same land Everard holds 3 hides, and he has there 3 ploughs, and
7 villans with 1 bordar and 5 slaves and 1 plough. Werlin, who held it TRE, 7
could not be separated from the church. It is worth £4. There are 9 acres of meadow.

● The church itself holds Bremhill. TRE it paid geld for 38 hides. There is land for 30 ploughs. Of this land 17 hides are in demesne, and there are 7 ploughs, and 12 slaves. There are 32 villans and 13 bordars with 20 ploughs. There are 2 mills rendering 30*s.*, and 12 acres of meadow, [and] woodland 2 leagues long and 2 furlongs broad. It was worth £14 when the abbot received it; now £16.

● Of the same land Edward holds 4 hides, and Theodric 4 hides. There is land for 7 ploughs, and there are as many ploughs, and 2 villans and 9 bordars and 7 cottars and 4 slaves. Among them there is a mill rendering 16*s.*, and 10 acres of meadow, and 4 acres of spinney, and woodland 1 furlong long and as much broad. Each [of these holdings] is worth 100*s.* Those who held these 8 hides TRE could not be separated from the church. Of the land of the villans the same Theodric holds 1 hide which the abbot gave him.

● Of the same [land] also, [. . .] Edward holds 2 hides of the king, and Gilbert [holds] of him. These a certain English abbot took away from the demesne of the church and gave to a certain reeve, and afterwards to a thegn, who could in no way be separated from the church. It is worth 40*s.* a year.

● William de Eu also holds of the same land 1 hide which the abbot leased to Ælfstan TRE. It is worth 6*s.*

● The church itself holds Purton. TRE it paid geld for 35 hides. There is land for 24 ploughs. Of this land 21½ hides are in demesne, and there are 2 ploughs, and 5 slaves. There are 20 villans and 12 bordars and 13 cottars with 19 ploughs. There is a mill rendering 5*s.*, and 60 acres of meadow, [and] woodland 2 leagues long and as much broad. In Cricklade a burgess belonging to this manor pays 6*d.* It was and is worth £16.

IX. WHAT [THE CHURCH OF] ST PETER OF WESTMINSTER HAS 2

● The Church of St Peter of Westminster holds the church of Cricklade, and has there many burgesses, and the third penny of the same vill. The whole together renders £9.

X. THE LAND OF THE ABBEY OF ST PETER OF WINCHESTER

● The Church of St Peter of Winchester holds Manningford Abbots. TRE it paid geld for 10 hides. There is land for 10 ploughs. Of this land 5 hides and half a virgate of land are in demesne, and there are 2 ploughs, and 5 slaves. There are 8 villans and 7 cotsets with 2½ ploughs. There is a mill rendering 12*s.* 6*d.*, and 10 acres of meadow, [and] pasture 4 furlongs long and 1 furlong broad. It was worth £6; now £8.

● The church itself holds Collingbourne Kingston. TRE it paid geld for 50 hides. There is land for 32 ploughs. Of this land 10 hides are in demesne, and there are 4 ploughs, and 13 slaves. There are 40 villans and 13 cotsets with 15 ploughs. There are 2 acres of meadow, woodland 1 league long and half a league broad, and as much pasture.

● Of the same land Croch holds of the abbot 10 hides and half a virgate of land and half a hide, and Fulchred 2 hides. Those who held [these lands] TRE could not be separated from the church. There are 8 ploughs. Of the thegnland the abbot has in his demesne 1 hide.

● The whole demesne of the abbot is now worth £28; what the men hold is worth £12; when received, it was worth 100*s.* less.

● The church itself holds Pewsey. TRE it paid geld for 30 hides. There is land for 24 ploughs. Of this land 6 hides and 1 virgate of land are in demesne, and there are 3 ploughs, and 6 slaves. There are 46 villans and 24 cotsets and 1 bordar with 18 ploughs. There are 7 mills rendering £4. 5*s*., and 15 acres of meadow, pasture 1 league long and as much broad, [and] woodland 3 furlongs long and half a furlong broad. Of the same land a thegn holds 2 hides less 1 virgate, and he could not be separated from the church; and Ernulf de Hesdin holds 2 hides of the king, which the abbot gave TRE to a thegn who, however, could not be separated from the church. It is worth 30*s*. The demesne of the abbot was worth £26; now it is worth £28.

● The church itself holds 2 hides in Addestone. There is land for 2 ploughs. Of this land 1 hide is in demesne, and 1 plough, and 3 slaves. There is 1 villan and 4 bordars with 1 plough, and 4 acres of meadow and 60 acres of pasture. It was worth 10*s*.; now 40*s*.

● The church itself holds Chiseldon. TRE it paid geld for 40 hides. There is land for 22 ploughs. Of this land 17 hides are in demesne, and 5 ploughs, and 6 slaves. There are 45 villans and 13 bordars with 10 ploughs. There is a mill rendering 40*d*., and 40 acres of meadow, pasture half a league long and 4 furlongs broad, [and] woodland 3 furlongs long and 2 furlongs broad. It was worth £18; now £24. 6 burgesses in Cricklade belonging to this manor pay 4*s*. 1*d*.

XI. THE LAND OF THE CHURCH OF CRANBORNE

● The Church of St Mary of Cranborne holds Ashton Keynes, and held it TRE, and it paid geld for 20 hides. There is land for 16 ploughs. Of this land 10 hides are in demesne, and there are 2 ploughs, and 5 slaves. There are 20 villans and 12 bordars and 4 cotsets with 13 ploughs. There is a mill rendering 5*s*., and 200 acres of meadow, [and] pasture 1 league long and half a league broad. The woodland is of like extent. It was and is worth £15.

● The church itself holds 1 hide in Damerham [Hants]. There is land for $1\frac{1}{2}$ ploughs. The abbot has there 1 plough, and 5 bordars with half a plough. It is worth 20*s*.

XII. THE LAND OF THE CHURCH OF SHAFTESBURY

● The Church of St Mary of Shaftesbury holds Beechingstoke, and Turstin holds it of the abbess. Hearding held it of the church TRE, and it paid geld for 5 hides. There is land for 5 ploughs. Of this land 3 hides are in demesne, and there are 2 ploughs, and 2 slaves. There are 6 villans and 6 cotsets with 3 ploughs. There is a mill rendering 12*s*., and 28 acres of meadow, and 40 acres of pasture. It was worth 60*s*.; now 100*s*. Hearding, who by agreement was entitled to hold this land in his own lifetime, of his own accord restored it to the church.

● The church itself holds Tisbury. TRE it paid geld for 20 hides. There is land for 40 ploughs. Of this land 5 hides are in demesne, and there are 3 ploughs. There are 40 villans and 50 bordars with 25 ploughs. There are 4 mills rendering 35*s*., and 40 acres of meadow, pasture 1 league long and half a league broad, [and] woodland 1 league long and as much broad.

2 Of the same land Turstin holds 3 hides of the abbess; Gunfrid 3 hides; Aubrey 2 hides. They have there 9 ploughs. Edward the sheriff has 3 ploughs in the land of the villans. The demesne of the abbess is worth £30; the knights' [land] £13.

● The church itself holds Donhead [St Andrew and St Mary]. TRE it paid geld for 40 hides. There is land for 32 ploughs. Of this land 12 hides are in demesne, and there are 2 ploughs. There are 35 villans and 25 bordars with 25 ploughs. There are 8 mills rendering 66*s*. 8*d*., and 15 acres of meadow, pasture 1 league long and as much broad, [and] woodland 6 furlongs long and 2 furlongs broad. Of the same land Turstin holds 6 hides, and a certain thegn 1 hide, and there are 6 ploughs. Those who held them TRE could not be separated from the church. The demesne of the abbess is worth £22; the men's [land] £10; and it was worth as much previously.

● The church itself holds Bradford on Avon. TRE it paid geld for 42 hides. There is land for 40 ploughs. Of this land 13 hides are in demesne, |[partly in margin]| and there are 8 ploughs, and 9 slaves |and 18| coliberts. There are 36 villans and 40 bordars with 32 ploughs, and there are 22 swineherds, and 33 burgesses paying 35*s*. 9*d*., and 1 sergeant rendering 7 sesters of honey. There are 2 mills rendering £3. The market renders 45*s*. There is an arpent of vineyard, and 50 acres of meadow, pasture 11 furlongs long and 3 furlongs broad, [and] woodland half a league long and 2 furlongs broad.

To the same manor of Bradford on Avon belongs "Alvestone" [? in Bradford on Avon]. TRE it paid geld for 7 hides apart from the 42 hides above-mentioned. There is land for 6 ploughs. Of this land 4 hides are in demesne, and there are 3 ploughs. The whole of Bradford on Avon, with its appendages, was and is worth £60.

● The church itself holds Liddington. TRE it paid geld for 38 hides. There is land for 16 ploughs. Of this land 24 hides are in demesne, and there are 4 ploughs, and 6 slaves. There are 23 villans and 17 bordars with 7 ploughs. There are 2 mills rendering 5*s*., meadow 4 furlongs long and 3 furlongs broad, [and] pasture half a league long and 4 furlongs broad. In Cricklade 1 burgess pays 6*d*. It was worth £18; now £22.

● The church itself holds Dinton. TRE it paid geld for 20 hides. There is land for 15 ploughs. Of this land 7 hides and 3 virgates of land are in demesne, and there are 2 ploughs, and 4 slaves. There are 21 villans and 10 bordars with 11 ploughs. There are 2 mills rendering 12*s*. 6*d*., and 20 acres of meadow, and as many acres of woodland, [and] pasture 1 league long and half a league broad. 2 burgesses pay 10*d*.

Of the same land Gunfrid holds 2 hides, and has there 2 ploughs. He who held them TRE could not be separated from the church. The demesne of the abbess was and is worth £18; Gunfrid's [holding] 40*s*.

XIII. THE LAND OF THE CHURCH OF WILTON

● The Church of St Mary of Wilton holds Stanton St Bernard. TRE it paid geld for 20 hides. There is land for 12 ploughs. Of this land 10 hides are in demesne, and there are 4 ploughs, and there are 8 slaves. There are 16 villans and 1 bordar and 21 cotsets with 8 ploughs. There are 2 mills rendering 12*s*. 6*d*., and 60 acres of meadow, and 3 acres of alder-wood, [and] pasture 1 league long and half a league broad. It was worth £16; now £24.

● The church itself holds North Newnton. TRE it paid geld for $13\frac{1}{2}$ hides and half a virgate of land. Of this land 3 hides are in demesne, and there are 2 ploughs, and 4 slaves. There are 13 villans and 16 cotsets with 5 ploughs. 10 ploughs can plough the whole manor. There is a mill rendering 12*s*. 6*d*., and 30 acres of meadow, pasture 4 furlongs long and 2 furlongs broad, [and] woodland 1 league long and as much broad.

Of the land of the villans the abbess gave to a knight $3\frac{1}{2}$ hides and half a virgate of land. He has there 2 ploughs, and his villans 1 plough.

Of the same land Ælfric the huntsman held of the abbess 1 hide and $1\frac{1}{2}$ virgates of land, on the condition that after his death it should return to the church because it was [part] of the demesne farm. Richard Sturmy holds it now. The whole manor was worth £14 when received; now £18.

● The church itself holds [Great and Little] Durnford. TRE it paid geld for 4 hides. There is land for 3 ploughs. Edward holds it of the abbess. 3 Englishmen held it TRE and they could not be
2 separated from the church. 2 of them paid 5*s*., and the third rendered service as a thegn. There are 6 oxen in the demesne plough, with 4 bordars. 2 Englishmen there have 2 ploughs. There is a mill rendering $7\frac{1}{2}$*s*., and there are 12 acres of meadow, [and] pasture 4 furlongs long and 1 furlong broad. It was worth 100*s*.; now £9.

● The church itself holds Swallowcliffe. TRE it paid geld for 4 hides and 1 virgate. There is land for 2 ploughs. There is 1 villan and 2 bordars, and 2 acres of meadow. It was and is worth 40*s*.

● The church itself holds Chilmark. TRE it paid geld for 20 hides. There is land for 14 ploughs. Of this land 8 hides are in demesne, and there are 2 ploughs. There are 15 villans and 12 bordars and 12 coliberts with 12 ploughs. There is a mill rendering 10*s*., and 5 acres of meadow, and 10 acres of thicket, [and] pasture 1 league long and half a league broad. It was worth £14; now £15.

● The church itself holds 1 hide of land in Wardour, and Beorhtmær holds it of the abbess. There is land for 1 plough. This [plough] is there with 4 bordars, and 3 acres of meadow. [There is] pasture 1 league long and half a league broad, [and] woodland 2 furlongs long and 1 furlong broad. It is worth 20*s*.

● The church itself holds West Knoyle. TRE [it paid geld] for 10 hides. There is land for 7 ploughs. Of this land $4\frac{1}{2}$ hides are in demesne, and 3 slaves. There are 11 villans and 9 cotsets with 5 ploughs. There are 5 acres of meadow, and pasture half a league long and 3 furlongs broad, [and] woodland half a league long and as much broad. It was worth £6; now £8.

● The church itself holds West Overton. TRE it paid geld for 10 hides. There is land for 4 ploughs. Of this land 7 hides and half a virgate of land are in demesne, and there are 2 ploughs, and 2 slaves. There are 3 villans and 8 bordars with 2 ploughs. There is a mill rendering 10*s*., and 5 acres of meadow, and 20 acres of pasture, and 20 acres of woodland. It is worth 100*s*.

● The church itself holds Chalke [Bowerchalke and Broad Chalke]. TRE it paid geld for 77 hides. There is land for 66 ploughs. Of this land 10 hides are in demesne, and there are 10 ploughs, and 20 slaves. There are 86 villans and 50 bordars and 10 coliberts having 50 ploughs. There are 5 mills rendering 65*s*., and 12 acres of meadow, pasture 3 leagues long and 1 league broad, and as much woodland.

Of the same land Gerard holds 3 hides. He who held them TRE could not be separated from the church. There are 2 ploughs. It is worth £3. The demesne of the abbess is worth £67.

Of the same land Richard Puignant holds $7\frac{1}{2}$ hides of the king. Of these, Æthelgifu held 2 hides TRE, and the men of the church held the others, rendering service as villans. The abbess claims them. Richard has there 5 ploughs; and it is worth £7.

● The church itself holds South Newton. TRE it paid geld for 19 hides and 3 virgates of land. There is land for 14 ploughs. Of this land 2 hides are in demesne, and there are 2 ploughs, and 6 coliberts. There are 20 villans and 16 bordars with 12 ploughs. There are 2 mills rendering 40*s*., and 20 acres of meadow, and 150 acres of pasture and 200 acres of woodland. To this manor belongs [the right] by custom to have in Melchet Wood [Hants] 80 cart-loads of wood |and fodder for 80 pigs,| and what may be necessary for the repair of the houses and fences. § |[partly in margin]|

● The church itself holds Wylye. TRE it paid geld for 10 hides. There is land for 5 ploughs. Of this land 5 hides are in demesne, and there are 2 ploughs, and 2 slaves. There are 9 villans and 10 bordars with 3 ploughs. There is a mill rendering 10*s*., and 12 acres of meadow, and 100 acres of pasture and 10 acres of scrubland. It was worth £6; now £8.

§South Newton is worth £16.

● The church itself holds Little Wishford. TRE it paid geld for 4 hides. There is land for 3 ploughs. Of this land 2 hides are in demesne, and there are 2 ploughs. There is 1 villan and 16 bordars with 1 plough. There are 2 mills rendering 24*s*., and 8 acres of meadow and 9 acres of pasture. It was worth £3; now £4.

● The church itself holds Little Langford. TRE it paid geld for 3 hides. There is land for 2 ploughs. These [ploughs] 2 Englishmen have there with 2 bordars and 2 slaves. There is a mill rendering 5*s*., and 25 acres of meadow and 20 acres of pasture. It was worth 40*s*.; now 50*s*. The father of those who now hold it, held it TRE, and could not be separated from the church.

● The church itself holds Ugford. TRE it paid geld for 4 hides. There is land for 3 ploughs. Of this land 3 hides are in demesne, and there is 1 plough. There are 2 villans and 4 bordars with 1 plough. There is a mill rendering 5*s*., and 6 acres of meadow. It was worth 40*s*.; now 60*s*. The church itself has half a hide of land in Ditchampton. It is worth 30*d*.

● The church itself holds Burcombe. TRE it paid geld for 6 hides. There is land for 4 ploughs. Of this land 2 hides are in demesne, and there are 2 ploughs. There are 13 bordars, and a mill rendering 15*s*., and 18 acres of meadow, [and] pasture 8 furlongs long and 1 furlong broad. It is worth 100*s*. Of the same land Edward holds 1 hide which cannot be alienated from the church. It is worth 15*s*.

● The church itself holds Baverstock. TRE it paid geld for 3 hides. There is land for 3 ploughs. Of these 2 hides are in demesne, and there is 1 plough, with 1 slave; and 4 bordars with 2 ploughs, and 6 acres of meadow and 4 acres of pasture. It is worth 60*s*.

● The church itself holds Washern. TRE it paid geld for $8\frac{1}{2}$ hides. There is land for 7 ploughs. Of this land 2 hides are in demesne, and there is 1 plough. There are 9 villans and 10 coliberts with 6 ploughs. There are 12 acres of meadow, [and] pasture 8 furlongs long and 6 furlongs broad. In Melchet Wood [Hants] [there is] pasture for 80 pigs, and 80 cart-loads of wood, and what is necessary for [repairing] the houses and fences. It is worth £7. 10*s*.

● The church itself holds Fovant. TRE it paid geld for 10 hides. There is land for 7 ploughs. Of this land 5 hides are in demesne, and there are 2 ploughs, and 7 coliberts. There are 8 villans and 7 bordars with 5 ploughs. There are 2 mills rendering 17*s*. 6*d*., and 8 acres of meadow, pasture 4 furlongs long and 1 furlong broad, [and] woodland 2 furlongs long and 1 furlong broad. It is worth £7. 10*s*.

● The church itself holds Laverstock. TRE it paid geld for 2 hides. There is land for 3 ploughs. Of this land 1 hide is in demesne, and there is 1 plough. There are 6 villans and 8 bordars with 2 ploughs. There is a mill rendering 7*s*. 6*d*., and 18 acres of pasture. It was worth 100*s*.; now £6. Of this land a fourth part has been put in the king's forest.

● The church itself held 2 hides TRE, which Thorth had given there with his 2 daughters, and from them they were always clothed, until the Bishop of Bayeux unjustly took them away from the church. [2]

● All the rents which the church has from this borough of Wilton are valued at £10. 17*s*. 6*d*. [2]

XIIII. THE LAND OF THE CHURCH OF ST MARY OF WINCHESTER

● The Church of St Mary of Winchester holds Urchfont. TRE it paid geld for 30 hides. There is land for 20 ploughs. Of this land 6 hides are in demesne, and there are 7 ploughs, and 17 slaves. There are 33 villans and 26 bordars and 6 cottars with 9 ploughs. There are 3 mills rendering 21*s*. 3*d*., and 64 acres of meadow, pasture 1 league long and half a league broad, and as much woodland. Of the same land Edward holds $1\frac{1}{2}$ hides and the third part of half a hide; Walter 1 hide; Englishmen hold 2 hides and 2 parts of half a hide. Of the 6 hides which are in demesne, the abbess's reeve held 2 hides TRE. Afterwards, however, he restored them to the church with all his livestock and they are now in demesne. When the abbess received the manor, it was worth £15; now what she has in demesne [is worth] £27; what the knights [hold] £3.

● The church itself holds All Cannings. TRE it paid geld for 18 hides and $1\frac{1}{2}$ virgates of land. There is land for 15 ploughs. Of this land 4 hides are in demesne, and there are 5 ploughs, and 8 slaves. There are 27 villans and 17 bordars and 6 cottars with 10 ploughs. There is a mill rendering 13*s*., and 108 acres of meadow, pasture 1 league long and 4 furlongs broad, [and] woodland 4 furlongs long and 2 furlongs broad. It was worth £20; now £30.

XV. THE LAND OF THE CHURCH OF ROMSEY

● The Church of St Mary of Romsey holds Edington. TRE it paid geld for 30 hides. There is land for $35\frac{1}{2}$ ploughs. Of this land $2\frac{1}{2}$ hides are in demesne, and there are 7 ploughs, and 10 slaves. There are 21 villans and 23 bordars and 10 coliberts with 15 ploughs. There are 2 mills rendering 19*s*., and 100 acres of meadow, pasture 1 league long and half a league broad, [and] woodland 10 furlongs long and 5 broad.

Of the same land William holds $4\frac{1}{2}$ hides; Osmund 4 hides; Hervey 2 hides; Englishmen 5 hides and 1 virgate of land. Those who held these 15 hides and 3 virgates TRE could not be separated from the church. There are $12\frac{1}{2}$ ploughs. The demesne of the church is worth £30; what the men hold £18.

● The church itself holds [Steeple and West] Ashton. TRE it paid geld for 40 hides. There is land for 37 ploughs. Of this land 10 hides are in demesne, and there are 9 ploughs, and 8 slaves. There are 40 villans and 30 bordars with 20 ploughs. There are 3 mills rendering 32*s*. 6*d*., and 100 acres of meadow, pasture 19 furlongs long and 1 furlong broad, [and] woodland 2 leagues long and half a league broad. Of the same land Edward holds 3 hides; William 1 hide; Englishmen 4 hides. Those who held them TRE could not be separated from the church. The demesne of the church is worth £30; [the holdings] of the men, £6. 13*s*. [2]

XVI. THE LAND OF THE CHURCH OF AMESBURY

● The Church of Amesbury holds Bulford. TRE it paid geld for 12 hides. There is land for 9 ploughs. Of this land 6 hides are in demesne, and there are 3 ploughs, and 13 slaves. There are 3 villans and 20 cotsets and 3 cottars with 5 ploughs. There are 2 mills rendering 65*s.*, and 35 acres of meadow, [and] pasture 1 league long and half a league broad. Of the same land Alweard holds 3 hides. He who held them TRE could not be separated from the church. The demesne of the abbess is worth £13; what the thegn holds is worth 15*s.*

● The church itself holds Boscombe. TRE it paid geld for 4 hides. There is land for 2 ploughs. Of this land $2\frac{1}{2}$ hides are in demesne, and there is 1 plough, with 1 slave. There are 2 villans and 5 cotsets and 2 cottars with 1 plough. There are 4 acres of meadow, [and] pasture 1 furlong long and half a furlong broad. It was and is worth £3.

● The church itself holds Allington [near Amesbury]. TRE it paid geld for 4 hides. There is land for 2 ploughs. Of this land 3 hides less 1 virgate are in demesne, and there is 1 plough, and 3 slaves. There are 3 villans and 5 cotsets and 1 cottar with 1 plough. There are 8 acres of meadow, [and] pasture 1 league long and 1 furlong broad. It was worth £3; now £4.

● The church itself holds Choulston, and Alweard holds it of the abbess. TRE it paid geld for $2\frac{1}{2}$ hides. There is land for $1\frac{1}{2}$ ploughs, and as many [ploughs] are there, with 2 slaves and 3 cotsets. There are 8 acres of meadow, [and] pasture 5 furlongs long and 1 furlong broad. It was worth 30*s.*; now 40*s.*

§ ● The church itself used to hold 2 hides TRE, and held them afterwards in the time of King William, and they are for the sustenance of the nuns. These [hides] the Count of Mortain holds unjustly.

● The church itself holds 6 hides in Rabson. There is land for 4 ploughs. Of this land 3 hides are in demesne, and there are 3 ploughs, and 2 slaves. There are 5 villans and 10 bordars with 1 plough. There are 3 acres of meadow, [and] pasture half a league long and as much broad. It was worth £4; now 100*s.*

● The church itself holds Maddington. TRE it paid geld for $4\frac{1}{2}$ hides. There is land for 2 ploughs. Of this land $2\frac{1}{2}$ hides are in demesne, and there is 1 plough. There are 4 villans and 4 bordars and 2 cottars with 1 plough. There are 8 acres of meadow and 10 acres of pasture. It was and is worth £4.

XVII. THE LAND OF SAINTE-MARIE OF BEC

● The Church of Sainte-Marie of Bec holds Brixton Deverill of the king. Beorhtric held it TRE, and it paid geld for 10 hides. There is land for 7 ploughs. Of this land $6\frac{1}{2}$ hides are in demesne, and there are 3 ploughs, and 8 slaves. There are 8 villans and 7 cotsets and 2 bordars with 4 ploughs. There is a mill rendering 30*d.*, and 4 acres of meadow, pasture 1 league long and 5 furlongs broad, [and] woodland 3 furlongs long and 2 furlongs broad. The church of the same manor has 1 hide of the same land. The whole manor is worth £12. It was worth £15 during the lifetime of Queen Matilda, who gave it to the same church.

XVIII. THE LAND OF GERALD OF WILTON

● Gerald of Wilton holds Upton Lovell of the king in alms. The same man held it TRE, and it paid geld for 10 hides. There is land for 6 ploughs. Of this land 6 hides and $1\frac{1}{2}$ virgates are in demesne, and there are 3 ploughs, and 4 slaves. There are 9 villans and 6 bordars and 4 cotsets with 3 ploughs. There is a mill rendering 20*s.*, and 15 acres of meadow, [and] pasture half a league long and 2 furlongs broad. It is worth £10.

[THE LAND] OF REGENBALD

● Regenbald the priest holds Latton and Eysey. 2 thegns held them as 2 manors TRE. Earl Harold joined them into 1, and it paid geld for 9 hides. There is land for 8 ploughs. Of this land 3 hides are in demesne, and 8 slaves. There are 15 villans and 6 bordars and 4 cotsets with 5 ploughs; and in demesne 3 ploughs. There are 2 mills, and 200 acres of meadow, [and] pasture 1 league long and half a league broad. It was and is worth £10.

XIX. [THE LAND OF] THE CANONS OF LISIEUX

● The Canons of Lisieux hold Kingston Deverill. Eadgifu held it TRE, and it paid geld for 4 hides. There is land for 3 ploughs. Of this $3\frac{1}{2}$ hides less 3 acres are in demesne, and there is 1 plough, and 2 slaves; and 6 cotsets with 1 villan have 1 plough. There are 3 acres of meadow, [and] pasture 4 furlongs long and 3 furlongs broad. It was worth 40*s.*; now 70*s.*

● Alweard the priest has 5 hides which belong to the church of Alderbury of the alms of the king. There is land for 3 ploughs. In demesne is 1 plough; and 4 villans and 8 bordars with 2 ploughs. There are 10 acres of meadow, and 4 furlongs of woodland in length and 4 in breadth. To this same church belongs 1 hide which has never paid geld. The whole is worth 70*s.*

● Osbern the priest has 2 hides of the king in the church of Alderbury. It is worth 20*s.*

● Agenulf holds Horningsham. His father held it of King Edward in alms. There is half a hide. [There is] land for 1 plough. There is 1 cotset, and 2 acres of meadow and 2 acres of woodland. It is worth 5*s.*

XX. THE LAND OF THE COUNT OF MORTAIN

● The Count of Mortain holds Conock, and [the Church of] Sainte-Marie of Grestain [holds] of him. TRE it paid geld for 10 hides. There is land for 4 ploughs. Of this land $6\frac{1}{2}$ hides are in demesne, and there are 2 ploughs, and 3 slaves. There are 6 villans and 9 bordars with 2 ploughs. There are 20 acres of meadow, [and]
[2] pasture half a league long and 3 furlongs broad. It was worth £8; now £9.

● The same count holds "Nechendune", and Gilbert [holds] of him. Godwine held it TRE, and it paid geld for 3 hides. There is land for 2 ploughs. Of this land 2 hides are in demesne, and there is
[2] 1 plough, and 2 slaves. There is 1 villan and 8 bordars with 1 plough. There are 20 acres of meadow and 15 acres of pasture. It was worth 30[*s.*]; it is now worth 40*s.*

● The same count holds [?]Clyffe Pypard, and Gilbert [holds] of him. Godwine held it TRE, and it paid geld for 3 hides. There is land for $1\frac{1}{2}$ ploughs. In demesne is 1 plough, and 2 slaves, and 10 acres of meadow. It was worth 20*s.*; now 40*s.*

● The same count holds [?]Clyffe Pypard, and Gilbert [holds] of him. Godwine held it TRE, and it paid geld for 4 hides less 1 virgate. There is land for $1\frac{1}{2}$ ploughs. There is 1 villan and 3 bordars, and 16 acres of meadow and 14 acres of pasture. It is worth 40*s.*

● The count himself holds Hanging Langford. Ketil held it TRE, and it paid geld for 5 hides. There is land for $2\frac{1}{2}$ ploughs. Of this land 4 hides and 1 virgate of land are in demesne, and there are 2 ploughs. There are 2 villans and 4 bordars with half a plough. There is half a mill rendering 30*d.*, and 20 acres of meadow and 30 acres of pasture. It was and is worth 100*s.*

● The count himself holds [? West] Winterslow. Hearding held it TRE, and it paid geld for $6\frac{1}{2}$ hides. There is land for 7 ploughs. Of this land 3 hides are in demesne, and there are 3 ploughs, and 6 slaves. There are 6 villans and 12 cotsets with 3 ploughs. There is a mill rendering 5*s.*, and 3 acres of meadow, pasture 1 league long and as much broad, [and] woodland 1 league long and half a league broad. It is worth £10. Of this manor the Abbess of Amesbury held 2 hides TRE. §

XXI. THE LAND OF EARL ROGER

● Earl Roger holds Castle Eaton. TRE it paid geld for 15 hides. There is land for 12 ploughs. Of this land half is in demesne, and there are $3\frac{1}{2}$ ploughs, and 6 slaves. There are 8 villans and 8 cotsets with 5 ploughs. There is a mill rendering 15*s.* 6*d.*, and 100 acres of meadow, [and] pasture 6 furlongs long and 3 furlongs broad. It was worth £15 TRE; now £12.

● The earl himself holds Milston. TRE it paid geld for $3\frac{1}{2}$ hides. There is land for 2 ploughs. Of this land 2 hides are in demesne, and there is 1 plough; and 3 villans and 5 cotsets with $1\frac{1}{2}$ ploughs. There are 8 acres of meadow, [and] pasture 1 league long and 3 furlongs broad. It was and is worth 70*s.* Turold holds these 2 manors of the earl. Osmund, a thegn, held them TRE.

● The same earl holds Poulton [near Cirencester, Glos.]. Siward held it TRE, and it paid geld for 5 hides. There is land for 8 ploughs. Of this land $3\frac{1}{2}$ hides are in demesne, and there are 4 ploughs, and 8 slaves; and 8 villans and 7 cotsets with 4 ploughs. There are 15 acres of meadow, [and] pasture 3 furlongs long and 1 furlong broad. It was worth £12; now £16.

XXII. THE LAND OF EARL HUGH

● Earl Hugh holds "Retmore", and William [holds] of him. TRE it paid geld for half a hide. There is land for 3 ploughs. In demesne are 2 ploughs with 1 slave. There is 1 villan and 3 bordars and 11 cotsets with 1 plough. There is a mill rendering 14*s.*, and 5 acres of meadow, pasture 3 furlongs long and 1 furlong broad, [and] woodland 3 furlongs long and 2 furlongs broad. It was worth 50*s.*; now 60*s.*

● The same earl holds [?]Wilsford [near Amesbury], and Hamo [holds] of him. TRE it paid geld for 1 hide. There is land for 1 plough, and this [plough] is in demesne, and 2 slaves and 3 cotsets. There are 6 acres of meadow, [and] pasture 8 furlongs long and 1 furlong broad. It is worth 40*s.*

● The same earl holds Hartham, and Edward [holds] of him. TRE it paid geld for 2 hides. There is land for 3 ploughs. Of this land 1 hide is in demesne, and there are 2 ploughs, and 2 slaves. There is
[2] 1 knight, and 3 cotsets, and 5 acres of meadow, and 3 acres of woodland and 12 acres of pasture. It is worth 40*s.*

● The same earl holds Burcombe, and Hamo [holds] of him. TRE it paid geld for 4 hides. There is land for 2 ploughs. Of this land 3 hides are in demesne, and there is 1 plough, with 1 slave. There is 1 villan and 4 bordars, and a mill rendering 10*s*., and 6 acres of meadow, and 10 acres of woodland and 20 acres of pasture. It was worth £3; now £4.

● The same earl holds CADENHAM, and William [holds] of him. TRE it paid geld for 2 hides. There is land for 2 ploughs. Of these [hides], 1 hide [is] in demesne, and 1 plough, and 2 slaves; and 8 bordars with 1 plough. There are 5 acres of meadow, [and] woodland 2 furlongs long and 1 furlong broad. It was worth 30*s*.; now 40*s*.

Eadnoth the steward held these 5 manors TRE.

● The same earl holds 'FISHERTON' [in Salisbury], and Hamo [holds] of him. Godric held it TRE, and it paid geld for 3 hides. There is land for 2 ploughs. In demesne are 2 hides of this land, and there is 1 plough, and 1 slave. There are 3 villans and 5 bordars, and a mill rendering 10*s*., and 40 acres of meadow and 40 acres of pasture. It was and is worth £3.

XXIII. THE LAND WHICH BELONGED TO EARL AUBREY

● EARL AUBREY held COMPTON [in Enford]. TRE it paid geld for 7 hides. There is land for 6 ploughs. Of this, 3 hides and 1 virgate of land are in demesne, and there is 1 plough, and 6 slaves. There are 5 villans and 5 cotsets with 3 ploughs. There is a mill rendering 10*s*., and 5 acres of meadow, [and] pasture 3 furlongs long and 1 furlong broad. It was and is worth £10.

● DURRINGTON paid geld TRE for 1½ hides. There is land for 1 plough. In demesne is 1 hide, and 4 cotsets have the rest of the land there. There are 5 acres of meadow. In this vill is 1 hide. [There is] land for 1 plough. A thegn held this TRE. There is 1 bordar, and 5 acres of meadow. These 2½ hides are worth £4.

● [? East] WINTERSLOW paid geld TRE for 2 hides. There is land for 2 ploughs. There is 1 villan and 3 bordars, and woodland 1 furlong long and half a furlong broad. It is worth 20*s*.

● ABLINGTON paid geld for 3 hides. There is land for 2 ploughs. Of this land 2½ hides are in demesne, and there is 1 plough, and 4 cotsets.
nargin]| There are 35 |acres| of meadow, and pasture 3 furlongs long and 1 furlong broad. It is worth £4.

● CHITTERNE paid geld TRE for 6 hides. There is land for 5 ploughs. Of this land 3 hides are in demesne, and there is 1 plough, and 4 slaves. There are 4 villans and 2 bordars with 2 ploughs. [There is] pasture 4 furlongs long and 2 furlongs broad. It was worth £4; now £6.

● TYTHERINGTON paid geld TRE for 2 hides. There is land for 2 ploughs. There is 1 villan, and half a mill rendering 30*d*., and 5 acres of meadow. It is worth 20*s*.

Hearding held these 6 estates TRE.

● ALLINGTON [near Amesbury] paid geld TRE for 4 hides. There is land for 2 ploughs. Of this land 2½ hides are in demesne, and there is 1 plough, and 3 slaves. There is 1 villan and 4 cotsets with 1 plough. There is a mill rendering 20*s*., and 5 acres of meadow, [and] pasture 3 furlongs long and 1 furlong broad. Earl Harold held this land. In the same vill are 4 hides of land which Harold unjustly took away from the Church of Amesbury, by the testimony of the thegns of the shire. The church, however, now has it.

● ELCOMBE paid geld TRE for 27 hides. There is land for 8 ploughs. Of this land 24 hides are in demesne, and there are 2 ploughs, and 6 slaves. There are 3 villans and 14 bordars with 3 ploughs. There are 60 acres of meadow, and as much pasture, and 20 acres of woodland. It was worth £27; now £20.

● STRATFORD TONY paid geld TRE for 13 hides. There is land for 7 ploughs. Of this land 9 hides and 1 virgate of land are in demesne, and there are 2 ploughs, and 7 slaves. There are 6 villans and 4 bordars and 10 cotsets with 4 ploughs. There are 2 mills rendering 17*s*. 6*d*., and 15 acres of meadow, and 2 acres of pasture near the river, and other pasture 1 league long and 6 furlongs broad. In Wilton, 1 burgess paying 20*d*. belongs to this manor. It is worth £20.

● GUSSAGE ST MICHAEL [Dorset] paid geld TRE for 10 hides. There is land for 12 ploughs. Of this land 4½ hides are in demesne, and there are 2 ploughs, and 8 slaves. There are 5 villans and 8 bordars with 4 ploughs. There are 40 acres of meadow, [and] pasture 1 league long and half a league broad, and as much woodland. It was worth £40 when Aubrey received it; now £10. Azur held these 3 manors TRE.

The whole of this land belonged to Earl Aubrey. It is now in the hand of the king.

THE RENDERS OF EDWARD OF SALISBURY

● EDWARD the sheriff has yearly from the pence which belong to the shrievalty, 130 pigs and 32 sides of bacon; of wheat, 2 modii and 8 sesters, and as much malt; of oats, 5 modii and 4 sesters; of honey, 16 sesters, or instead of honey 16*s*.; 480 hens; 1,600 eggs; 100 cheeses; 52 lambs; 240 fleeces; of corn in the field, 162 acres. He has also £80 in value between the reeveland and what he has from it. When the reeves' farm falls short, Edward must make it up from his own resources.

XXIIII. THE LAND OF THE SAME EDWARD OF SALISBURY

● EDWARD of Salisbury holds WILCOT of the king. TRE it paid geld for 15½ hides. There is land for 10 ploughs. Of this land 7 hides are in demesne, and there are 3 ploughs, and 6 slaves. There are 19 villans and 6 bordars and 12 cotsets. [. . .] There are 40 acres of meadow, and 20 acres of pasture, and 50 acres of scrubland, and a new church and an excellent house, and a good vineyard. It was worth £12; now £16.

● The same Edward holds ALTON BARNES. TRE it paid geld for 5 hides. There is land for 4 ploughs. In demesne are 2 ploughs, and 4 slaves. There are 3 villans and 1 bordar and 6 cotsets with 1 plough. There is a mill rendering 10*s*., and 25 acres of meadow, [and] pasture 3 furlongs long and 2 furlongs broad. It was worth 100*s*.; now £6.

● The same Edward holds ETCHILHAMPTON. TRE it paid geld for 7 hides. There is land for 4 ploughs. Of this land 4 hides are in demesne, and there are 3 ploughs. There are 12 bordars and 6 cottars and 2 Frenchmen holding 2 hides and 1 virgate of land and they have 2 ploughs. There are 6 acres of meadow and 50 acres of pasture. It was worth £6; now the demesne of Edward [is worth] £6½; the Frenchmen's [land] 40*s*.

● The same Edward holds HEDDINGTON. TRE it paid geld for 10 hides. There is land for 6 ploughs. In demesne are 3 ploughs, and 4 slaves. There are 9 villans and 2 cottars and 24 cotsets with 3 ploughs. There are 10 acres of meadow, and 8 acres of pasture, and 8 acres of woodland. It was worth £8; now £12. Earl Harold held it.

● The same Edward holds 6 hides in the HUNDRED of HIGHWORTH [at] LUS HILL, and it paid geld for 6 hides TRE. There is land for 3 ploughs. In demesne are 2 ploughs; and 4 villans and 2 cotsets with 1 plough. There is a mill rendering 18*d*., and 24 acres of meadow and 1 furlong of pasture. It was worth 100*s*.; now £6. Beorhtric held it. Huard holds it of Edward.

● The same man holds 1 hide in RATFYN. Ælfric held it TRE, and it paid geld for 1 hide. Hervey holds it of Edward. There is land for half a plough. There are 3 bordars, and 4 acres of meadow, [and] pasture half a furlong long and as much broad. It is worth 15*s*.

● The same Edward holds SHREWTON. Wulfgifu held it TRE, and it paid geld for 3 hides. There is land for 3 ploughs. Godfrey holds it of Edward. Of this land he holds 2 hides in demesne, and there are 2 ploughs, and 4 slaves. There are 4 villans and 4 bordars with 1 plough. There is a mill rendering 5*s*., and 6 acres of meadow, and 30 acres of woodland, [and] pasture 6 furlongs long and 4 furlongs broad. It was and is worth £3.

● The same Edward holds in WINTERBOURNE STOKE 1½ hides, and Walter holds of him. There is land for 1 plough, which [plough] is there. It is worth 30*s*.

● The same Edward holds in the same vill 1 hide. [There is] land for 1 plough. Walter holds of Edward. There he has 1 plough with 2 cottars, and 1 acre of meadow and 6 acres of pasture. It is worth 20*s*. Alwig, whose wife holds in the same place a hide [and] a half of the king, held it TRE.

● The same Edward holds SHREWTON. Alric held it TRE, and it paid geld for 13 hides and 3 virgates. There is land for 7 ploughs. Of this land 7 hides are in demesne, and there are 4 ploughs, and 7 slaves. There are 12 villans and 5 bordars with 3 ploughs. There are 10 acres of meadow, [and] pasture 1 league long and half a league broad. It was worth £6; now £10.

● The same Edward holds ORCHESTON; Hugh [holds] of him. Godric held it TRE, and it paid geld for 4½ hides. There is land for 2 ploughs. In demesne is 1 plough; and 4 bordars with 4 slaves have 1 plough. There is pasture 8 furlongs long and 2 furlongs broad. It was worth £3; now £4.

● William holds of Edward in Orcheston 2 hides. Alwine held them TRE. There is land for 1 plough, which [plough] is there with 1 bordar and 3 slaves, and 80 acres of pasture. It was worth 20*s*.; now 30[*s*.].

● Edward himself holds NORTH TIDWORTH. Alweard held it TRE, *North Tidworth [c.1300]*
and it paid geld for 4 hides. There is land for 2 ploughs. In demesne are 3 hides of the same [land], and there are 2 ploughs, and 3 slaves. There are 1 villan and 2 cotsets with half a plough, [and] pasture 4 furlongs long and 3 furlongs broad. It was worth 50*s*.; now 60*s*. In North Tidworth is 1 virgate of land which Croch proved ought to belong to him. This, however, Edward holds.

● Edward himself holds LUDGERSHALL. Alweard held it TRE, and it paid geld for 1 hide. There is land for 3 ploughs. In demesne are 2 ploughs, and 3 slaves; and 8 cotsets with 1 plough. There is pasture 3 furlongs long and 1 furlong broad, [and] woodland half a league long and 2 furlongs broad. It was worth 100*s*.; now £6. 10*s*.

● Osmund holds AMESBURY of Edward. Wulfmær held it TRE, and it paid geld for 1 hide. There is land for 1 plough. There are 3 cotsets, and 6 acres of meadow, [and] pasture 2 furlongs long and half a furlong broad. It was worth 10*s*.; now 20*s*.

● The same Osmund holds of Edward 3 virgates of land which belong to Amesbury. There is land for 1 plough, which [plough] is there, with 2 cotsets and 3 slaves. 1 Englishman holds $1\frac{1}{2}$ virgates of the same land, and has there half a plough, and 1 cotset and 3 slaves. The whole is worth 40*s*. Alric and Cola held it TRE.

● Edward himself holds HILL DEVERILL, and Adelelm [holds] of him. Sæwulf held it TRE, and it paid geld for 4 hides. There is land for 2 ploughs. In demesne [are] $2\frac{1}{2}$ hides of the same land, and there are 2 ploughs, with 1 slave. There is 1 villan and 9 cotsets with 1 plough. There are 2 acres of meadow, and 3 acres of woodland, [and] pasture 3 furlongs long and 2 furlongs broad. It was worth 40*s*.; now 60*s*.

● Edward himself holds BRADENSTOKE. Strami held it TRE, and it paid geld for 16 hides and 1 virgate. There is land for 10 [. . .] ploughs. Of this $7\frac{1}{2}$ hides are in demesne, and there are 4 ploughs, and 2 slaves. There are 8 villans and 16 borders and 16 cottars with 6 ploughs. There is a mill rendering 30*d*., and 4 acres of meadow, and 12 acres of pasture, [and] woodland half a league long and 3 furlongs broad. It was worth £6; now £10. To this manor belong 1 hide and 1 virgate of land, as the Englishmen have proved. This land William de Picquigny holds.

● Theodric holds of Edward $3\frac{1}{2}$ virgates of land in [? Great] SOMERFORD, and it paid geld for as much. There is land for 1 plough, which [plough] is there, with 3 bordars and 3 cotsets. There is part of a mill rendering 15*d*., and 5 acres of meadow and 7 acres of pasture. In Malmesbury 1 house renders 15*d*. It was worth 15*s*.; now 20*s*. Scirweald held it TRE.

● Robert holds BROAD BLUNSDON of Edward. Aki held it TRE, and it paid geld for 5 hides. There is land for 3 ploughs. Of this $4\frac{1}{2}$ hides are in demesne, and there are 2 ploughs; and 4 bordars with 1 plough. There is a mill rendering 25*d*., and 30 acres of meadow and as many of pasture. It was worth 40*s*.; now 60*s*.

● Edward himself holds CHITTERNE. Azur held it TRE, and it paid geld for 11 hides and 1 virgate of land. There is land for 14 ploughs. Of this 6 hides and 1 virgate of land are in demesne, and there is 1 plough, and 4 slaves and 11 coliberts; and 10 villans and 3 cotsets with 5 ploughs. There are 18 acres of meadow, and pasture 1 league long and half a league broad, and as much woodland. It was worth £20; now £30.

● Edward himself holds CHITTERNE. Cynewine held it TRE, and it paid geld for 5 hides. There is land for 4 ploughs. Of this 3 hides are in demesne, and there are 2 ploughs, and 4 slaves; and 5 villans and 3 cotsets with 2 ploughs. There are 8 acres of meadow, and pasture 5 furlongs long and 1 furlong broad. It was worth £8; now £10.

● Robert holds CHITTERNE of Edward. Wulfwynn held it TRE, and it paid geld for 5 hides. There is land for 4 ploughs. Of this $4\frac{1}{2}$ hides are in demesne, and there are 2 ploughs, and 4 slaves; and 4 villans and 2 bordars with 2 ploughs. There is pasture 6 furlongs long and 2 furlongs broad. It was worth 60*s*.; now 100*s*.

● Edward himself holds BOYTON. Alwine held it TRE, and it paid geld for $11\frac{1}{2}$ hides. There is land for 6 ploughs. Of this $8\frac{1}{2}$ hides are in demesne, and there are 3 ploughs, and 5 slaves; and 7 villans and 5 cotsets with 2 ploughs. There is a mill rendering 15*s*., and 10 acres of meadow, and pasture 4 furlongs long and 3 furlongs broad, [and] woodland 3 furlongs long and as many broad. It was worth £8; now £11. 10*s*.

● Adelelm holds BAYCLIFFE of Edward. Winegot held it TRE, and it paid geld for 1 hide. There is land for 2 ploughs, which are there in demesne, with 10 bordars, [and] woodland 3 furlongs long and 1 furlong broad. It was worth 20*s*.; now 40*s*.

● Azelin holds POOLE KEYNES [Glos.] of Edward. Wulfwynn held it TRE, and it paid geld for 5 hides. There is land for 5 ploughs. Of this 3 hides are in demesne, and there are 3 ploughs, and 6 slaves; and 6 villans and 2 bordars with 2 ploughs. There is a mill rendering 10*s*., and 60 acres of meadow, pasture 3 furlongs long and 2 furlongs broad, [and] woodland 1 league in length and breadth. It was worth 100*s*.; now £6.

● Edward himself holds BISHOPSTROW. Eadræd held it TRE, and it paid geld for 7 hides. There is land for 6 ploughs. Of this 4 hides are in demesne, and there are 3 ploughs, and 4 slaves; and 9 villans and 6 bordars and 2 cottars with 3 ploughs. There is a mill rendering 15*s*., and 8 acres of meadow, and 8 acres of woodland, [and] pasture 5 furlongs long and 3 furlongs broad. It was worth £7; now £11.

● Edward himself holds in MIDDLETON 3 virgates of land. Leofwine and Alric held them TRE, and it paid geld for as much. There is land for 1 plough, which [plough] is there, with 1 villan, and 4 acres of meadow, and 6 acres of pasture and 1 acre of woodland. It was and is worth 27*s*.

● Gilbert holds THICKWOOD of Edward. Swein held it TRE, and it paid geld for 2 hides. There is land for $2\frac{1}{2}$ ploughs. There are 2 ploughs in demesne, with 6 cotsets, and 3 acres of meadow and as many of pasture. It was worth 30*s*.; now 40*s*.

● Borel holds LANGLEY BURRELL of Edward. Wulfwig held it TRE, and it paid geld for 7 hides. There is land for 6 ploughs. Of this 2 hides are in demesne, and there are 2 ploughs, and 2 slaves; and 4 villans and 9 cottars and 7 cotsets with 3 ploughs. There are 8 acres of meadow and 6 acres of woodland. It was worth 40*s*.; now £4. The same Wulfwig holds 1 hide of the same land. It is worth 10*s*.

● Borel holds [East or West] TYTHERTON of Edward. Alric held it TRE, and it paid geld for 2 hides. There is land for 1 plough, which [plough] is there, and 2 slaves and 3 cotsets. There is the fourth part of a mill rendering 20*d*., and 6 acres of meadow. It was worth 10*s*.; now 20*s*.

● Edward himself holds LACOCK. Edwin held it TRE, and it paid geld for 7 hides. There is land for 9 ploughs. Of this $3\frac{1}{2}$ hides are in demesne, and there are 3 ploughs, and 7 slaves, and 12 villans and 16 cotsets and 3 cottars. There are 2 mills rendering 17*s*. 6*d*., and 20 acres of meadow, and half an acre of vineyard, [and] 1 league of woodland in both length and breadth. It was and is worth £7.

● Edward himself holds 1 hide in ROCKLEY. Azur held it TRE, [. . .]. There is land for 2 ploughs. In demesne is 1 plough; and 1 villan and 3 bordars with 1 plough, and 20 acres of pasture. It was and is worth 40*s*.

● Theobald holds SHREWTON of Edward. Alweard held it TRE, and it paid geld for 3 hides and 1 virgate of land and 4 acres. There is land for 2 ploughs. In demesne is 1 plough, with 1 villan and 6 bordars, and 13 acres of pasture. It was worth 30*s*.; now £4.

● Azelin holds 2 hides of land of Edward in DEPTFORD. Osweard and Godwine held them TRE, and it paid geld for as much. There is land for 2 ploughs. Of this $1\frac{1}{2}$ hides are in demesne, and there are 2 ploughs, with 1 villan and 3 bordars, and 2 cottars. There is a mill rendering 10*s*., and 8 acres of meadow and 16 acres of pasture. It was worth 20*s*.; now 40*s*. Those who held [this land] could go where they wished.

● Turchil holds of Edward 1 hide of land in HARTHAM. 2 thegns held it TRE, and it paid geld for as much. There is land for 6 oxen. There is 1 plough, with 1 slave and 4 cotsets, and 4 acres of meadow, and 12 acres of pasture, and 3 acres of scrubland. It was worth 10*s*.; now 15*s*.

● Godfrey holds NORTH WRAXALL of Edward. Baldwin held it TRE, and it paid geld for 7 hides. There is land for 9 ploughs. Of this 3 hides are in demesne, and there are 4 ploughs, and 3 slaves; and 16 villans and 5 bordars and 6 cotsets with 5 ploughs. There are 2 mills rendering 18*s*., and half an acre of meadow, [and] woodland 6 furlongs long and 4 furlongs broad; and 2 burgesses in Malmesbury pay 2*s*. It was worth 100*s*.; now £6.

● Aiulf holds TOLLARD ROYAL of Edward. Rozo held it TRE, and it paid geld for $2\frac{1}{2}$ hides. There is land for as many ploughs. Of this 2 hides and half a virgate of land are in demesne, and there are 2 ploughs; and 3 villans and 7 cotsets with half a plough. There is pasture 2 furlongs long and 1 furlong broad, and as much woodland. It was worth 40*s*.; now 50*s*.

● Peter holds 1 hide of Edward in PORTON. God held it TRE. There is land for 1 plough, which [plough] is there, with 1 slave and 1 bordar. There is a mill rendering 32*d*., and 2 acres of meadow, [and] pasture for 50 sheep. It is worth 20*s*.

● Edward himself holds WINTERBOURNE EARLS. Wulfwynn held it TRE, and it paid geld for 7 hides. There is land for 6 ploughs. Of this 3 hides are in demesne, and there are 2 ploughs, and 8 slaves; and 8 villans and 12 cotsets with 3 ploughs. There is a mill rendering 15*s*., and 13 acres of meadow, [and] pasture 5 furlongs long and 3 furlongs broad. It was worth £8; now £12.

● Letard holds of Edward 1 hide of land in LITTLE LANGFORD. Azur held it TRE, and it paid geld for as much. There is land for half a plough. There are 9 acres of meadow and 10 acres of pasture. It was and is worth 20*s*. The thegns adjudge this land to the Church of Glastonbury.

XXV. THE LAND OF ERNULF DE HESDIN

● ERNULF de HESDIN holds KEEVIL of the king. Beorhtsige held it
There is land for 16 ploughs
TRE, and it paid geld for 16 hides. Of this land 7 hides are in demesne, and there are 6 ploughs, and 10 slaves; and 18 villans and 14 bordars with 12 ploughs. There are 2 mills rendering 55*s*., and 16 acres of meadow, pasture 4 furlongs long and 4 broad, [and] woodland 1 league long and 2 furlongs broad. It is worth £26. When he received it, it was worth £20 apart from the farm of 2 thegns which was in the manor.

● The same Ernulf holds in POTTERNE 3 hides and 1 virgate of land, which paid geld with the Bishop of Salisbury's manor of Potterne TRE. Bishop Osmund claims this land. Algar, who held it TRE, could not be separated from the church. Robert holds it of Ernulf. There is land for 2 ploughs, and [2 ploughs] are in demesne;

and 1 villan has there half a plough; and 6 slaves and 3 bordars.
[1] There is a mill rendering 7*s*. 6*d*., and 14 acres of meadow, [. . .] 3 furlongs long and 1 furlong broad. It was worth £4; now 100*s*.

● Lethelin holds [? Little] CHEVERELL of Ernulf. Alweard held it TRE, and it paid geld for $3\frac{1}{2}$ hides. There is land for 3 ploughs. In demesne are 2 ploughs; and 12 bordars with 1 plough. There is half a mill rendering 30*d*., and 3 acres of meadow, [and] pasture 10 furlongs long and 1 broad. It was worth 60*s*.; now 100*s*.

● In ETCHILHAMPTON are 2 hides. [There is] land for 1 plough. Eadric held it TRE, and his wife holds it now of Ernulf, and has there 1 plough, and 7 bordars with 1 cottar. There are 12 acres of meadow and 12 acres of pasture. It was and is worth 40*s*.

● The same wife of Eadric holds CALSTONE WELLINGTON of Ernulf. Her husband held it TRE, and it paid geld for $2\frac{1}{2}$ hides. There is land for 3 ploughs. Of this 1 hide and 1 virgate is in demesne, and there is 1 plough; and 1 villan and 10 bordars and 18 cotsets with 1 plough. There is a mill rendering 15*s*., and 12 acres of meadow, and 6 acres of woodland, [and] pasture 3 furlongs long and 1 furlong broad. In Calne 1 burgess pays 11*d*. It was and is worth £4.

● In PEWSEY the same Ernulf holds 2 hides of the king. TRE a thegn held them of the Abbey of Winchester, and he could not be separated from it. It was and is worth 40*s*.

● Benzelin holds NORTH STANDEN [Berks.] of Ernulf. Beorhtric held it TRE, and it paid geld for 2 hides. There is land for 2 ploughs. In demesne is 1 [plough]; and a mill rendering 6*s*., and 4 acres of meadow, pasture 3 furlongs long and 3 broad, [and] woodland 3 furlongs long and 1 furlong broad. It is worth 40*s*.

● Ernulf himself holds [Great and Little] CHALFIELD. Waltheof held it TRE, and it paid geld for $2\frac{1}{2}$ hides. There is land for 2 ploughs. Of this $1\frac{1}{2}$ hides are in demesne, and there is 1 plough, with 1 slave and 4 bordars. There is half a mill rendering 18*d*., and 6 acres of meadow, and 6 acres of woodland and 8 acres of pasture. It was worth £4; now 50*s*.

● Ernulf himself holds in the same vill as much land, as 1 manor. Godwine held it TRE. It is reckoned at as much as is contained in the above [manor], and it is valued at as much.

● The same Ernulf holds 5 acres of land in BUTTERMERE.

● Robert holds [?]CLYFFE PYPARD of Ernulf. Ketil held it TRE, and it paid geld for 3 hides. There is land for 2 ploughs. Of this $2\frac{1}{2}$ hides are in demesne, and there are 2 ploughs, with 4 cotsets. There are 20 acres of meadow, and 15 acres of pasture and 4 acres of woodland. It was worth 30*s*.; now 40*s*.

● Robert holds "BICHENEHILDE" of Ernulf. Ketil held it TRE, and it paid geld for 1 hide. There is land for half a plough, which [half-plough] is there, with 1 cotset, and 6 acres of meadow, and 4 acres of woodland. It was worth 10*s*.; now 15*s*.

● Robert holds WITCOMB of Ernulf. Beorhtric held it TRE, and it paid geld for 2 hides. There is land for 2 ploughs. There are 7 cotsets with 1 plough, and 12 acres of meadow, and 6 acres of pasture and 12 acres of woodland. It was worth 20*s*.; now 30*s*.

● Robert holds HILMARTON of Ernulf. Eskil held it TRE, and it paid geld for 1 hide. There is land for 1 plough, which [plough] is there, with 3 cotsets. There is a mill rendering 7*s*. 6*d*., and 6 acres of meadow, and 1 acre of pasture and 8 acres of woodland. It was worth 15*s*.; now 30*s*.

● Wulfweard holds CHOLDERTON of Ernulf at farm. He himself held it TRE, and it paid geld for 1 hide and 4 acres. There is land for 1 plough, which [plough] is there in demesne, and pasture 2 furlongs long and 1 furlong broad. It was worth 25*s*.; now 40*s*.

● Ernulf himself holds CHOLDERTON. Sæwig held it TRE, and it paid geld for 1 hide. There is land for 1 plough, which [plough] is there, with 1 cotset, and pasture 2 furlongs long and 1 furlong broad. It was worth 25*s*.; now 40*s*.

● Godric holds 1 hide of Ernulf in CHOLDERTON. Alwine and Wulfric held it TRE as 2 manors, and it paid geld for 1 hide. There is land for $1\frac{1}{2}$ ploughs, and as many [ploughs] are there with 2 cotsets. There is pasture 2 furlongs long and 1 furlong broad. It was worth 20*s*.; now 40*s*.

● Robert holds "BECHENEHILDE" of Ernulf. Thorgot held it TRE, and it paid geld for 1 hide. There is land for half a plough. There is 1 cotset, and 6 acres of meadow and 6 acres of woodland. It was worth 10*s*.; now 15*s*.

● Urse holds "CHENEBUILD" of Ernulf. Wulfwith held it TRE, and it paid geld for $2\frac{1}{2}$ hides. There is land for 2 ploughs. In demesne is 1 [plough], and 2 slaves; and 6 acres of meadow and 2 acres of woodland. It was worth 20*s*.; now 25*s*.

● Ernulf himself holds CHEDGLOW. Wulfwig held it TRE, and it paid geld for 1 hide and $1\frac{1}{2}$ virgates. There is land for 1 plough, and $1\frac{1}{2}$ acres of meadow and 1 acre of woodland. It is worth 20*s*.

● In the same vill a thegn holds of Ernulf $2\frac{1}{2}$ virgates of land. This man, TRE, could go to what lord he pleased, and TRW of his own accord he turned to Ernulf. This land was worth 15*s*.; now 40*d*. which he pays to Ernulf as farm. [2]

● Urse holds [? Hill] DEVERILL of Ernulf. Wulfmær held it TRE, and it paid geld for $2\frac{1}{2}$ hides and half a virgate of land. There is land for 3 ploughs. Of this $1\frac{1}{2}$ hides are in demesne, and there are 2 ploughs, and 3 slaves; and 2 bordars and 6 cotsets with 1 plough. There is a mill rendering 5*s*., and 2 acres of meadow, pasture half a league long and 1 furlong broad, and as much woodland. It was worth 30*s*.; now 50*s*.

● Rainbald holds UPTON SCUDAMORE of Ernulf. Tous held it TRE, and it paid geld for $2\frac{1}{2}$ hides. There is land for 3 ploughs. Of this $1\frac{1}{2}$ hides are in demesne, and there are 2 ploughs, with 1 villan and 5 bordars. There are 4 acres of meadow and 3 acres of woodland. It is worth 40*s*. In this land is included half a hide which paid geld TRE, but has paid no geld since King William came into England.

Within the same land Ernulf holds half a hide of the land of William de Eu; and also, of the demesne land of the king, as much as is worth 1 hide.

● Nubold holds [?]BERWICK ST JAMES of Ernulf. Eadric held it TRE, and it paid geld for 1 hide and $2\frac{1}{2}$ virgates of land. There is land for 1 plough, which [plough] is there with 2 slaves, and 8 acres of pasture. It was worth 20*s*.; now 40*s*.

● Turchil holds HARDENHUISH of Ernulf. Alweard held it TRE, and it paid geld for 3 hides. There is land for 4 ploughs. There are 3 bordars, and 12 acres of meadow, [and] woodland 1 furlong long and 1 furlong broad. It was worth £4; now 40*s*.

● Ernulf himself holds EASTON [Easton Piercy and Lower Easton Piercy]. God held it TRE, and it paid geld for 5 hides. There is land for 3 ploughs. In demesne are 2 ploughs, with 1 slave and 3 bordars. There are 10 acres of meadow and 12 acres of pasture. It was worth 60*s*.; now 100*s*.

● Iudichael holds YATTON KEYNELL of Ernulf. 2 thegns held it TRE, and it paid geld for 5 hides. There is land for 3 ploughs. Of this $3\frac{1}{2}$ hides are in demesne, and there are 2 ploughs, and 2 villans and 6 bordars, and 20 acres of meadow, and as many of pasture, and 10 acres of woodland. It was worth 30*s*.; now 50*s*.

● Hubold holds 1 manor of Ernulf. Ælfric held it TRE, and it paid geld for 1 hide. There is land for 1 plough, and 3 acres of meadow. It was worth 5*s*.; now 10*s*.

XXVI. THE LAND OF ALVRED OF MARLBOROUGH

● ALVRED of MARLBOROUGH holds ALLINGTON [in All Cannings]. TRE it paid geld for $11\frac{1}{2}$ hides and 5 acres of land. There is land for 7 ploughs. Of this $7\frac{1}{2}$ hides are in demesne, and there are 4 ploughs, and 7 slaves; and 6 villans and 7 bordars with 1 plough. There are 20 acres of meadow, [and] pasture 6 furlongs long and 3 furlongs broad. Of this land a knight has 2 hides, and there is 1 plough. The whole was worth £12; now £15.

● William holds 18 hides, and Gilbert 1 hide, and Wulfgeat 1 hide, of Alvred [in] ROWDE. TRE it paid geld for 20 hides. There is land for 8 ploughs. In demesne are 4 ploughs, and 4 slaves; and 4 villans and 8 bordars and 11 cotsets and a priest with 4 ploughs. There are 2 mills of William's rendering 9*s*. 8*d*., and 20 acres of meadow, [and] woodland 6 furlongs long and $1\frac{1}{2}$ furlongs broad. The whole was worth £6; now £8.

● Alvred himself holds TEFFONT EVIAS. TRE it paid geld for $6\frac{1}{2}$ hides. There is land for 5 ploughs. Of this 4 hides are in demesne, and there are 2 ploughs, and 9 slaves; and 4 villans and 3 bordars and 1 Frenchman with 2 ploughs. There is a mill rendering 10*s*., and 6 acres of meadow, and 6 of pasture and 6 of woodland. It was and is worth £6.

● Hugh holds CROFTON of Alvred. TRE it paid geld for 8 hides. There is land for 5 ploughs. Of this 3 hides are in demesne, and there are 3 ploughs, and 3 slaves; and 2 villans and 5 cotsets with 2 ploughs. There is a mill rendering 30*s*., and 10 acres of meadow, and pasture 6 acres long and as many broad, [and] woodland 3 furlongs long and 1 furlong broad. It was and is worth £7.

● Alvred himself holds NEWTON TONY. TRE it paid geld for 11 hides. There is land for 7 ploughs. Of this 6 hides are in demesne, and there are 2 ploughs, and 6 slaves; and 6 villans and 4 bordars with 3 ploughs. There is a mill rendering 10*s*., and 3 acres of meadow, and pasture 3 furlongs long and 3 furlongs broad.

Of the same land Gerard has 3 hides, and there are 4 villans and 5 bordars with 2 ploughs. It was worth £10; now £18. By the English it is valued at £12.

● Edward holds of Alvred 1 hide in "WINTREBURNE". [There is] land for 1 plough, which [plough] is there, with 1 slave and 1 bordar. It was worth 10*s*.; now 20*s*.

● Alvred himself holds LYDIARD TREGOZE. TRE it paid geld for 7 hides. There is land for 7 ploughs. Of this 3 hides are in demesne, and there is 1 plough, and 3 slaves; and 8 villans and 10 cotsets with 4 ploughs; and 40 acres of meadow, and 30 acres of pasture, [and] woodland 1 league long and a half broad. It was worth £10; now £6. In Cricklade 7 burgesses pay 5*s*.

● Alvred himself holds in Swindon 1½ hides. [There is] land for 6 oxen. It is worth 12*s*.

● Albert holds Moredon of Alvred. TRE it paid geld for 6 hides. There is land for 4 ploughs. Of this 3 hides are in demesne, and there are 2 ploughs, and 3 slaves; and 3 villans and 5 bordars with 2 ploughs. There are 30 acres of meadow, [and] pasture half a league long and 2 furlongs broad. It was worth 100*s*.; now £4.

● Gunfrid holds [Lower and Upper] Widhill of Alvred. TRE it paid geld for 5 hides. There is land for 3 ploughs. Of this 4 hides are in demesne, and there are 2 ploughs; and 2 villans and 4 bordars with 1 plough. There is a mill rendering 25*d*., and 30 acres of meadow and as many of pasture. It was worth 40*s*.; now 60*s*.

● Ralph holds Upton Scudamore of Alvred. TRE it paid geld for 9 hides. There is land for 6 ploughs. Of this 5 hides are in demesne, and there are 2 ploughs, and 5 slaves; and 9 villans and 22 bordars with 4 ploughs. There is a mill rendering 20*s*., and 5 acres of meadow, and 30 acres of pasture, [and] woodland 3 furlongs long and 1 furlong broad. It was worth £8; now £9.

● Alvred himself holds Norton Bavant. TRE it paid geld for 11 hides. There is land for 8 ploughs. Of this 6 hides are in demesne, and there are 2 ploughs, and 2 slaves; and 12 villans and 8 bordars with 6 ploughs. There are 2 mills rendering 40*s*., and 10 acres of meadow, pasture 4 furlongs long and 2 furlongs broad, [and] woodland half a league long and 4 furlongs broad. It was worth £24; now £14. § It is worth £8.

2 ● Alvred himself holds Rockley. TRE it paid geld for 10 hides. There is land for 6 ploughs. Of this 6 hides and 3 virgates of land are in demesne, and there is 1 plough, with 1 slave. There are 7 villans and 12 bordars with 3 ploughs. There are 3 acres of meadow, [and] pasture half a league long and 4 furlongs broad. §

● Alvred himself holds Fifield Bavant. Ralph [holds] of him. TRE it paid geld for 5 hides. There is land for 4 ploughs. Of this 3 hides are in demesne, and there is 1 plough, and 3 slaves. There are 9 villans and 6 bordars with 2 ploughs. There are 2 acres of meadow, pasture half a league long and 2 furlongs broad, [and] woodland half a league long and half a furlong broad. It was worth £4; now 100*s*. There 1 forge renders 12*d*. a year. In Wilton 2 burgesses pay 18*d*.

Alvred himself holds 1 virgate of land in Lacock. There is land for 1 plough, which [plough] is there with 1 bordar, and 2 acres of meadow. It was worth 10*s*.; now 5*s*.

Karli held all these above-mentioned lands TRE.

● Roger holds Clevancy of Alvred. Godric and Theodger and Ælfric and Wulfric held it as 4 manors TRE, and it paid geld for 4 hides. There is land for 2 ploughs. In demesne is 1 plough, and 3 slaves and 2 cotsets. There are 24 acres of meadow, and 20 acres of pasture and 6 acres of woodland. It was worth 40*s*.; now 50*s*.

● Robert holds 2½ hides of Alvred in [?]Clyffe Pypard, and it paid geld for as much TRE. Sigar and Carlman held it. There is land for 1½ ploughs. There are 3 slaves with 1 bordar, and a mill rendering 5*s*., and 12 acres of meadow, and 20 acres of pasture and 50 acres of woodland. It was worth 20*s*.; now 30*s*.

● Siward holds Great Somerford of Alvred. Alnoth held it TRE, and it paid geld for 3 hides and 24 acres of land. There is land for 3 ploughs. Of this 2 hides are in demesne, and there is 1 plough, and 2 slaves; and 3 villans and 2 bordars and 8 cotsets with 2 ploughs. There is a mill rendering 5*s*., and 6 acres of meadow, [and] woodland 2 furlongs long and 1 furlong broad. It was and is worth 40*s*.

● Edward holds of Alvred in Chedglow 1 hide and 1 virgate of land. There is land for 1 plough. In demesne is half a plough, with 1 slave and 1 cottar, and 1 acre of meadow, and 1 acre of woodland in length and breadth. In Malmesbury half a house renders 6*d*. It was worth 40*s*.; now 10*s*. Besides this land Durand of Gloucester has half a virgate of land, which the same Edward held TRE. This Amalric de Dreux took from him unjustly, as all the thegns of the shire testify.

● Osmund holds of Alvred in Horningsham half a hide, and it paid geld for as much TRE. Kolsveinn held it, and he could go where he wished. There is land for 1 plough, which [plough] is there, with 4 bordars. There are 8 acres of woodland, and 1 league of pasture, and a mill rendering 7*s*. 6*d*. It was worth 5*s*.; now 10*s*.

● Alvred holds in West Kennett 13½ hides and 2 acres of land. Of these Nicholas has 2 hides; Turstin 3½ hides; Wulfgeat 2 hides; Leofric 3½ hides; Wulfmær 2½ hides and 2 acres of land. There is land for 6 ploughs. There are 4 ploughs, with 1 villan and 15 bordars. There is a mill rendering 12*s*., and 11 acres of meadow, and 106 acres of pasture and 7 acres of woodland. The whole was worth, when received, £4. 10*s*.; now £8. 10*s*. Wulfgeat, Alnoth, Eadmær, Leofric and Wulfmær held these hides in West Kennett TRE.

● William Durus holds West Tytherton of Alvred. Wulfgifu and Ælfgifu held it as 2 manors TRE, and it paid geld for 4 hides. There is land for 4 ploughs. Of this 2 hides are in demesne, and there is 1 plough, and 2 villans and 4 bordars and 2 cottars. [. . .] There are 2 parts of a mill rendering 40*d*., and 10 acres of meadow. It was and is worth 60*s*.

● Wulfmær holds 1 hide in Fifield Bavant of Alvred. The same man held it TRE. It was and is worth 10*s*.

XXVII. THE LAND OF HUMPHREY DE L'ISLE

● Humphrey de l'Isle holds Broughton Gifford of the king. 3 thegns held it in parage TRE, and it paid geld for 12 hides. There is land for 8 ploughs. Of this 4½ hides are in demesne, and there are 3 ploughs, and 2 slaves; and 17 villans and 4 bordars with 7 ploughs. There are 2 mills rendering 9*s*., and 12 acres of meadow, and 8 acres of pasture, [and] woodland 1 league long and 2 furlongs broad. It was worth £13; now £10.

● Pain holds Compton Bassett of Humphrey. Leofnoth held it TRE, and it paid geld for 5½ hides. There is land for 4 ploughs. Of this 2 hides and 1 virgate of land are in demesne, and there are 2 ploughs, and 4 slaves; and 4 villans and 4 cotsets with 2 ploughs. There is the third part of 2 mills rendering 10*s*., and 20 acres of meadow, and 10 acres of pasture and as many of woodland. It was and is worth £4. 10*s*.

● Humphrey himself holds Stert. Ælfric held it TRE, and it paid geld with its appendages for 5 hides and 1½ virgates. There is land for 3 ploughs. Of this 4 hides are in demesne, and there are 3 ploughs, and 6 slaves; and 15 bordars, and 1 Frenchman having 1½ virgates. There are 2 mills rendering 8*s*., and 30 acres of meadow, and 10 acres of pasture and 2 acres of woodland. It was worth 100*s*.; now £6.

● Blæcmann holds Burbage of Humphrey. Eadric held it TRE, and it paid geld for 2½ hides. There is land for 2½ ploughs. Of this 1½ hides are in demesne, and there is 1 plough; and 2 villans and 3 cotsets with 1 plough. There is woodland 3 furlongs long and 2 furlongs broad. It was worth 50*s*.; now 40*s*.

● Pain holds [Great and Little] Cumberwell of Humphrey. Leofnoth held it TRE, and it paid geld for 4 hides. There is land for 5 ploughs. In demesne are 2 ploughs, with 1 slave; and 2 villans and 4 bordars with 3 ploughs. There are 4 acres of meadow and 5 acres of woodland. It is worth £3. Of the same land the king has 1 hide in his demesne, and there is nothing there, and 1 Englishman holds half of it of the king. It is worth 8*s*.

● Gunter holds Lus Hill of Humphrey. Wulfric held it TRE, and it paid geld for 4 hides. There is land for 2 ploughs. In demesne is 1 [plough], with 2 bordars, and from a mill [are rendered] 12*d*., and [there are] 8 acres of meadow and half a furlong of pasture. It is worth 40*s*.

● Robert holds Wroughton of Humphrey. Alnoth held it TRE, and it paid geld for 10 hides. There is land for 4 ploughs. Of this 5½ hides are in demesne, and there are 2 ploughs; and 6 villans and 9 bordars with 2 ploughs; and there a Frenchman holds 2 hides of the same land. There is a mill rendering 15*d*., and 30 acres of pasture and 2 acres of woodland. It was and is worth 100*s*.

● Robert holds Salthrop of Humphrey. Wulfwine held it TRE, and it paid geld for 10 hides. There is land for 4 ploughs. Of this 8 hides are in demesne, and there are 2 ploughs, and 3 slaves; and 9 bordars with 1 plough. There are 20 acres of meadow and 30 acres of pasture. It was worth 100*s*.; now £4.

● Robert holds Clyffe Pypard of Humphrey. Edwin held it TRE, and it paid geld for 8 hides. There is land for 4 ploughs. Of this 6 hides are in demesne, and there are 2 ploughs, and 4 slaves; and 2 villans and 7 bordars with 2 ploughs. There are 20 acres of meadow and as much pasture; and 3 burgesses in Cricklade pay 3*d*. It was and is worth £4.

● Robert holds Great Somerford of Humphrey. Edwin held it TRE, and it paid geld for 3 hides and 24 acres. There is land for 3 ploughs. Of this 2 hides are in demesne. There 16 cotsets have
2 and 7 bordars 2 ploughs; and [there is] the third part of a mill rendering 8*s*., and 10 acres of meadow, [and] pasture 3 furlongs long and 1 furlong broad. In Malmesbury 1 burgess pays 12*d*. It was and is worth 60*s*.

● Elbert holds [Great and Little] Smithcot of Humphrey. Sæwine held it TRE, and it paid geld for 5 hides. There is land for 4 ploughs. Of this 2½ hides are in demesne, and there are 3 ploughs, and 2 slaves; and 3 villans and 4 bordars with 1 cotset have 2 ploughs. There is a mill [rendering] 5*s*., and 20 acres of meadow, [and] woodland 4 furlongs long and 1 furlong broad; and 1 burgess pays 8*d*. It was worth 40*s*.; now 60*s*.

● Ilbert holds Blunsdon St Andrew of Humphrey. Eadric held it TRE, and it paid geld for 5 hides. There is land for 2½ ploughs. Of this 2½ hides are in demesne, and there is 1 plough, with 1 slave; and 2 bordars with 1½ ploughs. It was worth 30*s*.; now 50*s*.

● Hugh and Gerald hold Groundwell of Humphrey. Ordwulf held it TRE, and it paid geld for 5 hides. There is land for 3 ploughs. Of this 4 hides are in demesne, and there are 2 ploughs, with 1 slave; and 1 villan and 2 bordars with 1 plough. There are 12 acres of meadow. It was worth 40*s*.; now 70*s*.

● Robert holds Ashton Gifford of Humphrey. Cynewig held it TRE, and it paid geld for 6 hides. There is land for 4 ploughs. Of this 3 hides are in demesne, and there are 2 ploughs, and 3 slaves; and 4 villans and 3 cotsets with 2 ploughs. There is half a mill rendering 6*s*. 3*d*., and 12 acres of meadow, [and] pasture 6 furlongs long and as much broad. It was worth £4; now £6.

• Humphrey himself holds BATHAMPTON. Ælfric held it TRE, and it paid geld for 3 hides and 3 virgates. There is land for 4 ploughs. Of this 1 hide and 1 virgate of land is in demesne, and there are 3 ploughs, and 12 slaves; and 2 villans and 6 cotsets with $1\frac{1}{2}$ ploughs. There is a mill [rendering] 15*s.*, and 10 acres of meadow, [and] pasture half a league long and as much broad. It was worth £3; now £4.

• Humphrey himself holds BATHAMPTON. Edwin held it TRE, and it paid geld for 3 hides. There is land for 2 ploughs. Of this 2 hides are in demesne, and there is 1 plough; and 2 villans and 1 cotset with 1 plough. There is a mill rendering 6*s.*, and 5 acres of meadow and 8 acres of pasture. It was worth 40*s.*; now 60*s.*

• Humphrey himself holds COLERNE. Leofnoth held it TRE, and it paid geld for 10 hides. There is land for 12 ploughs. Of this $4\frac{1}{2}$ hides are in demesne, and there are 3 ploughs, and 10 slaves; and 13 villans and 5 cotsets with 8 ploughs. There is a mill rendering 13*s.* 6*d.*, and 8 acres of meadow, [and] scrubland 1 league long and another broad. It was and is worth £10.

• Humphrey himself holds WINTERBOURNE BASSETT. 2 thegns held it TRE, and it paid geld for 10 hides. There is land for 6 ploughs. Of this 4 hides and 10 acres of land are in demesne, and there are 3 ploughs, and 8 slaves; and 4 villans and 8 bordars with 3 ploughs. There are 14 acres of meadow and 20 acres of pasture. It was and is worth £10.

• Humphrey himself holds POULTON [in Mildenhall]. Tovi held it TRE, and it paid geld for 10 hides. There is land for 4 ploughs. Of this 8 hides are in demesne, and there are 2 ploughs, and 2 slaves; and 2 villans and 7 bordars with 1 plough. There is a mill rendering 15*s.*, and 4 acres of meadow, and 10 acres of pasture and 8 acres of woodland. It was and is worth £8.

• Ranulph holds BROAD HINTON of Humphrey. Wulfgar held it TRE, and it paid geld for 10 hides. There is land for 4 ploughs. Of this 6 hides are in demesne, and there is 1 plough, with 1 slave; and 4 villans and 6 bordars with 2 ploughs. There are 12 acres of meadow and 14 acres of pasture. It was and is worth 100*s.*

• Turchil holds BIDDESTONE of Humphrey. Ælfric held it TRE, and it paid geld for 1 hide and 1 virgate. There is land [. . .]. There are 4 cotsets, and 3 acres of meadow and 2 acres of woodland. It was worth 10*s.*; now 20*s.*

• Hugh holds HARTHAM of Humphrey. Godric held it TRE, and it paid geld for 1 hide. There is land for half a plough. There are 2 cotsets, and 2 acres of meadow, and 7 acres of pasture and 2 acres of woodland. It was worth 8*s.*; now 12*s.*

• Humphrey himself holds CASTLE COMBE. Swein held it TRE, and it paid geld for 10 hides. There is land for 10 ploughs. Of this 5 hides less 1 virgate are in demesne, and there are 4 ploughs, and 13 slaves; and 5 villans and 7 bordars and 5 cottars with 6 ploughs. There are 3 mills rendering 31*s.* 6*d.*, and 12 acres of meadow, [and] woodland 1 league long and half a league broad. In Wilton 1 burgess pays 5*s.*, and 2 burgesses in Malmesbury pay 18*d.* It was and is worth £10.

• Robert holds SHERSTON of Humphrey. God held it TRE, and it paid geld for $6\frac{1}{2}$ hides. There is land for 5 ploughs. Of this $3\frac{1}{2}$ hides are in demesne, and there are 3 ploughs, and 2 slaves; and 3 villans and 9 bordars with 2 ploughs. There are 2 mills rendering 10*s.*, and 6 acres of meadow and 10 acres of scrubland. It was worth £3; now £4.

• Humphrey himself holds HURDCOTT [in Barford]. Ælfric held it TRE, and it paid geld for 3 hides. There is land for 4 ploughs. Of this 2 hides are in demesne, and there are 2 ploughs, with 1 slave; and 2 villans and 12 bordars with 2 ploughs. There is a mill rendering 6*s.*, and 6 acres of meadow and 8 acres of pasture. It was worth 40*s.*; now 60*s.*

• Humphrey himself holds 'FRUSTFIELD' [in Whiteparish]. Eadric held it TRE, and it paid geld for 3 hides. There is land for 4 ploughs. Of this 2 hides are in demesne, and there is 1 plough, and 3 slaves; and 4 villans and 2 bordars and 2 coliberts with 3 ploughs. There are 12 acres of meadow, [and] woodland 2 furlongs long and 1 furlong broad. It was worth 40*s.*; now 50*s.*

• Joscelin holds half a hide of land of Humphrey in MILFORD, and it paid geld for as much TRE. Sæweald and Sæweard held it. There is land for 1 plough. There are 6 cottars, and 3 acres of meadow. It was worth 15*d.*; now 7*s.* Half this land is in the king's forest.

XXVIII. THE LAND OF MILES CRISPIN

• MILES CRISPIN holds WOOTTON BASSETT of the king. Leofnoth held it TRE, and it paid geld for 12 hides. There is land for 12 ploughs. Of this 6 hides are in demesne, and there are 3 ploughs, and 5 slaves; and 11 villans and 14 bordars with 6 ploughs. There is a mill rendering 30*d.*, and 24 acres of meadow, and 33 acres of pasture, [and] woodland 2 leagues long and 1 league broad. In Malmesbury 1 house renders 13*d.* It was worth £10; now £9.

• Reginald holds CHILTON FOLIAT of Miles. Earl Harold held it TRE, and it paid geld for 10 hides. There is land for 12 ploughs. Of this $6\frac{1}{2}$ hides are in demesne, and there are 2 ploughs, and 2 slaves; and 7 villans and 10 cotsets with 5 ploughs. There are 2 mills rendering 40*s.*, and meadow 2 furlongs long and 1 furlong broad, and as much pasture, [and] woodland 1 league long and 2 furlongs broad. It was worth £12; now £10.

• Humphrey holds CLYFFE PYPARD of Miles. Harold held it TRE, and it paid geld for 5 hides. There is land for 2 ploughs. Of this $3\frac{1}{2}$ hides are in demesne, and there is 1 plough, with 1 slave. There are 3 villans and 4 bordars and 1 cottar with half a plough. There are 20 acres of meadow and 12 acres of pasture. It was worth 30*s.*; now 50*s.*

• In the same CLYFFE PYPARD Miles holds 1 hide. [There is] land for half a plough. It is worth 6*s.* He who held it TRE could go to what lord he wished.

• Turchil holds LITTLECOTT of Miles. Godric held it TRE, and it paid geld for 1 hide and 1 virgate. There is land for half a plough, which [half-plough] is there, with 1 bordar. There are 4 acres of meadow, and as many of pasture and as many of spinney. It is worth 10*s.*

• Reginald holds of Miles in WALCOT $2\frac{1}{2}$ hides. Alnoth held them TRE; and in the same place [are] 3 virgates of land which Leofnoth held TRE. The whole is worth 23*s.*

• Reginald holds DRAYCOT FOLIAT of Miles. Leofnoth held it TRE, and it paid geld for 10 hides. There is land for 6 ploughs. Of this 5 hides are in demesne, and there are 2 ploughs, with 1 slave; and 4 villans and 7 bordars with 3 ploughs. There are 18 acres of meadow and 40 acres of pasture. It was and is worth 100*s.*

• Humphrey holds BRINKWORTH of Miles. Toki held it TRE, and it paid geld for 5 hides. There is land for 3 ploughs. Of this 4 hides are in demesne, and there is 1 plough. There are 8 bordars and 8 cotsets with 1 plough. There are 24 acres of meadow, and 3 acres of pasture, [and] woodland 4 furlongs long and as much broad. It was and is worth 50*s.* This Toki could go where he wished.

⊠ • Reginald holds RODBOURNE of Miles. Vigot held it TRE, and it paid geld for 5 hides. There is land for 4 ploughs. Of this 2 hides are in demesne. [. . .] There are 3 villans and 5 bordars and 1 slave with 3 ploughs. [There is] meadow 6 furlongs long and 2 furlongs broad, [and] pasture 2 furlongs long and as many broad. It was worth 100*s.*; now £4.

• Siward, a thegn, holds CHEDGLOW of Miles. 2 thegns held it TRE, and it paid geld for 1 hide and $1\frac{1}{2}$ virgates. There is land for 6 oxen, which are at plough there, and [there is] 1 cottar and 1 slave. There is 1 acre of meadow, and $1\frac{1}{2}$ virgates and 1 acre of woodland. It was and is worth 10*s.* Those who held it TRE could go where they wished.

Besides this land Durand has half a virgate of land which Siward held TRE. Amalric de Dreux took this from him unjustly, as the thegns of the shire say.

• Miles himself holds OGBOURNE [? St Andrew]. Earl Harold held it TRE, and it paid geld for 10 hides. There is land for 8 ploughs. Of this 6 hides are in demesne, and there are 3 ploughs, and 4 slaves; and 11 villans and 4 bordars with 3 ploughs. There is a mill rendering 30*s.*, and 8 acres of meadow, [and] pasture half a league long and as much broad. It was and is worth £15.

• Reginald holds MANTON of Miles. Vigot held it TRE, and it paid geld for 3 hides. There is land for 3 ploughs. Of this 1 hide is in demesne, and there is 1 plough, and 2 slaves; and 5 villans and 5 bordars with 2 ploughs. There are 4 acres of meadow, and 40 acres of pasture and as many of woodland. It was and is worth £3.

• Reginald holds HAZELBURY of Miles. Leofnoth held it TRE, and it paid geld for 5 hides. There is land for 5 ploughs. Of this 1 hide is in demesne, and 2
there are 2 ploughs, and 2 slaves; and 5 villans and 13 cotsets and 2 cottars with 3 ploughs. There are 2 mills rendering 35*s.*, and 22 acres of meadow, and woodland 2 furlongs long and 1 furlong broad. It was and is worth £6.

XXIX. THE LAND OF GILBERT DE BRETEUIL

• GILBERT de BRETEUIL holds CHISBURY of the king. Eadric held it TRE, and it paid geld for 5 hides. There is land for 9 ploughs. In demesne are 4 ploughs, and 7 slaves; and 12 villans and 3 bordars and 14 cotsets with 5 ploughs. There are 2 mills rendering 20*s.*, and 15 acres of meadow, and 40 acres of woodland, [and] pasture 15 furlongs long and 3 furlongs broad. It was worth £8; now £12.

• The same Gilbert holds 5 hides in [?]BINCKNOLL. Hakun held it TRE. There is land for 2 ploughs. Of this 4 hides are in demesne, and there is 1 plough, and 4 slaves; and 1 villan and 3 bordars with 1 plough. There are 10 acres of meadow, and 12 acres of pasture and 4 acres of woodland. It was worth 40*s.*; now 50*s.*

• In the same vill Toli held 2 hides less 1 virgate TRE. [There is] land for 6 oxen. Gilbert has there 1 villan. It is worth 18*s.*

• In the same vill Sæwulf and Alwine held 3 hides and 1 virgate of land TRE. There is land for 10 oxen. Gilbert has there 2 villans, and 4 acres of meadow and 6 acres of pasture. It was worth 20*s.*; now 27*s.*

• Gilbert himself holds CLYFFE PYPARD. Ælfric and Burghelm and Godgifu held it TRE, and it paid geld for 16 hides less 1 virgate. There is land for 7 ploughs. Of the same land Ansfrid has 11 hides of Gilbert, and there are in demesne 3 ploughs, and [he has] 7 slaves; and 3 villans and 2 bordars and 10 cotsets with $2\frac{1}{2}$ ploughs. There is a mill rendering 5*s.*, and 50 acres of meadow, and 70 acres of pasture and 18 acres of woodland. One of these 11 hides, which lay in Clyffe Pypard TRE, is in THORNHILL.

There are in Clyffe Pypard 2 bordars and 2 slaves, and 16 acres of meadow and 17 acres of pasture, under Gilbert. This is worth 35*s*.; what Ansfrid holds is worth £6.

● Turstin holds MOREDON of Gilbert. Wulfgar held it TRE, and it paid geld for 3 hides less 1 virgate. There is land for 2 ploughs. Of this 1 hide and 1 virgate of land are in demesne, and there is 1 plough; and 2 villans and 4 bordars with 2 ploughs. There are 20 acres of meadow and 80 acres of pasture. It was and is worth 40*s*.

● Gilbert himself holds BROAD HINTON. Wulfgar held it TRE, and it paid geld for 11 hides and 1 virgate. There is land for 5 ploughs. Of this 9 hides and 1 virgate of land are in demesne, and there are 2 ploughs; and 4 villans and 5 bordars with 2 ploughs. There are 16 acres of meadow and 30 acres of pasture. It was worth 100*s*.; now £7.

● Ansfrid holds BECKHAMPTON of Gilbert. Eadric held it TRE, and it paid geld for 2 hides. There is land for 3 ploughs. Of this 1 hide is in demesne, and there are 2 ploughs; and 4 villans and 7 bordars and 3 cottars with 2 ploughs. There are 8 acres of meadow and 40 acres of pasture. It was and is worth £6.

● Ansfrid holds 'STANMORE' [in Preshute] of Gilbert. Bruning held it TRE, and it paid geld for 2½ hides. There is land for 2 ploughs. Of this 2 hides are in demesne, and there is 1 plough, and 2 slaves; and 1 villan and 3 bordars with half a plough. It was worth 20*s*.; now 40*s*.

XXX. THE LAND OF DURAND OF GLOUCESTER

● DURAND of GLOUCESTER holds CHIRTON of the king. Almær held it TRE, and it paid geld for 10 hides. There is land for 5 ploughs. Of this 7 hides with 1½ ploughs are in demesne; and 7 villans and 10 bordars with 2 ploughs. There is a mill rendering 10*s*., and 30 acres of meadow, [and] pasture half a league long and 3 furlongs broad. It was worth £11; now £10.

● Roger holds TOCKENHAM COURT of Durand. Dodda held it TRE of the Church of Malmesbury, and it could not be separated from it, and it paid geld for 5 hides. There is land [. . .]. In demesne is half a [. . .] and there are 2 ploughs, with 1 slave; and 7 villans and 3 bordars with 2 ploughs. There is a mill rendering 50*d*., and 12 acres of meadow, and 4 acres of pasture and 2 acres of woodland. It was worth 40*s*.; now £4.

● The same man holds 1½ hides in UFFCOTT. There is land for 1 plough. This [plough] is in demesne. It was and is worth 15*s*. Almær held it TRE.

● Durand himself holds [Lower and Upper] SEAGRY. 2 thegns held it TRE, and it paid geld for 5 hides. There is land for 4 ploughs. Of this 2 hides are in demesne, and there is 1 plough; and 3 villans and 2 bordars with 3 ploughs. There are 40 acres of meadow. It was worth 40*s*.; now 50*s*. 2 knights hold it of Durand. Those who held it TRE could go where they wished.

● Durand himself holds ASHLEY [Glos.]. Ealdræd held it TRE, and it paid geld for 5 hides less 1 virgate. There is land for 4 ploughs. Of these [hides], 3 hides are in demesne, and there are 2 ploughs, and 3 slaves; and 5 villans and 3 bordars with 2 ploughs and 2 cottars. There are 5 acres of meadow and 5 acres of woodland. It was and is worth £4. A knight of Miles Crispin claims 1 virgate of land in this vill.

● Durand himself holds LOCKERIDGE. Almær held it TRE, and it paid geld for 2 hides. There is land for 1 plough. Of this 1 hide is in demesne. There is 1 villan and 2 bordars with 1 slave, and 1 acre of meadow, and 12 acres of pasture and 6 acres of woodland. It was worth 40*s*.; now 30*s*.

● Herman holds LUCKINGTON of Durand. Earl Harold held it TRE, and it paid geld for 4 hides. There is land for 5 ploughs. Of this 2 hides are in demesne, and there are 2 ploughs, with 1 slave; and 6 villans and 8 bordars with 2 ploughs. There is a mill rendering 5*s*., and 10 acres of meadow, and 8 acres of pasture and 4 acres of woodland. It was worth 100*s*.; now £4.

XXXI. THE LAND OF WALTER GIFFARD

● WALTER GIFFARD holds MAIDEN BRADLEY of the king. Earl Tosti held it TRE, and it was assessed at 10 hides. There is land for 10 ploughs. Of this 4 hides are in demesne, and there are 2 ploughs, and 4 slaves; and 6 villans and 13 bordars with 6 ploughs. There are 2 mills rendering 12*s*. 6*d*., and 10 acres of meadow, pasture half a league long and 2 furlongs broad, [and] woodland 1 league long and 1 broad. It was worth £12; now £10.

XXXII. THE LAND OF WILLIAM DE EU

● WILLIAM de EU holds [Great and Little] DURNFORD of the king. TRE it paid geld for 16 hides. There is land for 14 ploughs. Of this 4 hides are in demesne, and there are 2 ploughs, and 2 slaves; and 26 villans and 37 bordars with 12 ploughs. There are 3 mills rendering 24*s*. 6*d*., and 30 acres of meadow, pasture 10 furlongs long and 2 furlongs broad, [and] woodland 4 furlongs long and 2 furlongs broad. In Wilton 4 houses render 4*s*. It was and is worth £24.

● William d'Audrieu holds LITTLETON PANNELL of William. TRE it paid geld for 6 hides and 1 virgate of land. There is land for 6 ploughs. In demesne are 2 ploughs, with 1 slave; and 3 villans and 21 bordars with 3 ploughs. There are 2 mills rendering 30*s*., and 12 acres of meadow, [and] pasture 10 furlongs long and 2 furlongs broad. It was worth £10; now £8.

TRE this land was thegnland of the Church of Salisbury. Ælfstan of Boscombe held it.

● The same William holds COMPTON BASSETT of William. TRE it paid geld for 6 hides. There is land for 4 ploughs. In demesne are 2 ploughs, and 5 slaves; and 3 villans and 11 bordars with 2 ploughs. There is the third part of 2 mills rendering 10*s*., and 24 acres of meadow, and 10 acres of pasture and as many of woodland. It was and is worth 100*s*.

● William Delamere holds BEVERSBROOK [Beversbrook or Lower Beversbrook] of William. TRE it paid geld for 2½ hides. There is land for 2 ploughs. Of this 1½ hides are in demesne, and there are 2 ploughs, and 2 slaves, and 1 villan and 8 bordars. It was and is worth 30*s*.

● Hugh holds 'CHARLTON' [in Hungerford, Berks.] of William. TRE it paid geld for 5 hides. There is land for 7 ploughs. Of this 4½ hides are in demesne, and there is 1 plough; and 2 villans and 7 bordars with half a plough. There are 2 mills rendering 8*s*. 4*d*., and 15 acres of meadow, pasture 4 furlongs long and 1 furlong broad, [and] woodland 6 furlongs long and 3 furlongs broad. It was and is worth 100*s*.

● The same Hugh holds [East or West] GRAFTON of William. TRE it paid geld for 1 hide. There is land for 1½ ploughs. There are 3 bordars, [and] pasture 2 furlongs long and 1 furlong broad. It was worth 60*s*.; now 40*s*.

● Edward holds BOSCOMBE of William. TRE it paid geld for 7 hides. There is land for 4 ploughs. Of this 4½ hides are in demesne, and there are 2 ploughs, and there are 2 slaves; and 3 villans and 4 cotsets with 1½ ploughs. There are 6 acres of meadow, [and] pasture 12 furlongs long and as many broad. It is worth £10.

● Bernard holds CHOLDERTON. TRE it paid geld for 3½ hides, less 4 acres. There is land for 2 ploughs. Of this 3 hides are in demesne, and there are 2 ploughs, and 2 slaves; and 5 bordars and 2 cotsets. There is pasture 6 furlongs long and 5 furlongs broad. It was worth 100*s*.; now £9.

● Ralph holds HILMARTON of William. TRE it paid geld for 9 hides. There is land for 8 ploughs. Of this 3 hides are in demesne, and there are 2 ploughs; and 7 villans and 10 bordars with 6 ploughs. There is a mill rendering 7*s*., and 50 acres of meadow and 40 acres of pasture. It was and is worth £7.

● Bernard holds CODFORD [? St Peter] of William. TRE it paid geld for 1½ hides. There is land for 2 ploughs. Of this 1 hide [is] in demesne, and there is 1 plough, with 1 slave; and 2 cotsets with 1 plough. There are 10 acres of meadow, and the fourth part of a mill rendering 3*s*., [and] pasture 4 furlongs long and 2 furlongs broad. It was worth £4; now £3.

● Warner holds DITTERIDGE of William. TRE it paid geld for 1 hide and 3 virgates of land. There is land for 1 plough, which [plough] is there in demesne, and 2 villans and 4 cotsets. There is half a mill rendering 5*s*., and 7 acres of meadow, and 15 acres of pasture and 17 acres of scrubland. It is worth 30*s*. A certain abbot of Malmesbury leased 1 hide of this land to Ælfstan.

● Ralph holds LACKHAM of William. TRE it paid geld for 7½ hides. There is land for 10 ploughs. Of this 1½ hides are in demesne, and there are 2 ploughs, and 2 slaves; and 10 villans and 4 bordars and 24 cotsets with 8 ploughs. There are 2 mills rendering 30*s*., and 15 acres of meadow, [and] woodland 1 league long and as much broad. It was worth £6; now the same.

● William holds SEVINGTON of William. TRE it paid geld for 10 hides. There is land for 7 ploughs. Of this 4 hides are in demesne, and there are 2 ploughs; and 10 villans and 5 bordars with 5 ploughs. There are 20 acres of meadow, [and] woodland 2 furlongs long and 1 furlong broad. It was worth £6; now £7.

● An Englishman holds YATTON KEYNELL of William. TRE it paid geld for 1 virgate of land. There is land for half a plough, which [half-plough] is there. It renders 5*s*.

Ælfstan of Boscombe held all these above-mentioned lands of William de Eu.

● Hugh holds SOPWORTH of William. Ælfric held it TRE, and it paid geld for 5 hides. There is land for 6 ploughs. Of this 3½ hides are in demesne, and there are 2 ploughs, and 6 slaves; and 3 villans and 5 bordars with 3 ploughs. It was worth £6; now £4.

● The same William holds TOLLARD ROYAL. Toli held it TRE as 1 manor, and it paid geld for 1 hide. There is land for 1 plough. There are [. . .] cotsets, and 5 acres of meadow and 1 furlong of woodland. It was and is worth 20*s*.

● Ansfrid holds UPTON SCUDAMORE of William. Toli held it TRE, and it paid geld for 3 hides. There is land for 2½ ploughs. Of this 2 hides are in demesne, and there is 1 plough; and 2 villans and 5 bordars with 1 plough. There is a mill rendering 5*s*., and 4 acres of meadow, [and] woodland 2 furlongs long and 1 furlong broad, and 20 acres of pasture. It was worth 15*s*.; now 60*s*.

It has not paid geld for half a hide since King William came into England; and Ernulf de Hesdin holds unjustly half a hide in the vill itself.

[. . .]

XXXIII. THE LAND OF WILLIAM DE BRAOSE

● William de Braose holds Shaw [in Overton] of the king. Alwine held it TRE, and it paid geld for 2 hides and $1\frac{1}{2}$ virgates of land. There is land for $1\frac{1}{2}$ ploughs. Of this 2 hides are in demesne. There is 1 villan and 2 bordars with half a plough. There are 40 acres of pasture, and woodland 1 league long and 3 furlongs broad. It was worth 10*s*.; now 20*s*. Robert holds it of William.

XXXIIII. THE LAND OF WILLIAM DE MOYON

● William de Moyon holds Sutton Veny of the king, and Walter [holds] of him. Cola held it TRE, and it paid geld for 5 hides. There is land for 4 ploughs. Of this 3 hides and 1 virgate of land are in demesne, and there are 2 ploughs, and 3 slaves; and 3 villans and 6 bordars with 2 ploughs. There is a mill rendering 4*s*., and 4 acres of meadow, and 2 acres of woodland, [and] pasture half a league long and 1 broad. It was worth £4; now 100*s*.

XXXV. THE LAND OF WILLIAM DE FALAISE

● William de Falaise holds of the king half a hide in Standlynch, and Alweard [holds] of him. There is land for half a plough, which [half-plough] is there, and 4 acres of meadow. It was worth 20*s*.; it now renders 10*s*. Lyfing held it TRE.

XXXVI. THE LAND OF WALTER DE DOUAI

● Walter de Douai holds "Celdewelle" of the king, and Godescal [holds] of him. Alsige held it TRE, and it paid geld for 5 hides. There is land for 3 ploughs. Of this 3 hides and 3 virgates of land are in demesne, and there is 1 plough, with 1 slave and 1 villan and 6 bordars with half a plough. There are 10 acres of meadow, and 7 acres of pasture and 8 acres of woodland. It was and is worth £3.

● Ralph holds Stourton of Walter. Ailwacre held it TRE, and it paid geld for 8 hides. There is land for 6 ploughs. Of this 5 hides are in demesne, and there are 2 ploughs, with 1 slave; and 6 villans and 13 cotsets and 8 cottars with 4 ploughs. There are 2 mills rendering 20*d*., and 60 acres of pasture, [and] woodland 1 league long and 1 broad. It was worth £4; now £7.

XXXVII. THE LAND OF WALERAN THE HUNTSMAN

● Waleran holds Codford [? St Mary] of the king. Herlebald held it TRE, and it paid geld for 6 hides. There is land for 6 ploughs. Of this 3 hides are in demesne, and there are 2 ploughs, and 3 slaves; and 7 villans and 6 bordars with 3 ploughs. There is a mill rendering 10*s*., and 10 acres of meadow, [and] pasture half a league long and 5 furlongs broad. It was worth £10; now £12.

● Walter holds Ansty of Waleran. Ælfric and Wulfweard held it TRE, and it paid geld for 7 hides. There is land for 4 ploughs. Of this 5 hides and 1 virgate of land are in demesne, and there are 2 ploughs, and 2 slaves; and 6 villans and 4 bordars with 2 ploughs. There is a mill rendering 5*s*., and 16 acres of meadow, and 15 acres of woodland, [and] pasture half a league long and 3 furlongs broad. It was and is worth 100*s*.

● Azelin holds Buttermere of Waleran. 8 thegns held it TRE, and it paid geld for 1 hide and 1 virgate of land. There is land for 2 ploughs. It is worth 20*s*.

● Waleran himself holds 1 hide in Standlynch. Cola held it TRE. There is land for half a plough. There are 6 acres of meadow. It was worth 5*s*.; now 10*s*.

● Richard holds East Kennett of Waleran. Leofdæg held it TRE, and and [*sic*] it paid geld for $1\frac{1}{2}$ hides and 1 virgate of land. There is land for 1 plough, which [plough] is there, with 1 slave and 2 bordars, and 1 acre of meadow and 4 acres of pasture. It was and is worth 20*s*.

● Azelin holds Stanley of Waleran. Selewine held it TRE, and it paid
2 geld for 1 hide and 3 virgates of land. There is land for 1 plough. There are 3 villans and 3 bordars, and 10 acres of meadow. It was worth 15*s*.; now 30*s*.

● Waleran himself holds Steeple Langford. Oswulf held it TRE, and it paid geld for 10 hides. There is land for 5 ploughs. Of this 5 hides are in demesne, and there are 2 ploughs, and 5 slaves; and 8 villans and 4 bordars with 3 ploughs. There is a mill rendering 15*s*., and 30 acres of meadow, [and] pasture half a league long and 2 furlongs broad. It was and is worth £10.

● Erenburgis holds Hanging Langford of Waleran. Northmann held it TRE, and it paid geld for 5 hides. There is land for 2 ploughs. Of this 4 hides are in demesne, and there is 1 plough, with 1 slave and 1 villan and 5 bordars with half a plough. There is half a mill rendering 30*d*., and 20 acres of meadow, [and] pasture 4 furlongs long and 1 furlong broad. It was and is worth 100*s*.

● Engenold holds half a hide of Waleran in Barford St Martin, and it paid geld for as much TRE. Bolla held it. There is land for half a plough. There are 2 bordars, and 3 acres of meadow. It was and is worth 7*s*.

● Robert holds of Waleran 3 virgates of land in [? Great] Wishford, and it paid geld for as much TRE. Bolla held it. There is land for half a plough. There are 2 bordars, and 4 acres of meadow. It was and is worth 10*s*.

● Herbert holds [East or West] Grimstead of Waleran. Aghmund held it TRE, and it paid geld for 3 hides. There is land for 3 ploughs. Of this $1\frac{1}{2}$ hides are in demesne, and there is 1 plough, and 2 slaves; and 5 villans and 7 cotsets with 3 ploughs. There are 10 acres of meadow, [and] woodland 5 furlongs long and 2 furlongs broad. It was and is worth 60*s*.

● Engenulf holds Whaddon [in Alderbury] of Waleran. Bolla held it TRE, and it paid geld for 2 hides. There is land for $1\frac{1}{2}$ ploughs. Of this $1\frac{1}{2}$ hides are in demesne, and there is 1 plough; and 4 cotsets with half a plough. There are 7 acres of meadow, [and] woodland 2 furlongs long and half a furlong broad. It was worth 15*s*.; now 25*s*.

● In Whaddon [in Alderbury] 2 knights hold $3\frac{1}{2}$ virgates of land less 2 acres. TRE 4 thegns held them, who could go where they wished. There is land for half a plough, which [half-plough] is there, with 2 cotsets, and $4\frac{1}{2}$ acres of meadow. It is worth 12*s*.

● Engenulf holds 1 virgate of land of Waleran in Alderbury, and has there 1 cotset. It is worth 2*s*. Boda held it TRE.

● Waleran himself holds West Dean. Godric held it TRE, and it paid geld for 2 hides and 1 virgate of land. There is land for 3 ploughs. Of this 1 hide is in demesne, and there are $1\frac{1}{2}$ ploughs, and 2 slaves; and 1 villan and 10 cotsets with $1\frac{1}{2}$ ploughs. There are $1\frac{1}{2}$ mills rendering 16*s*., and 5 acres of meadow, [and] woodland 1 furlong in both length and breadth. It was and is worth 60*s*.

● In Hurdcott [in Winterbourne Earls] [Waleran] holds half a hide. There is land for half a plough. He has there half a mill rendering 6*s*. The whole is worth 20*s*. Eadnoth held it TRE.

XXXVIII. THE LAND OF WILLIAM FITZGUY

● William fitzGuy holds Sutton Veny of the king. Alweald and his sister held it TRE, and it paid geld for 8 hides. There is land for 6 ploughs. Of this 4 hides are in demesne, and there are 2 ploughs, and 4 slaves; and 6 villans and 8 bordars with 4 ploughs. There are 2 parts of a mill rendering 13*s*. 4*d*., and 6 acres of meadow, [and] pasture 1 league long and 2 furlongs broad, and as much woodland. It was worth £8; now £10.

XXXIX. THE LAND OF HENRY DE FERRERS

● Henry de Ferrers holds Standen [Berks.] of the king. Godric held it TRE, and it paid geld for 1 hide. There is land for 5 ploughs. In demesne are 4 [ploughs], and 4 slaves, and 8 acres of meadow, and 10 acres of pasture and 6 acres of woodland. It is worth 100*s*. There is woodland belonging to [Great and Little] Bedwyn TRE.

● The same man holds [?]Clyffe Pypard. Godric held it TRE, and it paid geld for 5 hides less 1 virgate. There is land for 3 ploughs. Of this 4 hides and 1 virgate are in demesne, and there are 3 ploughs, and 6 slaves and 5 bordars, and 30 acres of meadow and 12 acres of pasture. It was and is worth £4.

XL. THE LAND OF RICHARD FITZGILBERT

● Richard son of Count Gilbert holds Sutton Mandeville of the king, and Berengar [holds] of him. Wulfweard held it TRE, and it paid geld for 10 hides. There is land for 6 ploughs. Of this 7 hides are in demesne, and there are 3 ploughs, and 5 slaves; and 6 villans and 9 bordars with 3 ploughs. There is a mill rendering 10*s*., and 12 acres of meadow, and 3 acres of woodland, [and] pasture 6 furlongs long and 3 furlongs broad, and 5 burgesses pay 50*d*. It was and is worth £6.

XLI. THE LAND OF RALPH DE MORTIMER

● Ralph de Mortimer holds Hullavington of the king. Earl Harold held it, and it paid geld for 20 hides. There is land for 14 ploughs. Of this 14 hides are in demesne, and there are 4 ploughs, and 8 slaves; and 19 villans and 8 cotsets with 6 ploughs. There are 12 acres of meadow, and 10 acres of pasture and 8 acres of woodland. It was and is worth £12. In Malmesbury 1 house renders 12*d*.

● Oidelard holds Tockenham of Ralph. Alwine held it TRE, and it paid geld for $2\frac{1}{2}$ hides. There is land for 3 ploughs. Of this 2 hides are in demesne, and there are 2 ploughs, with 1 slave; and 1 villan and 3 cotsets with half a plough. There are 12 acres of meadow, and as many of pasture and 2 acres of woodland. It was worth 30*s*.; now 50*s*.

● Edward holds Bradfield of Ralph. Beorhtwig and Alwig held it TRE, and it paid geld for $2\frac{1}{2}$ hides. There is land for 2 ploughs. Of this $1\frac{1}{2}$ hides are in demesne, and there are 2 ploughs, and 3 villans and 2 cotsets, and 12 acres of meadow. It was and is worth 30*s*.

● In Highway Ralph holds 1 hide, and has there 1 bordar, and 4 acres of meadow. It is worth 15*s*. Toti purchased it TRE of the Church of Malmesbury, for the lives of 3 men, and within that term could go with it to what lord he wished.

● Ralph himself holds Clatford. Alwine held it TRE, and it paid geld for 5 hides. There is land for 3 ploughs. Of this 3 hides are in demesne, and there are 2 ploughs, with 1 slave and 1 villan and 7 bordars with 1 plough. There is a mill rendering 20*s*., and 5 acres of meadow, pasture half a league long and 3 furlongs broad, [and] woodland half a league long and as much broad. It was and is worth 100*s*.

● Ralph himself holds Imber. Alwine held it TRE, and it paid geld for 2 hides. There is land for 2 ploughs. In demesne is 1 plough, and 2 slaves, and 1 villan and 4 bordars. There is pasture 3 furlongs long and 2 furlongs broad. It was worth £3; now £4.

● Richard holds [?]SURRENDELL of Ralph. Alwig held it TRE, and it paid geld for 5 hides. There is land for 6 ploughs. Of this 2½ hides are in demesne, and there are 2 ploughs, and 4 slaves; and 12 villans and 3 bordars with 4 ploughs. There are 7 acres of meadow. It was and is worth £7.

● Roger holds KINGTON ST MICHAEL of Ralph. Alwine held it TRE, and it paid geld for 1½ hides. There is land for 1 plough, which [plough] is there in demesne, with 1 slave and 2 bordars. There is a mill rendering 2*s*., and 4 acres of meadow and 6 acres of woodland. It was worth 20*s*.; now 30*s*. This Alwine held this land of the Church of Glastonbury and could not be separated from it, and rendered service to the abbot for it.

● Richard holds 3 hides of Ralph in ALDERTON, and Walter holds 1 hide in the same place. Alric, Godwine, Algar and Godric held them in parage TRE, and it paid geld for 4 hides. There is land for 4 ploughs. There are 4 villans and 5 bordars and
[2] 2 slaves, and a mill rendering 37*d*., and 25 acres of meadow. A burgess in Malmesbury pays 7*d*. It was and is worth 60*s*.

● Edward holds LUCKINGTON of Ralph. Alweard held it TRE, and it paid geld for 3 hides. There is land for 4 ploughs. Of this 2 hides less 1 virgate are in demesne, and there are 2 ploughs; and 2 villans and 4 bordars with 2 ploughs. There are 8 acres of meadow and 4 acres of woodland. It was and is worth £3.

XLII. THE LAND OF ROBERT FITZGERALD

● ROBERT fitzGERALD holds [?]WOODBOROUGH of the king. Sæwulf held it TRE, and it paid geld for 10 hides. There is land for 5 ploughs. Of this 7 hides are in demesne, and there are 4 ploughs, and 5 slaves; and 5 villans and 11 cotsets with 1 bordar have 1 plough. There is a mill rendering 12*s*. 6*d*., and 50 acres of meadow, and 50 acres of pasture and 10 acres of scrubland. It was worth £7; now £10. Joscelin holds it of Robert.

● Rainer holds FOSBURY of Robert. Vitalis held it TRE, and it paid geld for 10 hides. There is land for 5 ploughs. Of this 6 hides are in demesne, and there are 2 ploughs, and 2 slaves; and 7 villans and 2 bordars with 1½ ploughs. There is pasture 5 furlongs long and 3 furlongs broad, [and] woodland half a league long and 3 furlongs broad. It was and is worth 100*s*.

● Rainer holds FOSBURY of Robert. Alwine held it TRE, and it paid geld for 2 hides. There is land for 2 ploughs. There are 3 bordars with 1 plough, pasture 2 furlongs long and 1½ furlongs broad, [and] woodland 2 furlongs long and 2 furlongs broad. It was worth 15*s*.; now 30*s*.

● Robert holds BIDDESDEN. Cuthwulf held it TRE, and it paid geld for 1 virgate of land. There is land for 1 plough, which [plough] is there, with 1 villan and 2 bordars and 4 slaves, and pasture 2 furlongs long and 1 broad. It renders 30*s*.

● Robert holds BRIGMERSTON of Robert. Beorhtmær held it TRE, and it paid geld for 4 hides. There is land for 2 ploughs, which are there in demesne, with 11 bordars. There is a mill rendering 12*s*., and 10 acres of meadow, [and] pasture 12 furlongs long and 4 furlongs broad. It was worth 10*s*.; now £4.

[2] ● The same Robert holds MILSTON of Robert. Beorhtmær held it TRE, and it paid geld for 1½ hides. There is land for 1 plough, which [plough] is there, with 2 slaves and 4 cotsets. There is a mill rendering 18*s*., and 4 acres of meadow, [and] pasture 12 furlongs long and 1 furlong broad. It was worth 20*s*.; now 30*s*.

● Hugh holds [?]WILSFORD [near Amesbury] of Robert. Tovi held it TRE, and it paid geld for 1 hide. There is land for 1 plough, which [plough] is there, with 1 villan and 3 cotsets. There is a mill rendering 10*s*., and 6 acres of meadow, [and] pasture 9 furlongs long and 2 furlongs broad. It was worth 30*s*.; it is worth 60*s*.

● Rainer holds FITTLETON of Robert. Vitalis held it TRE, and it paid geld for 10 hides. There is land for 12 ploughs. Of this 5 hides and 1 virgate of land are in demesne, and there are 3 ploughs and 6 slaves; and 6 villans and 12 bordars with 3 ploughs. There is a mill rendering 22*s*. 6*d*., and 3 acres of meadow, [and] pasture 1 league long and half a league broad. It was and is worth £12.

● Hugh holds SHAW [in Overton] of Robert. Cuthwulf held it TRE, and it paid
[2] geld for 2 hides and 1½ virgates. There is land for 1 plough. There is 1 villan and 2 slaves, and 30 acres of pasture, [and] woodland 1 league long and 1 furlong broad. It was worth 20*s*.; now 40*s*.

● Robert holds EBBESBORNE WAKE of Robert. Alweard and Vitalis held it TRE as 2 manors, and it paid geld for 14 hides. There is land for 10 ploughs. Of this 10 hides are in demesne, and there are 6 ploughs, and 4 slaves; and 18 villans and 7 bordars with 4 ploughs. There are 14 acres of meadow, pasture 14 furlongs long and 4 furlongs broad, [and] woodland 2 leagues in both length and breadth. It was worth £12; now £14.

XLIII. THE LAND OF ROBERT FITZROLF

● ROBERT fitzRolf holds in MOREDON 1 hide and 1 virgate of land. Wulfgar held it TRE, and it paid geld for 5 virgates of land. There is land for 1 plough, which [plough] is there in demesne, with 1 slave and 1 villan, and 10 acres of meadow and 40 acres of pasture. It was and is worth 20*s*.

● Robert fitzRolf holds BROAD HINTON. Wulfgar held it TRE, and it paid geld for 9 hides less 1 virgate. There is land for 5 ploughs. Of this 6 hides are in demesne, and there are 2 ploughs, with 1 slave, and 5 villans and 6 bordars. There are 12 acres of meadow, [and] pasture 1 furlong long and as much broad. It was and is worth £6.

XLIIII. [THE LAND] OF ROGER DE COURSEULLES

● ROGER de COURSEULLES holds FISHERTON DE LA MERE of the king. Bondi held it TRE, and it paid geld for 10 hides. There is land for 10 ploughs. Of this 5½ hides are in demesne, and there are 3 ploughs; and 16 villans and 12 bordars and 14 cottars with 7 ploughs. There is a mill rendering 20*s*., and 12 acres of meadow, and 10 acres of woodland, [and] pasture half a league long and as much broad. It was and is worth £25.

XLV. [THE LAND] OF ROGER OF BERKELEY

Lacy [2] ● ROGER of Berkeley holds FOXLEY of the king. Ealdræd held it TRE, and it paid geld for 2 hides. There is land for 4 ploughs. Of this 1 hide is in demesne, and there are 2 ploughs, and 3 slaves; and 4 villans and 3 cotsets with 3 ploughs. There is a mill [rendering] 7*s*. 6*d*., and 4 acres of meadow, and 8 acres of pasture, and 1 house in Malmesbury. It was and is worth 40*s*.

● The same Roger holds 1 hide less half a virgate of the demesne farm of Chippenham. Celein held it TRE, on lease from Eadric the sheriff.

● Roger himself holds EASTON GREY. Alwig held it TRE, and it paid geld for 3 hides less half a virgate. There is land for 3 ploughs. Of this 2 hides are in demesne, and there are 2 ploughs, and 4 slaves; and 2 villans and 3 bordars with 1 plough. There is a mill rendering 6*s*. It was worth 30*s*.; now 40*s*.

XLVI. ● BERNARD Pauncevolt holds 'FRUSTFIELD' [in Whiteparish]. Godwine held it TRE, and it paid geld for 1½ virgates of land. There is land for half a plough. It is worth 5*s*.

XLVII. THE LAND OF BERENGAR GIFFARD

● BERENGAR Giffard holds FONTHILL GIFFORD of the king. Euing held it TRE, and it paid geld for 5 hides. There is land for 7 ploughs. Of this 1 hide is in demesne, and there are 3 ploughs, and 4 slaves; and 6 villans and 16 bordars with 4 ploughs. There is a mill rendering 5*s*., and 7 acres of meadow, pasture half a league long and 3 furlongs broad, [and] woodland 4 furlongs long and 2 furlongs broad. It was worth 100*s*.; now £6.

● The same man holds 1 hide in BARFORD ST MARTIN. Earl Harold held it TRE, and it paid geld for as much. There is land for 1 plough. There are 6 bordars, and 6 acres of meadow. It was worth 60*s*.; now 20*s*.

XLVIII. THE LAND OF OSBERN GIFFARD

● OSBERN Giffard holds ELSTON of the king. Dunna held it TRE, and it paid geld for 11 hides. There is land for 6 ploughs. Of this 9 hides are in demesne, and there are 4 ploughs, and 5 slaves; and 4 villans and 5 bordars with 2 ploughs. There are 6 acres of meadow, and pasture 9 furlongs long and 6 furlongs broad. It was worth £7; now £9.

● The same Osbern holds 2 hides in [?]ELSTON. There is land for 1 plough. There are 2 acres of meadow and 3 acres of pasture. It was worth 30*s*.; now 40*s*.

● The same Osbern holds 3½ hides in ORCHESTON. Wulfmær and Alwine held them TRE. There is land for 2 ploughs, which are there in demesne, and 3 slaves. [There is] pasture half a league and 40 acres long and broad. It was worth 40*s*.; now 50*s*.

● Osbern himself holds STANTON [Stanton St Quintin and Lower Stanton St Quintin]. Beorhtric held it TRE, and it paid geld for 18 hides. He has there 2 ploughs in demesne on 9 hides, and there are 7 slaves; and 9 villans and 3 cotsets with 6 ploughs. There are 6 acres of meadow, pasture 1 league long and 1 broad, [and] woodland 1 league long and 3 furlongs broad. It was worth £9; now £8.

● The Church of Saint-Etienne of Fontenay holds of Osbern 2 hides and 1 virgate of land in MIDDLETON. Dunna held it TRE, and it paid geld for as much. There is land for 2 ploughs, which are there in demesne, with 1 slave and 2 bordars. There are 5 acres of meadow, and 20 acres of pasture and 1 acre of woodland. It was worth 20*s*.; now 50*s*.

● Osbern himself holds CODFORD [? St Peter]. Ælfric held it TRE, and it paid geld for 1½ hides. There is land for 2 ploughs. Of this 1 hide is in demesne, and there are 1½ ploughs, and 2 slaves; and 6 cotsets and 1 cottar with half a plough. There is the fourth part of a mill rendering 3*s*. 1½*d*., and 10 acres of meadow, [and] pasture 4 furlongs long and 1 furlong broad. It was worth 50*s*.; now 60*s*.

● Osbern himself holds ORCHESTON. Trasmund held it TRE, and it paid geld for 5 hides. There is land for 3 ploughs. Of this 4 hides are in demesne, and there are 2 ploughs, and 3 slaves; and 4 villans and 3 cotsets and 5 cottars with 1½ ploughs. There is pasture 3 furlongs long and 1 furlong broad. It was worth £4; now 100*s*.

● Osbern himself holds HILL DEVERILL. Smala held it TRE, and it paid geld for 3 hides and half a virgate of land. There is land for 3 ploughs. Of this 2 hides are in demesne, and there are 2 ploughs, with 1 slave and 9 cotsets and 3 bordars. There is a mill rendering 30*d*., and 2 acres of meadow, and pasture 2 furlongs long and 1 furlong broad, [and] woodland half a league long and as much broad. It was worth 40*s*.; now 60*s*.

● Osbern himself holds KELLAWAYS. Dunna held it TRE, and it paid geld for 10 hides. There is land for 6 ploughs. Of this 9 hides are in demesne, and there are 3 ploughs, and 4 slaves; and 2 villans and 4 cotsets and 3 bordars with 3 ploughs. There are 10 acres of meadow. It was worth £4; now 100*s*.

● Osbern himself holds SHERRINGTON. Algar held it TRE, and it paid geld for 5 hides. There is land for 2½ ploughs. Of this 4½ hides are in demesne, and there are 2 ploughs, and 5 slaves; and 2 villans with half a plough. There is half a mill rendering 7*s*. 6*d*., and 6 acres of meadow, and 60 acres of pasture and 40 acres of woodland. It was worth £4; now 100*s*.

● Osbern himself holds SHERRINGTON. Smala held it TRE, and it paid geld for 5 hides. There is land for 2½ ploughs. Of this 4½ hides are in
[X] demesne, and there are 2 ploughs, and 5 slaves; and 2 villans with half a plough. There is half a mill rendering 7*s*. 6*d*., and 6 acres of meadow, and 60 acres of pasture, and 40 acres of woodland, and 1 burgess in Wilton paying 3*s*. It was worth £4; now 100*s*.

● Gunduin holds UGFORD of Osbern. Eadnoth held it TRE, and it paid geld for 2½ hides. There is land for 1 plough, which [plough] is there, with 1 slave and 1 bordar. There is a mill rendering 4*s*., and 4 acres
[7] of meadow and 10 acres of pasture. It was worth 30*s*.; now 40*s*. Earl Godwine took away this land from [the Church of] ST MARY of Wilton, and then Eadnoth recovered it.

XLIX. THE LAND OF DROGO FITZPONS

● DROGO fitzPons holds [Lower and Upper] SEAGRY of the king. Wigflæd held it TRE, and it paid geld for 5 hides. There is land for 4 ploughs. Of this 2 hides are in demesne,

ROGER de Lacy, and Turstin fitzRolf, and William Leofric hold 1 hide in COLESHILL [Berks.]. 3 thegns held it TRE. The share of all is worth £4.

and there is 1 plough; and 5 villans and 6 bordars and 5 cotsets with 1 plough. There are 2 mills rendering 22*s.* 4*d.*, and 30 acres of meadow. A house in Malmesbury renders 9*d.* It was worth 60*s.*; now 70*s.*

● Gilbert holds Easton [Easton Piercy and Lower Easton Piercy] of Drogo. Osweard held it TRE, and it paid geld for 5 hides. There is land for 3 ploughs. Of this 4 hides are in demesne, and there are 2 ploughs, and 2 slaves, and 1 villan and 4 bordars and 2 cotsets. There are 10 acres of meadow, [and] woodland 2 furlongs long and 2 furlongs broad. It was worth 40*s.*; now 50*s.*

● Hugh holds Alderton of Drogo. Eadric held it TRE, and it paid geld for 3 hides. There is land for 3 ploughs. Of this 2 hides and 3 virgates of land are in demesne, and there is 1 plough, with 1 slave and 2 bordars. From part of a mill [comes] 22*d.*; and [there are] 15 acres of meadow. It was and is worth 60*s.*

L. THE LAND OF HUGH L'ASNE

● Hugh L'Asne holds 1 hide of land and 3 virgates of the king in Shalbourne, and William holds of him. A thegn held it of King Edward, and it paid geld for as much. There is land for 2 ploughs. There is 1 villan and 4 cotsets with 1 plough. There is 1 arpent of meadow, and 2 acres of woodland. It is worth 30*s.*

● Harold holds Westlecott of Hugh. Leofric held it TRE, and it paid geld for 5 hides. There is land for 2 ploughs. Of this 4 hides are in demesne, and there are 1½ ploughs, with 1 slave; and 3 villans and 6 bordars with half a plough. There is a mill rendering 5*s.*, and 25 acres of meadow and 30 acres of pasture. It was and is worth 40*s.*

● Hugh himself holds 2 hides in [?]Clyffe Pypard. Godgifu held it as 1 manor. There is land for 1 plough. There is 1 cotset, and 12 acres of meadow. It is worth 12*s.*

● William holds Corton of Hugh. Dene held it TRE, and it paid geld for 6 hides. There is land for 4 ploughs. Of this 4 hides are in demesne, and there are 1½ ploughs, and 2 slaves; and 4 bordars with half a plough. There is a mill rendering 20*s.*, and 6 acres of meadow, pasture 3 furlongs long and 2 furlongs broad, and as much woodland. It was worth 100*s.*; now £6.

● The Church of St Mary of Winchester holds [? East] Kennett of Hugh for his daughter. Hunwine held it TRE, and it paid geld for 2 hides less 1 virgate. There is land for 1 plough, which [plough] is there in demesne, with 2 bordars, and 1 acre of meadow and 6 acres of
§1 pasture. It was worth 10*s.*; now 20*s.*

LII. [THE LAND] OF HUMPHREY THE CHAMBERLAIN

● Humphrey the chamberlain holds Shorncote [Glos.] of the king. Alweard held it TRE, and it paid geld for 5 hides. There is land for 4 ploughs. Of this, 2½ hides are in demesne, and there are 2 ploughs, and 3 slaves; and 8 villans with 2 ploughs. There are 50 acres of meadow, and pasture 2 furlongs long and 1 furlong broad. It was worth 40*s.*; now 60*s.*

LIII. THE LAND OF GUNFRID MAUDUIT

● Gunfrid Mauduit holds Calstone Wellington of the king. Algar held it TRE, and it paid geld for 2 hides and 1 virgate of land. There is land for 2 ploughs. Of this 5 virgates of land are in demesne, and there are 2 ploughs, and 3 slaves; and 6 bordars with half a plough. There is a mill rendering 15*s.*, and 8 acres of meadow, [and] pasture 2 furlongs long and 1 furlong broad. It was worth 40*s.*; now 50*s.*

● The same Gunfrid holds Whitley. Api held it TRE, and it paid geld for 1 hide. There is land for 2 ploughs, which are there in demesne, with 1 slave and 6 bordars. There are 8 acres of meadow, [and] woodland 3 furlongs long and 1 furlong broad. It was worth 40*s.*; now 50*s.*

LIIII. THE LAND OF ALVRED D'EPAIGNES

● Alvred d'Epaignes holds Yatesbury of the king. Alwig held it TRE, and it paid geld for 5 hides. There is land for 4 ploughs. Of this 3½ hides are in demesne, and there are 2 ploughs, and 2 slaves; and 7 bordars and 1 knight with 1 plough. There are 20 acres of pasture. It was worth £3; now £4.

LV. [THE LAND] OF AIULF THE SHERIFF

● Aiulf the sheriff holds 5 hides and half a hide of the king in
☒ Tollard Royal. 5 thegns held it TRE, and it paid geld for 5½ hides. There is land for 4 ploughs. Of this 4 hides are in demesne, and there are 2 ploughs, and 2 slaves, and 3 villans and 14 bordars. There are 2 arpents of vineyard, and 20 acres of pasture and 4 acres of woodland. It was worth £4; now £6.

● The same Aiulf holds half a hide in Bemerton. There is land for half a plough. It renders 12*s.* Radulf held it TRE.

LVI. THE LAND OF NIGEL THE PHYSICIAN

● Nigel the physician holds Stratton St Margaret of the king. TRE it paid geld for 30 hides. There is land for 14 ploughs. Of this 5 hides are in demesne, and there are 3 ploughs, and 2 slaves; and 24 villans and 18 bordars with 12 ploughs. There is a mill rendering 2*s.*, and meadow 8 furlongs long and 5 furlongs broad, [and] pasture 1 league long and 5 furlongs broad. It was worth £18; now £16.

● The same Nigel holds [East and West] Chisenbury. TRE it paid geld for 8 hides. There is land for 5 ploughs. Of this 4½ hides are in demesne, and there are 2½ ploughs, and 2 slaves; and 8 villans and 12 bordars with 2 ploughs. There is a mill rendering 7½*s.*, and 20 acres of meadow, and pasture 1 league long and 5 furlongs broad. It was and is worth £13.

☒ ● The same Nigel holds 1 hide in Netheravon, and Durand [holds] of him. There is land for 1 plough. There are 3 bordars with half a plough, and 6 acres of meadow, [and] pasture 4 furlongs long and 2 furlongs broad. It was and is worth £3. These 3 manors belong to the Church of Netheravon.

● The same Nigel holds 4 hides in Sutton Veny, and it paid geld for as much TRE. There is land for 3 ploughs. [The Abbey of] Sainte-Marie of Montebourg holds it of Nigel. Of this land 2 hides are in demesne, and there is 1 plough, and 3 slaves; and 5 villans and 5 bordars with 2 ploughs. There is the third part of a mill rendering 6*s.* 8*d.*, and 3 acres of meadow, pasture half a league long and 1 furlong broad, [and] woodland 1 league long and 1 furlong broad. It was worth £4; now 100*s.* Spirites the priest held these 4 manors TRE.

● Nigel holds half a hide in Beversbrook [Beversbrook or Lower Beversbrook], and it paid geld for as much TRE. He has there 1 villan and 1 bordar; and woodland 1 furlong long and half a furlong broad. It is worth 7*s.*

● The same Nigel holds Hazelbury. TRE it paid geld for 1 virgate of land. There is land for 6 oxen. There are 3 bordars, and 3 acres of meadow, [and] pasture 4 furlongs long and 1 furlong broad. It is worth 10*s.* Alsige the priest held these 2 estates TRE.

LVII. THE LAND OF OSBERN THE PRIEST

● Osbern the priest holds Homington. Alsige held it TRE, and it paid geld for 2 hides. There is land for 1 plough. There are 2 cotsets, and 3 acres of meadow and 6 acres of pasture. It is worth 30*s.*

LVIII. THE LAND OF RICHARD PUIGNANT

● Richard Puignant holds Calstone Wellington of the king. Gunnar held it TRE, and it paid geld for 4 hides less 1 virgate. There is land for 4 ploughs. Of this 2 ploughs [*sic*] and 1 virgate are in demesne, and there are 3 ploughs, and 2 slaves; and 16 cotsets and 3 bordars with 1 plough. There are 2 mills rendering 33*s.* 6*d.*, and 15 acres of meadow, and as many of pasture, [and] woodland 3 furlongs long and 2 furlongs broad, and in Calne 2 burgesses pay 20*d.* It was worth £4; now 100*s.*

● The same Richard holds Trow. TRE it paid geld for 7½ hides. There is land for 4 ploughs. Of this 5 hides are in demesne, and there are 3 ploughs. There are 3 villans with 1 plough, and 2 acres of meadow, pasture 4 furlongs long and 3 furlongs broad, [and] woodland 6 furlongs long and 3 furlongs broad. It was worth 100*s.*; now £7.

[The Church of] St Mary of Wilton held this land TRE, and it could not be alienated from the church. [2]

LIX. THE LAND OF ROBERT MARSHAL

● Robert Marshal holds Market Lavington of the king. Queen Edith held it, and it paid geld for 15 hides. There is land for 10 ploughs. Of this 7 hides are in demesne, and there are 4 ploughs, and 7 slaves; and 14 villans and 17 bordars with 5 ploughs. There are 2 mills rendering 16*s.* 4*d.*, and 20 acres of meadow, and 12 acres of woodland, [and] pasture 1 league long and as much broad. It was and is worth £20.

● The same Robert holds Gore. Osweard held it TRE, and it paid geld for 3 hides. There is land for 3 ploughs. Of this 2 hides are in demesne, and there are 2 ploughs, and 6 slaves; and 3 villans and 1 bordar with 1 plough, and 40 acres of pasture. It was worth 30*s.*; now 50*s.*

LX.

● Robert the Fair holds West Lavington of the king. Aki held it TRE, and it paid geld for 10 hides. There is land for 7 ploughs. Of this 1 hide and 1 virgate are in demesne, and there is 1 plough. 2 sons-in-law of his hold 7 hides and 1 virgate of him, and they have there 5 ploughs with their men. There is a mill rendering 5*s.*, and pasture 1½ leagues long and 4 furlongs broad. It was worth £15; now £12.

LXI. THE LAND OF RICHARD STURMY

● Richard Sturmy holds Cowesfield of the king. Ælfric held it TRE, and it paid geld for 2 hides. There is land for 2 ploughs. Of this 1 hide is in demesne, and there is 1 plough; and 2 villans and 8 cotsets with 2 ploughs. There is pasture 2 furlongs long and 1 furlong broad, and as much woodland. It was worth 15*s.*; now 30*s.*

LXII. [THE LAND] OF REGINALD CANUTE

● Reginald Canute holds 1 hide in Chippenham of the king. Toki held it TRE. There is land for 1 plough. 2 bordars there have half a plough, and [there are] 20 acres of meadow, and half a mill rendering 15*s.* The whole was and is worth 20*s.*

LXIII. THE LAND OF MATTHEW DE MORTAGNE

● Matthew de Mortagne holds Maddington of the king. Wulfweard held it TRE, and it paid geld for 4 hides. There is land for 2 ploughs. Of this 2 hides are in demesne, and there is 1 plough, with 1 slave; and 2 villans and 4 bordars with 1 plough. There is pasture 4 furlongs long and as much broad. It was worth 40*s.*; now 60*s.*

LXIIII. [THE LAND] OF JOSCELIN RIVIERE

● Joscelin Riviere holds Zeals of the king. Almær held it TRE, and it paid geld for 2½ hides. There is land for 3 ploughs. In demesne is 1 plough, and 2 slaves; and 5 villans and 3 cotsets with 2 ploughs There is a mill rendering 40*d.*, and 3 acres of
☒ meadow, pasture 3 furlongs long and 3 broad, [and] woodland half a league long and as much broad. It was and is worth 30*s.*

LXV. [THE LAND] OF GODESCAL

● Godescal holds Winterbourne [? Gunner] of the king. Alwig held it TRE, and it paid geld for 2 hides. There is land for 2 ploughs. In demesne is 1 plough, and 3 slaves, and 4 bordars and 5 cotsets. There is half a mill rendering 3*s.* 9*d.*, and half an acre of meadow, [and] woodland 2 furlongs long and as much broad. It was worth 30*s.*; now 40*s.*

● The same Godescal holds half a hide which Guthmund held TRE, and it paid geld for as much. There is 1 cotset. It is worth 12*s.* § f.74v

LXVI. [THE LAND OF] THE KING'S SERGEANTS

● Herman de Dreux holds "Etone" of the king. Eadric held it TRE, and it paid geld for 2 hides. There is land for 2 ploughs. In demesne is 1 plough; and 2 bordars and 2 cotsets and 1 villan with 1 plough. There are 2 acres of meadow, [and] woodland 2 furlongs long and 1 furlong broad. It was and is worth 30*s.*

§1

LI. THE LAND OF HUGH FITZBALDRIC

● Hugh fitzBaldric holds Marden, and Walter, his son-in-law, [holds] of him. Wynsige held it TRE, and it paid geld for 10 hides. There is land for 8 ploughs. In demesne are 2 ploughs, and 4 slaves; and 9 villans and 14 cotsets and 2 bordars with 5 ploughs. There is a mill rendering 7½*s.*, and 24 acres of meadow, [and] pasture 3 furlongs in length and 2 furlongs broad. A house in Wilton renders 10*d.* It was worth £7; now £10.

● Amalric de Dreux holds Manningford Bohune of the king. Godric held it TRE, and it paid geld for 3½ hides. There is land for 1½ ploughs. There are 4 bordars, and the third part of a mill rendering 50*d.*, and 12 acres of meadow, [and] pasture 4 furlongs long and 1½ furlongs broad. It was worth 30*s.*; now 60*s.*

● Ansger the cook holds Hilperton. 3 thegns held it in parage TRE, and it paid geld for 4 hides and 1 virgate and 6 acres. There is land for 3 ploughs, which are there in demesne, with 1 slave and 9 cotsets. There are 12 acres of meadow and 20 acres of pasture. It was worth £4; now 10*s.* less.

● William Corniole holds Hilperton of the king. 4 thegns held it in parage TRE, and it paid geld for 5 hides and 1 virgate of land. There is land for 5 ploughs. In demesne are 2 ploughs; and 1 villan with 1 plough, and 12 acres of meadow and 20 acres of pasture. It renders 40*s.*

● Fulchred holds 3 virgates of land in Gillingham [Dorset]. Algar held them TRE. There is land for 2 ploughs, which are there, with 1 bordar. It was and is worth 15*s.*

● Stephen the carpenter holds 1 hide and 1 virgate of land in
[2] Earlscourt. Oda held it TRE. There is land for 2 ploughs, which are there, with 1 slave and 3 villans and 2 bordars. There are 30 acres of meadow, and 8 acres of pasture, and in Cricklade a garden renders 2*d.* It was worth 30*s.*; now 60*s.*

● The same Stephen holds 3 hides. Aki held them TRE. There is land for 1 plough, which [plough] is there, with 1 villan and 4 bordars. There is pasture half a league long and 3 furlongs broad. It was worth 20*s.*; now 40*s.*

● Osmund holds 1 hide in Pomeroy. Alnoth held it TRE. There is land for 1 plough, which [plough] is there in demesne. It was worth 5*s.*; now 10*s.*

LXVII. THE LAND OF ODA AND OTHER KING'S THEGNS

● Oda of Winchester holds Calcutt of the king. There are 5 hides. TRE it paid geld for half a hide. There is land for 3 ploughs. Of this 4½ hides are in demesne. There 1 villan and 4 bordars with 1 slave have 1 plough; and [there are] 60 acres of meadow. In Cricklade 3 burgesses pay 21*d.* It is worth £4.

● Beorhtric holds Coulston of the king. TRE it paid geld for 5 hides. There is land for 4 ploughs. In demesne are 2 ploughs, and 6 slaves; and 5 villans and 3 bordars with 2 ploughs. There is a mill rendering 10*s.*, and 30 acres of meadow and 5 furlongs of pasture. It is worth 100*s.*

● Beorhtric holds in Swallowcliffe 1 hide and 1½ virgates of land. There is land for 1 plough, which [plough] is there, with 2 villans. It is worth 15*s.*

● Beorhtric holds 1 hide in Trowle. There is land for 1 plough, which [plough] is there, with 1 villan. It is worth 10*s.*

● Beorhtric holds Monkton Farleigh, and his brother [holds] of him. TRE it paid geld for 5 hides. There is land for 4 ploughs. In demesne is 1 plough, and 4 slaves; and 5 villans and 3 bordars with 3 ploughs. There are 20 acres of pasture and 3 acres of woodland. It is worth 70*s.*

● Beorhtric holds Oaksey. His father held it TRE, and it paid geld for 10 hides. There is land for 6 ploughs. In demesne are 2 ploughs, and 10 slaves; and 6 villans and 12 cotsets with 4 ploughs. There is a mill rendering 5*s.*, and 40 acres of meadow, and 30 acres of pasture, [and] woodland 1 league long and half a league broad. It was worth £8; now £6.

● Beorhtric holds Trowbridge. His father held it TRE, and it paid geld for 10 hides. There is land for 9 ploughs. In demesne are 2 ploughs, and 7 slaves; and 11 villans and 6 cotsets with 7 ploughs. There is a mill rendering 10*s.*, and 10 acres of meadow, and 12 acres of pasture, [and] woodland 5 furlongs long and 3 furlongs broad. It was worth £4; now £8.

● Beorhtric holds Staverton. His father held it TRE, and it paid geld for 5 hides. There is land for 3 ploughs. In demesne are 2 ploughs, and 7 slaves; and 3 villans and 2 cotsets with 1 plough. There is a mill rendering 20*s.*, and 20 acres of meadow and 20 acres of pasture. It is worth 70*s.*

● Beorhtric holds Odstock. His father held it TRE, and it paid geld for 12 hides. There is land for 6 ploughs. In demesne is 1 plough, and 3 slaves; and 9 villans and 16 cotsets with 2½ ploughs. There is a mill rendering 7*s.* 6*d.*, and 40 acres of meadow, pasture 1 league long and 3 furlongs broad, and in another part 5 acres of pasture, [and] woodland 3 furlongs long and 3 furlongs broad. 1 burgess in Wilton pays 12*d.* It is worth £10.

● Beorhtric and his brother Alwig hold Cowesfield. TRE it paid geld for 1½ hides. There is land for 1 plough, which [plough] is there, with 3 cotsets. There are 2 furlongs of scrubland. It is worth 10*s.*

● Alweard holds 3 hides in Potterne. TRE it paid geld with the bishop's manor. There is land for 3 ploughs. In demesne is 1 [plough]; and
[1] 3 villans and 4 bordars with 2 ploughs. There is [. . .] 4 furlongs long and 3 furlongs broad. It is worth 70*s.* Bishop Osmund claims it.

● Alweard holds 1 hide in Tilshead. There is land for 1 plough, which [plough] is there, and 1 furlong of pasture. It is worth 20*s.*

● Alweard holds Swallowcliffe. TRE it paid geld for 3 hides less half a virgate. There is land for 1½ ploughs. The villans hold it. It is worth 30*s.*

● Alweard Colling holds Knook. TRE it paid geld for 4 hides. There is
[2] land for 3 ploughs. In demesne is 1 plough, and 3 slaves; and 4 villans and 3 bordars with 2 ploughs. There is a mill rendering 15*s.*, and 5 acres of meadow, [and] pasture half a league long and 1 furlong broad. It is worth £4.

● Ælfric of Melksham holds Wilsford [near Pewsey] of the king. Beorhtmær held it TRE, and it paid geld for 5 hides. There is land for 2½ ploughs, which are there, with 10 bordars. There are 8 acres of meadow, [and] pasture 5 furlongs long and 1 furlong broad. It was worth 100*s.*; now 8*s.* Edward holds it in pledge.

● Ælfric holds Monkton Farleigh. Beorhtmær held it TRE, and it paid geld for 5 hides. There is land for 4 ploughs. In demesne is 1 plough, and 4 slaves; and 5 villans and 3 bordars with 3 ploughs. There are 20 acres of pasture and 3 acres of woodland. It is worth 70*s.*

● Ælfric holds Whaddon [in Semington]. He himself held it TRE, and it paid geld for 3 hides. There is land for 2 ploughs. In demesne is 1 [plough], and 3 slaves and 3 cotsets. There is a mill rendering 5*s.*, and 8 acres of meadow, [and] 1 furlong of pasture in length and breadth. It is worth 20*s.*

● Ælfric the Little holds 2½ virgates of land in Tilshead. There is land for half a plough. It is worth 7*s.* 6*d.*

● The same man holds 1 hide in Hilmarton. There is land for 1 plough, and he has there 1 slave. It is worth 15*s.*

● The same man holds 1 hide in Tockenham, and it paid geld for as much. There is land for 1 plough. There are 6 acres of meadow and 6 acres of pasture. It is worth 13*s.*

● The same man holds 2 hides less 1 virgate which 2 thegns held TRE. There is land for 6 oxen. It is worth 15*s.*

● Alwine the priest holds [? Great] Somerford. TRE it paid geld for 2½ virgates of land. There is land for half a plough. There are 2 cotsets and 1 cottar, and part of a mill rendering 15*d.*, and 4 acres of meadow and 4 acres of pasture. It is worth 11*s.*

● In the same vill Alwig holds 2½ virgates of land, and it paid geld for as much TRE. There is land for half a plough. There are 2 cotsets, and part of a mill [rendering] 15*d.*, and 4 acres of meadow and 4 acres of pasture. It was and is worth 8*s.*

● In the same vill Edward holds half a hide. There is land for half a plough. It is worth 40*d.*

● In the same vill Sægifu holds 2½ virgates of land. There is land for half a plough. There is 1 cotset and 1 cottar. Part of a mill renders 15*d.*, and [there are] 4 acres of meadow and 4 acres of pasture. It is worth 11*s.*

● Alwig the son of Thorbiorn holds half a hide in Standlynch. There is land for half a plough. There are 4 acres of meadow. It is worth 5*s.*

● Alric holds half a hide paying geld in Tockenham. There is land for half a plough. There are 3 acres of meadow and 3 acres of pasture. It is worth 7*s.*

● Azur holds 2 hides in 'Barley' [in South Wraxall]. Dunna held them TRE. There is land for 4 ploughs. In demesne are 2 ploughs, with 1 bordar and 2 villans. It was and is worth 40*s.*

● Ælfstan holds half a hide of land in Tilshead. It is worth 5*s.*

● Almær holds 2½ virgates of land in Tilshead. It is worth 5*s.*

● Algar holds 1 hide paying geld in Tockenham. There is land for 1 plough. He has there half a plough, with 1 bordar; and 6 acres of meadow and as many of pasture. It is worth 13*s.*

● Ælfgeat holds Zeals. TRE it paid geld for 2½ hides. There is land for 3 ploughs. In demesne is 1 plough, and 4 slaves; and 8 villans and 9 bordars with 2 ploughs. There is a mill rendering 3*s.*, and 4 acres of meadow, and 40 acres of pasture, [and] woodland half a league long and half a league broad. It is worth 30*s.*

● Azur holds 1 hide in Corsley. There is land for 1 plough, which [plough] is there in demesne, with 4 bordars. There is a mill rendering 40*d.*, and woodland 1 furlong long and half a furlong broad. It is worth 20*s.*

● Ealdræd holds Bemerton. He himself held it TRE, and it paid geld for 2 hides. There is land for 2 ploughs. There is 1 villan and 3 bordars, and 4 acres of meadow, and a mill rendering 12*s.* 6*d.* It is worth 40*s.*

● Ealdræd holds Alderstone. He himself held it TRE, and it paid geld for 1 hide. There is land for 2 ploughs. There is 1 plough, with 1 villan and 3 cotsets. There is pasture 1 furlong long and 1 broad, [and] woodland 2 furlongs long and 1 furlong broad. It is worth 10*s.*

● Ealdræd holds Winterbourne [? Gunner]. Godwine held it TRE, and it paid geld for 1½ hides. There is land for 1 plough. There is half a plough, with 1 villan and 1 bordar, and part of a mill rendering 22½*d.*, [and] pasture 2 furlongs long and as much broad. It is worth 30*s.*

● Cuthwulf holds [?]Rollestone. He himself held it TRE. He has there 6 hides. There is land for 3 ploughs. In demesne are 2 ploughs; and 5 slaves with 1 villan and 2 bordars have 1 plough. There are 4 acres of meadow and half a league of pasture. It is worth £3.

● Ketil holds 1 hide in Malmesbury. Godwine held it TRE. There is land for 1 plough, which [plough] is there, with 2 bordars. There are 6 acres of meadow, [and] pasture 3 furlongs long and half a furlong broad. It is worth 20*s.*

● Cypping holds Hazelbury. He himself held it TRE, and it paid geld for 1 virgate of land. There is land for 1 plough, which [plough] is there, and woodland 2 furlongs long and 1 furlong broad. It is worth 7*s.*

● Cola holds [East or West] Grimstead. His father held it TRE, and it paid geld for 1½ hides. There is land for 1 plough. There are 4 villans. It is worth 15*s.*

§ Ealdræd holds 3 hides in Ansty. There is land for 2 ploughs, which are there, with 1 slave and 1 villan and 3 bordars. There is a mill rendering 25*d.*, and 5 acres of woodland, and 5 acres of meadow and 2 furlongs of pasture. It is worth 30*s.* Ealdræd holds 10 hides in Wroughton. There is land for 4 ploughs, which are there, with 5 slaves and 3 villans and 3 bordars. It was and is worth 100*s.* Beorhtnoth and Alwine held these 2 estates TRE.

● GRIMBALD the goldsmith holds MANNINGFORD BRUCE. Edward held it TRE, and it paid geld for 6½ hides. There is land for 4 ploughs. In demesne are 2 ploughs; and 1 villan and 10 cotsets and 2 bordars with 1 plough. There are 2 parts of a mill rendering 12*s*. 6*d*., and 20 acres of meadow, [and] pasture 12 furlongs in length and breadth. It was worth 100*s*.; now £6.

● The same Grimbald holds STANTON FITZWARREN. Langa held it TRE, and it paid geld for 10 hides. There is land for 6 ploughs. In demesne are 2 ploughs, and 2 slaves; and 4 villans and 10 cotsets with 3 ploughs. There are 3 acres of meadow, [and] pasture 6 furlongs long and 4 broad. It is worth £12.

● GODRIC the huntsman holds 1 virgate of land paying geld in MERE. There is land for half a plough. He has there 1 cotset, and half an acre of meadow. It is worth 5*s*.

● GODRIC holds HARTHAM. His father held it TRE, and it paid geld for 3½ virgates. There is land for half a plough. There are 2 acres of meadow and 3 acres of pasture. It is worth 10*s*.

● GODWINE Clec holds 1 virgate of land in HILPERTON. It is worth 2*s*.

● GODE holds 1 hide in STITCHCOMBE. She herself held it TRE. There is land for 3 ploughs. In demesne is 1 plough; and 2 villans and 5 bordars with 2 ploughs. There is a mill rendering 15*s*., and 50 acres of woodland. It is worth 50*s*.

● ERLKING holds 1½ virgates of land in ETCHILHAMPTON. There is land for 2 oxen. It is worth 7*s*. 6*d*.

● EADRIC holds 1 hide in PEWSEY. There is land for 1½ ploughs. It is worth 20*s*.

● EDWIN holds CHEDGLOW. He himself held it TRE, and it paid geld for 1½ virgates of land. There is land for half a plough, which [half-plough] is there. It is worth 3*s*.

● EDGAR the priest holds half a hide in [? Hill] DEVERILL. Algar held it TRE, and it paid geld for as much. There is land for half a plough. He has there 2 cotsets. [There is] pasture 3 furlongs long and 1 broad. It is worth 12*s*.

● EADRIC the Blind holds HARTHAM. He himself held it TRE, and it paid geld for 1 virgate of land. There is land for 2 oxen, which are there. It is worth 30*d*.

● EDWARD holds WITHERINGTON. His father held it TRE, and it paid geld for 3 hides. There is land for 3 ploughs. In demesne is 1 plough; and 4 villans and 5 cotsets and 3 bordars with 1 plough. There is a mill rendering 10*s*., and 20 acres of meadow and 3 furlongs of woodland. It was worth £3; now £4.

● EDMUND holds half a virgate of land in BRAMSHAW [Hants]. It is worth 30*d*.

● EDMUND holds PLAITFORD [Hants]. Algar held it TRE, and it paid geld for 1 virgate of land. There is land for half a plough, which [half-plough] is there, with 2 bordars and 2 cotsets. There is a mill rendering 10*d*., [and] woodland 3 furlongs long and 1 furlong broad.

● The same Edmund holds 1 virgate of land, in which he has half a plough, and 4 bordars and 2 cottars. These 2 estates together are worth 40*s*.

● EDMUND son of Æthelwulf holds 1 hide in BRITFORD. It renders 12*s*. 6*d*.

● The son of Æthelwulf holds [East or West] GRIMSTEAD. His father held it TRE, and it paid geld for 1½ hides. There is land for 2 ploughs. In demesne is 1 plough, with 1 villan and 2 cotsets and 2 cottars. There is a mill rendering 10*s*., and 14 acres of meadow, and 4 furlongs of pasture, [and] woodland 4 furlongs long and 4 furlongs broad. It is worth 40*s*.

● HEARDING holds 'KNIGHTON' [in Durrington] of the king. He himself held it TRE, and it paid geld for 11 hides. There is land for 6 ploughs. In demesne are 2 ploughs, and 6 slaves; and 7 villans and 6 cotsets with 3 ploughs. There is a mill rendering 10*s*., and 20 acres of meadow, [and] pasture 12 furlongs long and 3 furlongs broad. It is worth £11.

● HEARDING holds FIGHELDEAN. He himself held it TRE, and it paid geld for 11½ hides. There is land for 5 ploughs. In demesne is 1 plough, and 6 slaves; and 7 villans and 8 bordars with 4 ploughs. There is a mill rendering 15*s*., and 24 acres of meadow, [and] pasture 12 furlongs long and 3 furlongs broad. It is worth £9.

Of this land Earl Aubrey had 4½ hides. The king now holds them.

● HEARDING holds OGBOURNE [? Maizey]. He himself held it TRE, and it paid geld for 5 hides. There is land for 3 ploughs. In demesne is 1 plough, with 1 slave; and 3 villans and 4 bordars with 1 plough. There are 2 acres of meadow, [and] pasture 2 furlongs long and 1 furlong broad. It is worth £4.

● THORKIL holds [land] in COMPTON BASSETT. He himself held it TRE, and it paid geld for 6 hides. There is land for 4 ploughs. In demesne is 1 plough, and 4 slaves; and 5 villans and 10 cotsets and 3 bordars with 2 ploughs. There is the third part of 2 mills rendering 10*s*., and 24 acres of meadow, and 10 acres of pasture and 10 acres of woodland. It is worth 100*s*.

● ULF holds 1 hide in BUDBURY. There is land for 1 plough. There are 4 bordars and 3 slaves, and 3 acres of woodland. It is worth 10*s*.

● WULFRIC holds 1 hide and 1 virgate of land in SHALBOURNE. Ordweald held it TRE, and it paid geld for as much. There is land for 1½ ploughs, and there are 3 bordars. It is worth 20*s*.

● WULFRIC holds 3 virgates of land in [?West] WINTERSLOW, and 1 virgate of land in WEST TYTHERLEY [Hants]. His father held it TRE, and it paid geld for 1 hide. There is land for 1 plough. This [plough] 4 peasants have there. [There is] woodland 4 furlongs long and 1 furlong broad. It is worth 20*s*.

● WULFRIC holds 3½ hides in UFFCOTT. His father held it TRE. There is land for 1½ ploughs. It is worth 30*s*.

● WULFRIC holds MERE. Ællic held it TRE, and it paid geld for 1½ virgates of land. There is land for half a plough, which [half-plough] is there, with 4 bordars, and half an acre of meadow and 1 acre of pasture. It is worth 7*s*. 6*d*.

● WULFRIC holds 1 hide and 1 virgate of land in SWINDON. There is land for half a plough. It is worth 7*s*.

● WULFRIC holds 1 hide in BRITFORD. There is land for half a plough. It is worth 12*s*. 6*d*.

● WULFRIC holds 1 hide in 'FRUSTFIELD' [in Whiteparish], and has there 6 bordars. It is worth 20*s*.

● WULFRIC holds PORTON. His father held it TRE, and it paid geld for 2 hides. There is land for 2 ploughs. In demesne is 1 plough, with 1 slave; and 2 villans and 3 cotsets with 1 plough. There are 6 acres of meadow and 3 furlongs of pasture. It is worth 40*s*.

● WULFWEARD holds 4 hides in [?West] WINTERSLOW. There is land for 3 ploughs. In demesne is 1 plough, and 2 slaves, and 1 villan and 3 bordars, [and] woodland 3 furlongs long and 1 furlong broad. It is worth 40*s*.

● WULFWEARD the king's purveyor holds 2 hides in SWINDON. There is land for 6 oxen. It is worth 15*s*.

● WULFRIC Waula holds half a hide in [?] CLYFFE PYPARD. There is land for half a plough. It is worth 4*s*.

● WULFNOTH holds 1 hide in MERE, and it paid geld for as much TRE. There is land for 1 plough, which [plough] is there, with 6 cottars, and 4 acres of meadow and 1 acre of pasture. It is worth 20*s*.

● WULFGEAT the huntsman holds LONGFORD. TRE it paid geld for 4 hides. There is land for 2 ploughs. In demesne is 1 plough, with 1 slave, and 2 villans and 6 bordars and 3 cottars. There is a mill rendering 5*s*., and 20 acres of meadow, [and] pasture 5 furlongs long and 2 furlongs broad. It is worth 60*s*.

● WULFNOTH holds half a hide paying geld in BRAMSHAW [Hants]. His father held it. There is land for half a plough. It is worth 10*s*.

● WULFGEAT holds half a hide in MILFORD. There is land for 2 oxen. It is worth 2*s*. Half this land is in the forest.

● The wife of WYNSIGE holds TIDCOMBE. Her husband held it TRE, and it paid geld for 2 hides. There is land for 3 ploughs. In demesne is 1 plough, with 1 slave; and 2 villans and 6 bordars with 2 ploughs. There is a mill rendering 15*s*., and 4 acres of woodland, [and] pasture 5 furlongs long and 2 furlongs broad. It is worth 70*s*.

● WADO holds 1 hide in BARFORD ST MARTIN. He himself held it TRE. There is land for 1 plough, which [plough] is there, with 1 bordar, and 6 acres of meadow. It is worth 15*s*.

● ASGOT holds half a hide in SHALBOURNE. There is land for half a plough. It is worth 5*s*.

● ODOLINA holds 1 hide in MARTEN. There is land for 1½ ploughs. There are 30 acres in both meadow and pasture. It is worth 40*s*.

● SÆWULF holds 1 hide paying geld in "GATEGRAM". His father held it. There is land for half a plough. It is worth 10*s*.

● THORKIL holds 2 hides in OGBOURNE [? Maizey]. His father held them. There is land for 1 plough. There are 30 acres of pasture. It is worth 10*s*.

● LEOFGYTH holds KNOOK. Her husband held it TRE, and it paid geld for 3½ hides. There is land for 2½ ploughs, which are there, with 1 slave, and 4 villans and 4 bordars. There is a mill rendering 15*s*., and 5 acres of meadow, [and] pasture half a league long and 1 furlong broad. It is worth £3. This Leofgyth made and makes the gold fringe of the king and the queen.

● ÆLFHILD holds HARTHAM. Her husband held it TRE, and it paid geld for 1 virgate. There is land for half a plough, which [half-plough] is there, and 1 acre of meadow. It is worth 3*s*.

● SÆGIFU holds 1 virgate of land paying geld. Alwig held it TRE. There is land for 2 oxen. There is 1 acre of meadow. It is worth 3*s*.

● LIDHSMAN holds 3 hides in MELKSHAM. He himself held it TRE, and it paid geld for as much. There is land for 2½ ploughs. In demesne is 1 plough; and 4 villans and 3 bordars and 3 cottars with 1 plough. There are 10 acres of meadow, and 5 acres of pasture and 5 acres of woodland. It is worth 30*s*.

● EALDHILD holds 1 hide and 6 acres of land in HILPERTON. Her husband held them TRE. There is land for 1 plough. There is 1 bordar, and 4 acres of meadow. It is worth 8*s*.

● OSWEARD holds 1 hide paying geld in BRITFORD. There is land for half a plough. His father held it. It is worth 12*s*. 6*d*.

● ODA holds LANDFORD. His father held it TRE, and it paid geld for 2 hides. There is land for 2 ploughs. There are 6 bordars, and a mill rendering 20*d*. There is pasture 1 league long and half a league broad, [and] woodland 4 furlongs long and 4 furlongs broad. It is worth 15*s*.

● ESBERN holds 1 virgate of land in 'FRUSTFIELD' [in Whiteparish]. It is worth 15*d*.

● SWEIN holds STAPLEFORD. His father held it TRE, and it paid geld for 10½ hides. There is land for 10 ploughs. In demesne are 2 ploughs, with 1 slave; and 17 villans and 10 bordars with 8 ploughs. There are 2 mills rendering 30*s*., and 40 acres of meadow, pasture half a league long and as much broad, [and] woodland 1 league long and half a league broad. It is worth £12.

● SÆRIC holds WINTERBOURNE [? Gunner]. Alwine held it TRE, and it paid geld for 1½ hides. There is land for 1 plough, which [plough] is there in demesne, with 1 villan and 4 cotsets. There is part of a mill rendering 22½*d*., [and] woodland 2 furlongs long and 1 furlong broad. It is worth 30*s*.

● SÆRIC holds LAVERSTOCK. Gestr, his brother, held it TRE, and it paid geld for half a hide. There is land for half a plough, which [half-plough] is there. It is worth 10*s*.

● SÆWEARD holds 3 hides in BROUGHTON GIFFORD. Alweald held them TRE. There is land for 2 ploughs, which are there. It is worth 40*s*.

● RAGNBURH holds a manor which Godric held TRE, and it paid geld for 5 hides. There is land for 3 ploughs, which are there, and 5 slaves, and 6 villans and 1 bordar, and 4 acres of meadow, [and] pasture 5 furlongs long and 2 furlongs broad. It was worth £4; now 100*s*.

● The king's FORESTERS hold 1½ hides in the forest of Grovely. It is worth 30*s*.

LANG held [? Broad] Blunsdon of King Edward, and it was assessed at 2 hides. Edward the sheriff now holds it in the hand of the king, and there are 3 bordars. It was worth 20*s*.; now 7*s*.

§f.73

LXVIII. THE LAND OF THE KING'S SERVANTS

● HERVEY OF WILTON holds 1 hide in EDINGTON of the king. Osweard held it TRE. There is land for 1 plough. There are 3 bordars, and as much meadow and pasture as is sufficient for 1 hide. It is worth 30*s.*

● Hervey holds 1½ hides. Edwin held this TRE. There is land for 1 plough. There are 4 acres of pasture. It was and is worth 30*s.* This is in NETHERAVON.

● RICHARD Sturmy holds 1 hide and 1½ virgates of land in HUISH. There is land for 3 ploughs. In demesne is 1 plough, and 4 slaves; and 3 villans and 4 cotsets with 2 ploughs. There are 4 acres of meadow, and woodland 1 league long and 4 furlongs broad. It was worth 30*s.*; now 60*s.*

● The same Richard holds BURBAGE, and William [holds] of him. Ælfric held it TRE, and it paid geld for 2½ hides. There is land for 2 ploughs, which are there, with 1 slave and 1 villan and 4 cotsets. There are 2 arpents of meadow, and woodland 4 furlongs long and 2 furlongs broad. It is worth 30*s.*

● The same man holds 1 hide in [East or West] GRAFTON. It is worth 20*s.*

● The same man holds 1½ hides in HARDING, and Robert [holds] of him. Ælfric held them TRE. There is land for 1 plough, which [plough] is there in demesne. It is worth 10*s.*

● The same man holds 1 hide and 3 virgates of land in SHALBOURNE. Ordweald held them TRE, and it paid geld for as much. There is land for 3 ploughs. In demesne are 2 ploughs, and 4 slaves; and 3 villans and 3 cotsets with 1 plough. There are 3 arpents of meadow, and woodland 4 furlongs long and 2 furlongs broad. It is worth 40*s.*

● ROBERT fitzRalph holds 1 hide and 2½ virgates of land in [East or West] GRAFTON. Wulfmær held them TRE. There is land for 2 ploughs, which are there in demesne, with 1 slave and 5 cotsets, and 2 arpents of woodland. It is worth 30*s.*

● RALPH de Hauville holds 3 hides and 1½ virgates of land in [East or West] GRAFTON. Alwine, and Alweald, and Leofwine and Ceolstan held of him TRE. There is land for 4½ ploughs. In demesne are 3 ploughs, and 3 slaves; and 4 cotsets with 1½ ploughs. There is pasture 2 furlongs long and half a furlong broad. It is worth £7.

● The same Ralph holds 1 hide in MARTEN. 2 thegns held it TRE. There is land for 1 plough, which [plough] is there in demesne, with 2 slaves and 2 cotsets. There are 2 arpents of meadow and 2 acres of pasture. It is worth 40*s.*

● The same Ralph holds in BURBAGE 2 hides and 1 virgate of land. Alric held it TRE. There is land for 2 ploughs, which are there with 1 slave, and 2 villans and 1 bordar. [There is] woodland 3 furlongs long and 2 furlongs broad. It is worth 30*s.*

● In WOLFHALL he has 4 hides. Thorold and Alwine held them TRE, and it paid geld for as much. There is land for 3 ploughs, and [there is] no livestock. There is a mill rendering 16*s.*, and 4 villans and 4 cotsets, [and] woodland 2 furlongs long and as much broad. It is worth 30*s.*

● THORBERT holds 1 hide in MARTEN. Leofwine held it TRE, and it paid geld for as much. There is land for 1 plough. There are 2 cotsets, and 6 acres of meadow and 10 acres of pasture. It was and is worth 40*s.*

● CROCH holds NORTH TIDWORTH. 3 thegns held it TRE, and it paid geld for 3 hides. There is land for 1½ ploughs. Of this, Croch holds 3 virgates of land, and a knight of his 2 hides. There is 1 plough, and 2 bordars and 1 villan, and pasture 2 furlongs long and 1 furlong broad. It was worth 20*s.*; now 50*s.* Edward the sheriff holds 1 virgate of land which belongs to these 3 hides.

● HERVEY holds RATFYN. Earl Harold held it TRE, and it paid geld for 2 hides. There is land for 1 plough, which [plough] is there in demesne, and 5 bordars. There are 8 acres of meadow, and pasture 2 furlongs long and 1 furlong broad. It was worth 30*s.*; now 40*s.*

● THEOBALD and Humphrey hold [Lower and Upper] WIDHILL. Robert fitzWimarc held it, and it paid geld for 5 hides. There is land for 5 ploughs. In demesne are 2 ploughs and 2 slaves, and 6 bordars. There are 50 acres of meadow and 60 acres of pasture. It was worth 20*s.*; now 40*s.*

● ANSKETIL holds BUTTERMERE. Godwine held it TRE, and it paid geld for half a virgate of land. There is land for 2 oxen. It is worth 40*d.*

● JOHN the doorkeeper holds ALTON [in Figheldean]. Godric and Bolla held it TRE, and it paid geld for 5 hides. There is land for 4 ploughs. In demesne are 2 ploughs, and 3 slaves; and 4 villans and 2 cottars with half a plough. There are 8 acres of meadow, and pasture 3 furlongs long and 2 furlongs broad. Of this land Turstin holds 1 hide, and Frawine 1 hide. There is 1 bordar and 1 cottar with half a plough, and 2 acres of meadow. [There is] pasture 4 furlongs long and 2 furlongs broad. The whole is worth 100*s.*

● The same man holds half a hide in BARFORD ST MARTIN. Ælfric held it TRE. There is land for 1 plough. There is 1 bordar with 1 slave, and 8 acres of meadow. It was and is worth 10*s.*

● WILLIAM Scudet holds WESTBURY. Wulfweard held it TRE, and it paid geld for 4½ hides. There is land for 7 ploughs. In demesne are 4 ploughs, and 4 slaves; and 20 bordars with 3 ploughs. There are 20 acres of meadow, and 4 acres of woodland, and 2 mills rendering 25*s.* It was and is worth £8.

● GEOFFREY holds DRAYCOT CERNE. Eadric held it TRE, and it paid geld for 5 hides. There is land for 5 ploughs. In demesne are 2 ploughs, and 4 slaves; and 7 villans and 10 cotsets with 3 ploughs. There is a mill rendering 5*s.*, and 40 acres of meadow, pasture 2 furlongs long and 1 furlong broad, [and] woodland 4 furlongs long and 2 furlongs broad, and 1 burgess pays 12*d.* It is worth 100*s.*

● WILLIAM fitzAnsculf holds THORNHILL. Strami held it TRE, and it paid geld for 7½ hides. There is land for 5 ploughs. In demesne are 2 ploughs; and 5 villans and 5 bordars and 5 cotsets with 3 ploughs. There is a mill rendering 5*s.*, and 11 acres of meadow, and 10 acres of woodland, and pasture 2 furlongs long and 2 broad. It was and is worth 100*s.*

● WILLIAM holds 2 hides near those above-mentioned 7 hides. One belongs to Bradenstoke, the manor of Edward the sheriff, and the other to Clyffe Pypard, the manor of Gilbert de Breteuil, according to the testimony of the thegns. They are worth 20*s.*

● WIBERT holds [?]CLYFFE PYPARD. This was of the land of Wulfgifu [of] Beslow, and it paid geld TRE for 5 hides and 1 virgate of land. There is land for 3 ploughs. In demesne are 2 ploughs; and 3 villans and 1 bordar and 1 cotset with 1 plough. A house in Cricklade renders 3*d.* There are 42½ acres of meadow, and 84 acres of pasture and 24 acres of woodland. It was worth 20*s.*; now £3. 10*s.*

● ODIN the chamberlain holds SWINDON. Thorbert held it TRE, and it paid geld for 12 hides. There is land for 6 ploughs. In demesne are 2 ploughs, and 2 slaves; and 6 villans and 8 bordars with 3 ploughs. There is a mill rendering 4*s.*, and 30 acres of meadow and 20 acres of pasture. It was worth 60*s.*; now 100*s.* Of this land Miles Crispin holds 2 hides, and has there 1 plough. Odin claims them.

● TURSTIN the chamberlain holds [?]CLYFFE PYPARD. Alwine held it TRE, and it paid geld for 4 hides. There is land for 1½ ploughs. In demesne is 1 plough, with 1 slave and 4 cotsets. There is a mill rendering 5*s.*, and 12 acres of meadow and 8 acres of pasture. It is worth 50*s.*

● AUBREY the chamberlain holds 'SMALLBROOK' [in Warminster]. Mainard held it TRE, and it paid geld for 2 hides. There is land for 3 ploughs. In demesne is 1 plough; and 1 villan and 12 bordars with 2 ploughs. There are 6 acres of meadow and 9 acres of woodland. It was worth 30*s.*; now 40*s.*

● AUBREY the chamberlain holds [? Hill] DEVERILL. 2 thegns held it TRE, and it paid geld for 1 hide. There is land for 1 plough. There are 8 cotsets with 1 plough, and a mill rendering 4*s.*, and 1 acre of meadow. [There is] pasture 4 furlongs long and 2 furlongs broad, [and] woodland 5 furlongs long and 1 furlong broad. It was worth 40*s.*; now 29*s.*

● GUNDUIN the keeper of the granaries holds WHITECLIFF. Alwig held it TRE, and it paid geld for 2 hides. There is land for 1 plough, which [plough] is there in demesne, with 1 slave and 1 cotset. There are 2 acres of meadow, and pasture 4 furlongs long and 1 furlong broad, [and] woodland 1 furlong long and another broad. It was worth 20*s.*; now 35*s.*

● WARIN the crossbowman holds CHELWORTH [in Cricklade]. Eadric held it TRE, and it paid geld for 2 hides. There is land for 2 ploughs. In demesne is 1 plough, with 4 bordars. There are 8 acres of meadow and 10 acres of woodland. It was and is worth 40*s.*

● CROCH holds half a hide in BRADENSTOKE. There is land for half a plough. It is worth 10*s.*

● WILLIAM Corniole holds [? Great] WISHFORD. Æfic held it TRE, and it paid geld for 2 hides. There is land for 2 ploughs. There are 3 villans and 3 bordars with 1 plough, and a mill rendering 15*s.* There are 8 acres of meadow. It was and is worth 40*s.*

● EDWARD holds 1 virgate of land in ALDERBURY. Boda held it TRE. It is worth 40*d.*